PERFORMING DREAMS

Discourses of Immortality Among the Xavante of Central Brazil

Laura R. Graham

Fenestra Books

Performing Dreams:
Discourses of Immortality Among the Xavante of Central Brazil

Second Edition

Second edition (2003) published by Fenestra Books™
610 East Delano Street, Suite 104, Tucson, Arizona 85705, U.S.A.
www.fenestrabooks.com

All author earnings from this edition of *Performing Dreams*, as with earnings from previous editions, are sent to the Xavante Association of Pimentel Barbosa to support community projects.

Publisher's Cataloguing-in-Publication Data

Graham, Laura R., 1956–
    Performing dreams : discourses of immortality among the Xavante of central Brazil / Laura R. Graham. – 2nd ed.
    p. cm.
    Includes bibliographical references and index.
    LCCN: 2002116088
    ISBN: 1-58736-172-8

    1. Xavante Indians–Folklore. 2. Xavante Indians–Rites and ceremonies. 3. Xavante Indians–Social conditions. 4. Oral tradition–Brazil–Pimentel Barbosa Reserve. 5. Folklore–Brazil–Pimentel Barbosa Reserve–Performance. 6. Discourse analysis, Narrative–Brazil–Pimentel Barbosa Reserve.   I. Title.
F2520.I.A4G73 2003
306'.089'984–dc20

Contents

Preface and Acknowledgments   ix

Notes on Xavante Orthography and Transcription   xiii

1. Introduction: Performing Dreams   1

2. Descendants of the First Creators   19

3. Sounds of Time, the Time of Sounds   64

4. Singing Dreams, Dreams of Singing   103

5. Depersonalizing the Dream:
the Politics of Narrative Performance   137

6. Becoming a Creator   175

7. Performing the Dream   207

Epilogue   227

Appendix: Musical Transcriptions   237

Notes   251

References   267

Index   285

MAPS

1. Brazil 26

2. Area of Xavante Reserves 30

3. Pimentel Barbosa Indigenous Reserve 33

ILLUSTRATIONS

1. Warodi Telling His Dream to the Elders 3

2. Lino Tsere?ubudzi Shopping with His Son 14

3. "Saving the Whites," Rio das Mortes 34

4. Xavante Leader Celestino en Route to
a Federal Ministry Building, 1980 56

5. Sõrupredu Haranguing FUNAI President
Romero Jucá Filho, 1987 58

6. Warodi's Granddaughter Jacoro 68

7. Intonational Contours of Xavante Interrogative
and Declarative Sentences 85

8. Warodi and Sibupa Conversing on Warodi's Bed 88

9. Da-ño?re Performers Move around the Village in Either a Clockwise
or Counterclockwise Direction 111

10. Pre-initiate Wapte Performing Da-ño?re
with Their Tsimñohu Sponsors 113

11. Some ?ritai?wa Novitiates Performing Da-ño?re 119

12. Da-ño?re Transcription, Benedito's Song (Da-hipɔpɔ) 120

13. Warã Seating Arrangements after the 1985
Tsada?ro Age-set Da-tsi-tɔ 148

14. Elder Men Listening to the *Warā* Men's Council   153

15. Warodi Fitting the *Buriti* Fiber Robe to His Brother's Son   210

16. Women Applying Body Paint in Preparation for Performance   213

17. The Dream Performance in the Village Center   215

18. Women and Men Dance in Adjacent Sections   216

19. Warodi Was the Only Performer Who Did Not Paint   216

20. Riridu Singing with the Tape-recorded Version of the *Hedza* He "Received" from the Immortals   233

In memory of
Warodi Xavante
Tsiʔutõriʔõ (Never Ending)
1930?–1988

Preface and Acknowledgments

This book is based on research I carried out among the Xavante in Brazil between 1981 and 1991, mostly in the community known in Portuguese as Pimentel Barbosa. Soon after I began this research, however, it became unclear whether I would be able to work there, or even among the Xavante at all.

In December 1981, after I had spent nearly two months in Xavante communities located near the Kuluene River, in what is now the Parabubure Reserve (see Map 2), the National Indian Foundation's (FUNAI) regional administrator relocated me to the Pimentel Barbosa Reserve. Although members of the community welcomed me when I arrived, the FUNAI agent, whom I shall call Boanergis da Viega, attempted to sabotage my work from the outset. In addition to commanding me to live in a dilapidated, bat-infested room at the FUNAI post a quarter mile from the community, he mandated the hours I could visit the Xavante and dictated whom I could talk to and when. I was dismayed over these conditions, which made ethnographic research nearly impossible.

I was not the only one dissatisfied with the situation: Boanergis's inhospitable stance fueled resentments that many in the community already felt toward him. The elders objected to my having to live at the government post and, countering Boanergis's mandate, invited me to live in an empty house in the village. The day after I accepted their invitation, Boanergis, who evidently perceived me as a threat, implicated me in a land dispute between the Xavante and local ranchers. Thus he engineered my expulsion from the Reserve. On January 26, Boanergis sent this short-wave radio message—which he showed me and I copied—to his superior, whom I shall call Osvaldo Santano, the senior administrator at FUNAI's regional headquarters: "Situation in PI [Indigenous Post] continues tense. Anthropologist Laura Graham residing in indigenous village, inciting Indians toward violence against ranch. Request permission to evacuate subversive influence."

Santano sent this response: "Inform you to proceed with removal of said researcher according to noncompliance with Item B of authorization [the condition that stipulates investigators will not interfere in internal political affairs] as well as according to the serious problems at the level of security in the area."

At that time, of course, I understood very little about the Xavante's internal political situation or about the the tensions between them and the rancher. Nevertheless, I was expelled from the reserve. For several months after my expulsion it was not clear that I would be allowed back to Pimentel Barbosa or permitted into any Xavante reserve. However, thanks to the efforts of Lux Vidal and Eunice Durham, then president of the Association of Brazilian Anthropologists, and to the moral support of Sylvia Caiuby Novaes and Greg Urban, I was able to return to Pimentel Barbosa after about a month to continue my research.

Even though the particulars of my story are specific to my experience, my story is not exceptional. Nearly every anthropologist I know who has done research among indigenous peoples in Brazil has, at some time during the course of her or his study, encountered difficulty with representatives of the National Indian Foundation. Because the trauma I experienced occurred just as I was beginning to develop a relationship with the community, and at a time when their relations with FUNAI were tense, this episode influenced the way in which the people of Pimentel Barbosa perceived me. Except for a few youths—Boanergis's acolytes—people welcomed me as an ally.

Since 1982 I have returned to Pimentel Barbosa several times. I spent two months there in 1984, before returning from December 1985 to December 1987 to conduct my doctoral research. I made my most recent visit in June–August 1991. Since my first field trip, as FUNAI administrators have come and gone, I have been treated very well by FUNAI staff. I appreciate the support they have lent to my work.

I am grateful to many people for their inspiration, encouragement, and support of my research and writing; it is a pleasure to thank them here. I am especially grateful to Doug Schwartz and his staff for helping to provide the wonderful atmosphere and time for uninterrupted thought and writing which I enjoyed as a National Endowment for the Humanities Resident Scholar at the School of American Research during 1992–1993. The stimulating conversations I shared with other scholars at the School helped to shape the manuscript into its present form. It owes much to long walks and ski trips with Paul Stoller and Richard Waller, as well as to the careful readings, thoughtful comments, and spirited encouragement of Jenny White, Richard Waller, T. M. Scruggs, and Jane Kepp, who read the entire manuscript. Special thanks to my advisor, Greg Urban, for giving me his unwavering support throughout all phases of my work and for reading various versions of this material.

I wish also to thank Kirin Narayan for her beautiful ethnographic writing, which has been an inspiration to me, as well as Holly Carver and Theresa May for their valuable support and encouragement. T. M. Scruggs, who has accompanied me to visit the Xavante and who carried a tapir across the central plaza to marry me in the Xavante way, has been especially important. I thank him for sharing in the experience of my work and writing about the Xavante and for living the joys and hardships of fieldwork and commuting. I am grateful to have a relationship that inspires my thinking, research, and writing.

Many thanks to others who have discussed ideas or read parts of earlier versions of this manuscript, especially my dissertation and articles that appeared in the *American Ethnologist,* parts of which appear in Chapters 4 and 5. I wish to thank members of the anthropology and linguistics faculty at the University of Texas at Austin, especially Richard Bauman, Steve Feld, Joel Sherzer, Katie Stewart, and Anthony Woodbury, for the challenges and insights they provided while I was a graduate student. Don Brenneis, Charles Briggs, Steve Caton, Sylvia Caiuby Novaes, Janet Chernela, Beth Conklin, Alessandro Duranti, Aracy Lopes da Silva, David Maybury-Lewis, Alcida Ramos, Anthony Seeger, Milton Singer, Barbara Tedlock, and Terry Turner may recognize threads of conversations that provided valuable insights. I am grateful for them all and for the comments offered by the University of Texas Press's anonymous readers.

I am especially appreciative of the encouragement I received from those who preceded me in working with the Xavante. From the outset, David Maybury-Lewis, Nancy Flowers, and Aracy Lopes da Silva welcomed my interest and contributions. I am fortunate to share in the wonderful collegial atmosphere of those who work among the Xavante, as well as those who work among Gê peoples.

For fond memories, friendship, and their hospitality during my stays in Brazil, I thank many who welcomed me into their homes. Special thanks to Sylvia Caiuby Novaes, Jorge Leal Medeiros, Nina Villas Boas, André Villas Boas, Mônica Lobos and Diô, Guillerme Carrãno, Lucia Andrade, Jean Jacques Vidal, Lux Vidal, Regina Müller, Valerie Mitchell, Marcos Lazarin, Robin Bradley, Bart Fibelkorn, Selma Parreira, Aracy Lopes da Silva, and Rômulo de Sousa.

I am indebted to the Centro Ecumênico de Documentação e Informação, especially Ricardo Alberto and Marco Antonio Gonçalves, for navigating the bureaucratic labyrinths that led to permission to use photographs from the archives of the Museu do Indio and the Brazilian newspapers *O Globo* and *Jornal do Brasil.* Thanks also to Richard Graham for his courier services between Brazil and the United States, Eliza Willis for her assistance in calculating dollar values for Xavante Project budgets, Joseph Ryan Rodriguez for help with graphic art, and Victoria Gitman for her drawing. I also want to thank Marc Walker and John Cotter for lending their map-drawing skills and T. M. Scruggs for his help with musical transcriptions.

None of this work would have been possible without the institutional and financial support I have received over the years. I am grateful to the Brazilian institutions FUNAI and Conselho Nacional de Desenvolvimento Científico e Tecnológico, to the Universities of São Paulo and Brasília, which facilitated my research in Brazil, and to those institutions which have generously supported my research. Grants from the Fulbright-Hayes Doctoral Dissertation Research Abroad Program, the Social Science Research Council, the National Science Foundation (#BNS-8507-401), the Inter-American Foundation, the Tinker Foundation, the University of Texas at Austin, and the University of Iowa have made it possible for me to return repeatedly to the Xavante for short as well as extended periods. A Charlotte W. Newcombe Dissertation Writing Fellowship and President's Fellowships from the University of Texas at Austin supported the writing of my dissertation. My thanks to these institutions and the members of their staffs.

Last, but most important of all, my most heartfelt thanks extend to the people of Pimentel Barbosa and to Lino Tsere?ubudzi of São Marcos. Of all these people, it is to Warodi that I owe the greatest thanks. May he continue always living.

Notes on Xavante Orthography and Transcription

I n transcribing the Xavante language in this book I have adopted the phonetic notation system developed by Summer Institute of Linguistics missionaries who worked among the Xavante in the 1970s, which is also used by Xavante themselves. To simplify, I substitute ɔ for ó, ε for é, and ñ for nh. To conform to the conventions of English punctuation, upper-case characters are used when Xavante words appear in sentence-initial position. Upper-case E is used for ε. I also use upper-case letters for Xavante names, so that, for example, apöwẽ is written Apöwẽ. Although s and c are not part of the phonetic inventory, I write personal names such as Sibupa and Cipassé the way these individuals write their names.

The consonants p, b, t, d, m, n, w, and h should be pronounced as they are in English. To pronounce the affricate sounds ts and dz, the reader should briefly raise the tongue to the roof of the mouth just before making the English sounds s or z. The letter r is a tap; the tongue momentarily touches the roof of the mouth. The character ʔ is a glottal stop, the sound English speakers make before the vowels in the utterance "uh uh." The letter ñ is pronounced like the ñ of the Spanish piñata.

Xavante distinguish between long and short vowels and nasalized and non-nazalized vowels. Two vowels together indicate a long vowel, as in ĩĩ. The diacritic ~ denotes nasalized vowels. Non-nasal vowels are pronounced similarly to the vowels of the following English words, although many English vowels differ in that they are diphthongs:

i—an unrounded high front vowel, as the e in "feet"
e—an unrounded mid-front vowel, similar to the a of "The Hague"
ε—an unrounded low-mid-front vowel, as the e of "hen"
ö—an unrounded mid-central vowel, a sound similar to the "reduced vowel" [ə], as in some pronunciations of the initial e in "receive"

u—a rounded high back vowel, as the *o* of "who"

o—a rounded mid-back vowel, similar to the *o* in "only"

ɔ—a rounded low-mid-back vowel, as *ou* in "bought"

a—an unrounded low back vowel, as the *a* in "father"

ʌ—a low central vowel, as the *u* of "uh huh"; found only in the speech of elders.

Unless noted otherwise, the transcribed texts that appear in this book are excerpted from Warodi's dream narrative. The full text appears in Graham (1990). In the transcriptions, lines are determined on the basis of pause structure and grammatical markings. New sentences begin at the left margin; continuations of a sentence are indented; and successive indentions denote additional pauses within the same sentence. In some translations I have added commas to facilitate comprehension; they do not indicate pauses. Three dots (. . .) indicate that material has been omitted, except in Example 1 in Chapter 5, which is explained in the text. Square brackets across lines denote simultaneous or overlapping utterances. In English translations I have left two Xavante sounds, *ã* and ʌ, as they occur. These sounds are used rhetorically—to mark the ends of phrases, for example—and do not translate.

I

Introduction: Performing Dreams

On the morning of August 8, 1984, seven elder men in the Xavante village of Eteñitɛpa, known as Pimentel Barbosa in Portuguese, slipped quietly from their houses.[1] Each followed the path that passes behind the arc of beehive-shaped houses, discretely making his way to the *marã*, a secluded forest clearing used for ritual preparations. The night before, Warodi had told me that the celebration would take place today. As we sipped the precious coffee that I had brought to Pimentel Barbosa, I eagerly awaited some sign that preparatory activities had begun. Rising from his seat near the cookfire and preparing to go, Warodi beckoned me to follow. Hurriedly, I gathered up my notebook and equipment, the tools of my ethnographer's trade. With tape recorder and camera in hand, I accompanied him to the forest clearing.

The others—Sibupa, Wadzaʔe, Eduardo, Raimundo, Daru, Aiʔrere, and Etɛ̃pa—had seated themselves in a circle around the coals of a small fire whose glow took the chill off the Central Brazilian Plateau's crisp morning air. As the sun's rays crested over the trees, Warodi took his place among the elders. The gathering was small: it was the dry season when a number of families were off on trek, the extended hunting trips typical of the traditional Xavante seminomadic life-style. Because no major celebrations such as the male initiation ceremonies or the ceremonials of the *waiʔa* were scheduled this year, the trekking groups would not return until sometime in September. Nevertheless, among those present were some of the community's eldest and most committed leaders of ceremonial life. These eight men talked quietly among themselves, paying no attention to the adolescent novitiates who worked nearby clearing brush to enlarge the forest opening. No one paid heed as I set up my tape recorder and microphone in the center of their circle.

The soft murmur of their conversation blended into the sounds of the waking forest. From time to time loud birdcalls punctuated the cicada's buzzing drone. Suddenly Warodi cleared his throat loudly, spat, and began singing very quietly. His singing was at first almost imperceptible. As he softly repeated the song's patterned phrases, the others joined in, also with hushed voices. There was a moment's silence when the song finished. Only the sound of the novitiates rustling in the brush and the early morning bird calls disturbed the calm.

After a brief pause Warodi recommenced his singing, this time at full volume. As the others joined him their deep, mature voices resounded in the forest clearing. When they stopped, Warodi whispered, "This is öwawẽ-ʔwa's [the one who created the sea's]. It is his." He then went on to sing two more songs—at first softly, then once again loudly after the others joined him. When the elders had learned the three songs according to this pattern, Warodi led them through the entire set singing at full volume. In this way Warodi taught the others the songs he had learned in a dream.

Immediately after finishing the third song, Warodi began to speak, very quietly. I moved the microphone closer to him and adjusted the record levels to pick up the soft voice and rhythmic cadences of his speech (Fig. 1). From time to time others added their voices; frequently several elders spoke at the same time. Punctuated with clicks and emphatic glottal sounds, their simultaneous utterances, their staggered and overlapping phrases produced a soft but acoustically spectacular murmur in the forest clearing. It was difficult for me to make out what Warodi was saying; his voice was barely audible even without the constant voice-over contributions of his neighbors.

Echoed by affirmations, questions, asides, and comments, Warodi recounted his dream to the elders. In truly polyvocal discourse, Warodi told of his participation in a gathering of immortals.[2] Among those present were the ancestors responsible for the Xavante creation—the two parinaiʔa, boys who had created animals, insects, fish, and foods; the wedehu date da-waʔre (the one whose foot was pierced by a stick), who augmented the Xavante population; and the boy whose stomach burst, the öwawẽ-ʔwa, who created the sea and the whites.[3] These creators, Warodi reported, had given him their songs—gifts to the living—so that, performing them, the Xavante would continue as Xavante forever.

Thus began a unique celebration that was itself a performance of Warodi's dream. That morning Warodi sat among the elders of Pimentel Barbosa as he had sat among the ancestors of his dream. He taught the creators' songs and shared their thoughts with the living in the same way that, in the dream, the creators had shared their thoughts with him. As Warodi recounted his vision, he and the others made plans for the dream performance, a performance that would include the entire community. These plans merged into Warodi's dream narrative, blurring the distinction between the present and the time of the mythic creators who had appeared to Warodi. Down to the last detail the elders designed their celebration to

1. Warodi (left) telling his dream to the elders in the *marã* (forest clearing). Seated next to him is Etẽpa. (Photo by Laura Graham, 1984.)

represent the dream activities as Warodi reported them. They discussed their body paint, for example, as the ancestors had done. They chose designs to replicate those the immortals wore in the dream. With these designs, as Warodi's brother Sibupa pointed out, the performers would *be* the immortals themselves.

The elders then summoned three of the community's young men. With body paint and *buriti* palm (*Mauritia* sp.) fiber robes they metamorphosed the three into the creator figures who had appeared in Warodi's dream as birds. Two young men, one from each exogamous moiety, represented the *parinaiʔa* creators. The elders blackened their eyes with charcoal, then encircled them with red *urucum* (*Bixa orellana* L.). With painted eyes, woven fiber robes, and headdresses, these two appeared as jabiru storks (*Jabiru mycteria*). This form, of all the transformations that the *parinaiʔa* underwent when making the creation, is the one Xavante associate with the creators' incarnation in the present time (*parinaiʔa* is the name of a wasp's nest, one of the creators' metamorphoses). To the oiled body of the third young man the elders applied just a bit of red paint, making him appear as the creator he represented. Outfitted in a palm-fiber robe, he too appeared in the form of a bird, as Warodi had envisioned him in his dream.[4]

When the creators were ready and the men, having completed their preparations, were well appointed with body paint, they summoned the women to join them. Once all the members of the community except small children, the sick, and the very old had assembled, Warodi led them through a rehearsal of his dreamed songs. Again he recounted his dream and prescribed their body paint so that their designs would conform to his vision. Supported by the other elders, Warodi was moving the members of the community toward a performance of his dream—a performance that would bring the voices and embodied images of the immortals and creators into the world of the living.

As the sun moved across the sky, the momentum of the preparatory activities increased. The participants immersed themselves in expressive behaviors—narrative, song, dance, and body decorating—and paved the way for their climactic transformation into the immortals of Warodi's dream. Accumulating over a period of eight hours, by 4:00 PM, when the preparations were complete, this momentum swept up the participants in its embrace. It carried them into the central plaza, the scene of the public performance, the climax of the day's events. In their bird costumes, the creator figures stood in the center of a large circle of dancers. Following Warodi's lead, those around them joined hands to sing and dance the three songs. As they sang and danced, the creator figures moved their arms in imitation of storks flapping their wings in flight. In performance the participants became the immortals of the dream. The performance crystallized the transformations that had been budding through various expressive practices rehearsed during the long day. The past merged with the present and the immortals lived through the actions of the living. Through their singing and dancing, the living brought the immortals into the present, into the realm of the living.

THE EXPRESSIVE PERFORMANCE OF DREAMS

This extraordinary performance, which took place soon after I returned to Pimentel Barbosa for the second time, forms the centerpiece of this book. It was clear to me that Warodi had orchestrated this event in part because I was there; through it he was attempting to teach me, an outsider, something he considered tremendously important. But he could not have succeeded in enlisting the support of the other elders and members of the community had he designed the performance only for my benefit. The others invested themselves in this performance because it partook of the content and conventions of other significant performances. For the participants, this unique performance took on meanings through the expressive practices embedded within it: *da-ñoʔre* song and dance, narrative, and myth telling. In turn, my own understanding of the performance depended upon comprehending the meanings of these same expressive practices in this and other contexts. Developing an understanding of the central role of these expressive practices in Xavante society and of the processes by which meanings unfold in performance—in this performance particularly—is the objective of this book. Chapters 2 and 3 provide a historic and ethnographic matrix for the ensuing chapters, which are devoted to analysis of the expressive practices embedded in the dream rehearsal and in the performance itself.

I take the performance as well as the preparations for it as a whole, that is, as an event in which, as Richard Bauman and Richard Schechner have stressed, rehearsal and performance must be considered together as a single complex.[5] In preparation for the performance, Warodi shared his dream—in the form of narrative, myth telling, song, and dance—with members of the community. Then, in the performance, these people re-presented Warodi's dream. Through this process, Warodi moved his dream experience outward, so that it could be experienced by others.[6] Both in performance and in making arrangements for it, Warodi socialized his dream.

In considering the forms in which individuals such as Warodi choose to publicly re-present their dreams I envisage dream sharing as a form of social action. In a very Bakhtinian sense the representational forms that circulate within communities influence the ways in which "inner experiences" such as dreams are externalized. These publicly circulating expressive forms perhaps even influence the way in which dream experience is brought forth to consciousness (see Chapter 4). My approach to dreams reflects a shift that is currently under way in the anthropological orientation toward dreams, a shift away from the focus on content—the result of the dominant Freudian perspective—toward a perspective that views dreams as communicative process.[7] This reorientation enables me to consider instances of dream sharing as potentially multifunctional expressive acts. For example, dream sharing may establish as well as reflect a particular form of trust or bond between participants, as in the case of Western psychoanalysis or that of young Xavante males who sing and dance each other's dreams. Or (though certainly not exclusively) dream sharing may be a way of establishing social prestige, a way of spreading more of oneself throughout a community.

Warodi's dream performance and the preparations for it showcased expressive practices which Xavante use to establish individual and social identities, beliefs about the world, and understandings of ways of acting in it. These practices foster a sense of cultural continuity in the midst of changing historical circumstances. The expressive forms *da-ñoʔre* song and dance, narrative, and myth telling that are embedded within the dream performance are means by which participants construct and express their sense of identity as individuals and as members of social groups. Moreover, through the movements and sounds of these expressive forms, participants create and reaffirm their links to those who have performed them in the past. Performance thus engenders a subjective sense of continuity. By linking themselves to past performers, individuals sense the continuity of a distinctive Xavante identity, a way of being and acting in the world. Shaped by and reaffirmed through expressive performance, this feeling of continuity enables Xavante to experience a sense of control over their present circumstances. Furthermore, this sense of connection with the past empowers them as they move into the future.

In dealing with expressive practices, it is important to distinguish between the content of a message or expression and discourse practice, the form in which a message is expressed in the process of cultural transmission. Along with a number of other scholars of language use and expressive performance,[8] I am concerned with actual utterances—instances of language use and song, for example—which I consider to be, in themselves, forms of social action. This perspective differs from those that focus on a cognitive point of view which posits that cultural transmission involves passing on a set of shared beliefs, values, and ideas about the world which are understood to be embodied within the content of a message—for example, in the content of a myth. The message is considered to be of utmost importance, while the form in which the message is communicated is hardly relevant.

In contrast, by adopting a perspective that focuses on discourse practice I am able to posit that processes of cultural transmission involve the replication of discursive forms over time. The practice of passing a set of discourse forms from one generation to the next promotes feelings of cultural continuity, even though the messages encoded in those forms may change over time. This is not to say that the content of a message is unimportant; the point is to emphasize the significant part that discursive practice plays in processes of cultural transmission. The continuity of *form* promotes feelings of persistence, even in societies such as the Xavante, who, as we shall see in Chapter 2, are experiencing dramatic changes in their traditional ways of life.

Moreover, by directing our analytical attention to actual instances of discourse and expressive behavior, rather than exclusively to messages that are disembodied from the contexts of their expression, we can see that the process of constructing identities, beliefs, values, and ideas about the world is situated in expressive acts, the most important of which are discursive acts.[9] Indeed, it is only possible to speak of culture, conceived of as a system of meanings, social categories, beliefs, values, and myths, as having an existence independent of its expressive manifestations insofar as culture is understood to be the history of past expressive performances that persist in memory. The "system" is a precipitate of past expressive performances. It is the sediment of past performances that settles in memory, creating the illusion of a systematized set of beliefs, values, ideas, and so forth. But the "system" itself is ephemeral, dependent on actual behaviors for its very existence. The Saussurean system of *langue*, for example, is no more than a precipitate of instances of *parole* (speech) that have sedimented in memory.

An individual is able to interpret instances of discourse and expressive performance by making associations, or interpretive moves, between behaviors within the immediate context, as well as between those and others she or he has experienced over time. To analyze the processes by which social actors make these interpretive moves, imbuing actions and instances of discourse with meaning, I adopt the framework of Peircian semiotics, building on the work of scholars such as Michael Silverstein and Greg Urban, who introduced and integrated this paradigm into studies of language and other cultural phenomena.[10] According to Peircian semiotics, social actors interpret signs based on perceived relationships between a sign and its object, or meaning.[11] The notion of "interpretive moves" or of a similar one, that of "networks of association," is not specific to those who work in the Peircian tradition.[12] However, the Peircian framework, as it has been taken up to explain the processes by which instances of discourse operate as complex, multifunctional signs, offers a more analytically specific paradigm than do other interpretive approaches.

The interpretive frameworks that individuals build up over the course of their lives through exposure to meaningful behaviors provide them with the ability to imbue actions, words, and material objects with significance. A framework's existence and particular form depend on the individual's history as an interpreter of signs. Each individual thus possesses a unique interpretive frame that is the product of her or his historical experience. Notably, one's ability to interpret meaningful behaviors changes over time. Histories of experience differentiate young people from their seniors, men from women, and, of course, any individual from another. No one in a society interprets an action in exactly the same way as anyone else.[13] Nevertheless, to the degree to which individuals share similar histories of exposure to and interpretation of meaningful behaviors, they share similar interpretive frameworks. Social memories depend on shared histories of experience, and these inevitably vary within any social group.[14] Among the Xavante, young and old, men and women have different histories of exposures and different ways of understanding what it means to be and act in the world, different ways of conceiving of and experiencing reality. And these are different from mine.

To have meaning for participants, each new performance necessarily reflects the history of expressive performances that have come before it. Performance in this sense is, as Richard Schechner points out, "never for the first time." [15] Yet simultaneously, each new performance is itself a creative act; its essence lies in processes of decontextualization and recontextualization, in the dynamic tension between the "ready-made" and the emergent. [16] Each instance of expressive performance therefore opens up the possibility for change.

By focusing on specific performances we can examine processes of change and creative adaptation as they take place at very micro levels. For example, by focusing on instances of myth telling we comprehend that a myth is not an entity that has an abstract existence within the mind apart from its connection with past tellings. A myth has a life that is born through its tellings. And each new telling has the potential to vary, even in the most minute way, details of previous tellings. Each telling teases the tensions between decontextualizing and recontextualizing discourse, the processes of extracting ready-made discourse from a previous context and fitting it to another. This tension, as Richard Bauman asserts, is an essential mechanism of social and cultural continuity. [17] Chapters 4 through 6 present microanalyses of the expressive forms Warodi embeds in the dream performance to reveal meanings that participants draw upon in their interpretation of the dream performance. They also demonstrate that Warodi and his collaborators employ these forms to achieve personal as well as community goals.

In Chapter 6, for example, I examine details of the myth tellings that Warodi embeds, or recontextualizes, in his dream narrative. I compare these with other instances of myth telling to illustrate ways in which Warodi varies his tellings according to features of the context, particularly the audience. This focus on details of the performance reveals that, while certain elements appear to form a repeatable core from one telling to the next, there is a good deal of variability between one performance and another. Elders present at Warodi's telling contribute individual perspectives to the polyvocal development of the tale and even contest details of Warodi's telling. The variation in opinion among participants, as well as the variation that exists between tellings by the same narrator, illustrates that a myth is neither a static nor a homogeneous entity. Myths are dynamic precisely because they come into existence through tellings. Tellings enable people to change and adapt their myth tellings to new circumstances, to recontextualize them over time, and to attain personal goals through telling. Yet at the same time, the act of telling, replicating the repeatable forms of past tellings, creates a subjective, albeit dynamic, sense of continuity.

Dreamed songs, *da-ño?re* (Chapter 4), clearly manifest the tension between existing forms that circulate within a community and the creative innovation of individual composition. The fashion in which the songs are learned and then individually reshaped to express individual subjectivity illustrates Vološinov's proposed dialectic between inner and outer speech.[18] Even though individual compositions change over time, repetition of the forms in regular performances lends sonic continuity to the Xavante soundscape. Yet, since each new composition is an individual creation, reflecting the subjectivity of individual composers, the performances manifest the dynamic elasticity of Xavante expressive forms.

Because Warodi's dream performance reflects a history of past myth tellings, representations of dreams, song and dance performances, and men's council gatherings in which narrative and discussion occurred (Chapter 6), participants were able to fill the performance with meanings. It therefore expresses continuity. But this performance was also a creative adaptation, designed in part to address me and to harness the technological potential that Warodi and others perceived to inhere in my ethnographic tools—in my ability to record the performance with my camera and tape recorder and in writing. The performance thus expresses a creative response to new opportunities—and new means—of promoting continuity. This ability to adapt creatively to new circumstances is the force which has enabled the Xavante to maintain a sense of themselves over time; it has given them their remarkable sense of cultural continuity. Creative adaptation is, in fact, the key to their very cultural survival, their ability to continue as Xavante forever.

WARODI

I first met Warodi during my initial field trip to the Xavante in 1981–1982. Warodi, through the personal relationship I developed with him and the members of his family, helped to shape my fieldwork. Doing fieldwork involves a great deal of negotiation between the ethnographer and members of the community where she chooses to work.[19] This negotiation is itself an ongoing process that begins the minute she arrives in the community and lasts until the end of the field stay. In many cases it continues beyond. Most of the choices I made involved Warodi in one way or another. His own personal, spiritual, and political objectives and the ways in which he endeavored to accommodate these through my presence in the community influenced the course of my research and ultimately my current understanding of Xavante and Xavante worldviews. Furthermore, owing to my early difficulties with government agents in the area, without Warodi's support during my first field trip I might not have been able to continue my research in Pimentel Barbosa.

When I met Warodi he was a calm, peaceful elderly man. He was the

eldest son of the formidable leader Apöwẽ, the man responsible for the
Xavante's first peaceful contacts with representatives of Brazilian national
society in 1946. Just a few years later, when David Maybury-Lewis came
to conduct the first anthropological research among the Xavante, Warodi's father took him under his wing. Maybury-Lewis, who knew Warodi
as a young man, described him as a rather surly, cunning character. In
fact, Maybury-Lewis suspected that Warodi might have been responsible
for the disappearance of his prized *wamñoro* dance masks, although Warodi never confessed to it.[20] But the Warodi I came to know had grown
into a mature leader and respected guardian of historical, spiritual, and
cultural knowledge.

Xavante as well as Brazilians regard Warodi as an astute political leader
of his time. In the late 1970s Warodi led the Xavante of Pimentel Barbosa
in an impressive battle to reclaim lands that had been illegally swept from
their jurisdiction. As the community's representative, he made multiple
arduous trips to the capital, Brasília, to negotiate with officials of the government Indian agency, Fundação Nacional do Indio (FUNAI). When ultimately these negotiations proved futile, the Xavante of Pimentel Barbosa
attacked and burned ranches in their area. Warodi then summoned representatives and leaders from the other Xavante reserves; together these
men cut down a line of trees through a forested area to demarcate the
reserve's contested border according to Xavante claims.[21] The gathering
Warodi convened constituted the first politically coordinated action of
representatives from the different Xavante reserves and cemented Warodi's reputation as a bold political actor.

In July 1982, medical doctors diagnosed Warodi with prostate cancer.
David and Pia Maybury-Lewis, who were visiting the community at the
time, accompanied Warodi to Goiânia, where he underwent surgery for
this condition.[22] After his operation, Warodi continued to play a leading
role in the community's political and ceremonial life, although he did not
have the energy he once had. In 1985, his younger brother Milton, who
had acted as one of Warodi's assistants (known as "secretaries" in Portuguese), replaced him as the community's officially recognized leader for
dealings with FUNAI and as manager of financial affairs.

Even though following his illness Warodi rarely attended the evening
men's council, he continued to be a central figure in community politics.
From morning until dusk men visited Warodi's house to discuss community business and private matters with him. Warodi's two assistants, Milton and Sõrupredu, came daily to report on the past evening's men's council and to plan for the upcoming session. Of all the visitors, Warodi's
closest classificatory brother, Sibupa, and his wife's brother, Aiʔrere, came
most frequently. Lying on their backs by Warodi's side for hours—the
way men often spend much of their day talking together—they discussed

political affairs and business issues related to FUNAI. These elders also shared their intimate thoughts and dreams.

As I came to know Warodi better, I began to appreciate his wisdom and spiritual qualities as well as his political astuteness. Warodi exhibited magnificent knowledge of Xavante history and the past; his speech resonated with information about the creation of the world. Warodi had so immersed himself in discourse of the Xavante's past that he filtered his experience of the present through a template of his and his community's relationship to the first creators, the architects of the Xavante creation. For example, when he and his brother Sibupa discussed government plans to asphalt the road that runs next to the reserve's western border, Warodi spoke of the ways this project fit into the first creators' work. One of his nephews aptly characterized him as "one whose head seems always to be with the creators, the *höimanaʔuʔö* [always living] ancestors."

FIELDWORK AS COLLABORATIVE PROCESS

When I planned my research among the Xavante, I envisioned a project that would focus on instances of discourse as they emerged in the context of ongoing activities. David Maybury-Lewis's descriptions of "antiphonal speech" in men's council meetings piqued my curiosity; I wondered what this could be, what it sounded like, and what social information speakers communicated using it. I was curious to know what other linguistic resources speakers in this small-scale Gê society had to draw upon and how these might compare with speech patterns ethnographers had observed in other Gê groups.[23]

The groundwork laid by previous studies of the Xavante, particularly the solid foundation provided by studies in Xavante social organization, made work with the Xavante attractive.[24] Moreover, working on discourse among a Gê group had special appeal, for it promised an ideal potential for comparative analyses, as the Harvard Central Brazil Project and subsequent studies of Gê social organization have demonstrated.[25] Possibilities for comparative analyses in the area of expressive culture were ripening at the time I was making plans for my research. Desidério Aytai was completing a pioneering study of formal aspects of the Xavante's musical system, and Anthony Seeger was working on the analysis of Suyá (Northern Gê) music. Greg Urban was engaged in studies of the discourse patterns of the Xokleng, a Southern Gê group.[26] Work in the area of discourse and expressive performance among the Xavante, members of the central branch of the Gê, would enable us to develop a comparative profile of expressive performance and discursive practices.

I became frustrated, however, when, after I had been in the community only a short time, Warodi began to summon me to bring the tape recorder so that he could make a speech or tell a story. My enthusiasm for documenting naturally occurring discourse led me initially to discount anything that appeared to be contrived. At first I stubbornly resisted his invitations, or I made recordings without appreciating that these discourses had exceptional value. I then came to realize that Warodi was adapting a traditional pattern of interaction to conform to a new situation and to my technology. As a Xavante father summons his son to his sleeping mat in the afternoon to tell him some bit of family history or a tale, Warodi called me to impart some of his knowledge to me. He wanted me to record it, write it, and tell others about his thoughts and his community.

Eventually I found myself soliciting tales from Warodi and other elders, both men and women, in order to understand the many oblique references to traditional tales that appeared elsewhere in naturally occurring speech and in the dream narrative in particular. Ultimately I realized that Warodi's and my own objectives complemented each other. Warodi's attitude toward me and my work offered me opportunities to pursue my goals. For example, when I asked him questions to advance my comprehension of the dream narrative or other behaviors, he frequently broke into narratives as a way of answering my queries. Similarly, my work tape-recording and writing complimented his objectives. Over time, in subtle ways, we developed an understanding that accommodated both of our needs. I may have been an outsider in the community, but I was an outsider whose interests allied with those of the community's elders, especially with Warodi's. Relative to most other non-Xavante, I was regarded by members of the community as an insider. My status, like that of many anthropologists, was something akin to that of an outside-insider.[27] Ever since Warodi and the members of his household adopted me in 1982, I have been considered a member of his family. By extension I belong to a kin network and an age-set. When I return to the community I continue to live in Warodi's household and I increasingly maneuver through daily life using Xavante.

Since I tape-recorded discourse in all situations, from music and formal speech to everyday conversations, as well as ambient sounds—crickets and frogs, for example—it must have appeared that I possessed endless supplies of cassette tapes and batteries. I always arrived in Pimentel Barbosa tremendously laden. My luggage invariably weighed in on the extraordinarily heavy side; besides recording equipment and, later, solar panels, my burden consisted of coffee and sugar. Clearly, I possessed the means to document a great deal of the community's oral traditions.

Warodi and all the members of the community encouraged me in my efforts to learn and speak Xavante and took pride in my progress as a speaker. Warodi was especially impressed with my ability to write the language. Having dealt extensively with FUNAI government bureaucracy—whose officials display copious amounts of paperwork to indigenous leaders from oral societies to justify their policies—Warodi attached tremendous significance to writing and to written documents. He knew the power of his signature on written documents. Nearly every afternoon he pushed open the thatch of his house to form a window, took out a carefully guarded notebook and pen, and practiced signing his name.

Once I began to build up a corpus of tape-recorded discourse, the problem arose as to who would be appropriate to assist me in the task of making translations. This was not a straightforward issue: Warodi and I, along with other members of the community, had to negotiate over the various candidates. Especially at the outset, I needed to work with an individual who had at least a reasonable command of Portuguese. This requirement narrowed the pool of candidates significantly, for in Pimentel Barbosa only a handful of young men (and no women) speak Portuguese with any fluency. During my first trip Warodi proposed two young men who refused to help. They belonged to a group whom the local FUNAI post chief at that time had, for reasons discussed in the Preface, influenced against me and my work. Their lack of cooperation left Warodi and me frustrated and dismayed. No individual capable of assisting agreed to help me transcribe and translate a myth performance Warodi and the members of his family staged in 1982.[28]

Later, when I left Pimentel Barbosa, I found someone who was enthusiastic, willing, and able to do this type of work. This person was Lino Tsereʔubudzi (Fig. 2), a youth who was completing his junior high school education with FUNAI sponsorship in the Brazilian town of Barra do Garças (see Map 2), the seat of the regional FUNAI administration. Lino is a Xavante intellectual who, from the outset, enjoyed grappling with the puzzles and problems we encountered. Lino, however, is from São Marcos, the Catholic mission village that is a historic rival to Pimentel Barbosa. Because of this rivalry, Warodi had mixed emotions when I returned to him with Lino's translation of the myth performance. It displeased him that the work had been done by someone from São Marcos. At the same time, he was delighted that the work had been completed and the narrative was recorded in writing.

Warodi met with his brothers and affines to discuss this problem. These men, like Warodi, were distressed that their sons and other community youth had refused to help. Ultimately they agreed that I should continue to work with Lino and justified their position on the basis of kinship: Lino could be classified as a brother's son. After that, Lino called Warodi ñimama ãmo (my other father, or uncle, FB), and Warodi called him aibö (man), the appropriate term of address for an adult classificatory son. Lino continued to work with me from 1982 to 1987, and during the course of this research Lino and Warodi developed an independent relationship of mutual respect. Warodi came to appreciate Lino's talent as an

2. Lino Tsereʔubudzi of the comparatively Westernized community of São Marcos, shopping with his son in the Brazilian city of Goiânia. (Photo by Laura Graham, 1987.)

interpreter and Lino continued to value Warodi's wisdom and eloquence. The three of us, as well as others, constantly engaged in dialogue over our translations.

In translation sessions with assistants I used a special technique that linguistic anthropologists are now adopting in field research. This involved two tape recorders: one to play back instances of the dream narrative and other contextually situated discourse; the other to record my assistants' explanations and their responses to questions I posed about language use as we listened to the in-context recordings. In this way I recorded my assistants' translations and explanations of what was happening with the language, as well as their responses to elicited sentences. Sometimes there were discrepancies between what my assistants told me was correct and what actually occurred in practice, in the naturally occurring speech recorded on tape. I looked for regularities in the occurrence of such discrepancies to determine elements of Xavante speech patterning that assistants could not describe, at least not at the outset. The technique helped me to identify such significant pragmatic phenomena as Warodi's pronominal switching in the dream narrative (Chapter 5) and patterns of honorific speech. This kind of information has immense significance for the interpretation of the multiple meanings within any body of discourse. Not surprisingly, it is the sort of information that ethnographers who look *through* discourse—to discover underlying meanings—instead of *at* discourse itself easily miss.[29]

Although I worked steadily with Lino, the situation with other assistants continued in flux during my subsequent trips to Brazil from 1984 through 1987. Warodi and I continually discussed our options. Happily, by 1984 the previously unsupportive post chief had departed. The young men who had been hostile toward my work came forward with generous offers of assistance. Despite their willingness to help, I still had difficulties finding assistants in Pimentel Barbosa who could work on a more or less consistent basis. By 1986, those individuals who spoke the best Portuguese were frequently absent, accompanying leaders on trips to Brasília to act as translators in dealings with FUNAI. At the same time, internal factionalism created problems in identifying appropriate help for particular translations. One young man, for example, agreed to help with translations only if we worked on narratives and speeches by his faction's leaders. Another, whose father rivaled Warodi for leadership, refused to translate Warodi's narratives.

Together Lino and I completed the translations of the majority of Warodi's dream narrative. I followed him to Brasília in 1986 and then, in 1987, to Goiânia, where he attended high school and worked for FUNAI as a nurse's assistant. In Goiânia, we added Warodi's two nephews from Pimentel Barbosa, Cipassé and Jurandir, also students in Brazilian secondary schools, to our team.[30] During this period Warodi and Sibupa visited frequently to counsel their nephews. In Goiânia, Warodi and Sibupa stayed with me. During their visits, or else on my regular visits to Pimentel Barbosa, Lino and I went over the translations with them. We posed questions about the narrative and performance that we had saved up since our last collective discussion. We also enlisted the help of other elders who occasionally visited Goiânia for health care or administrative reasons. In this way the endeavor of translating the dream narrative evolved as a collaborative process.

DISCOURSES OF IMMORTALITY

Gradually I began to appreciate the strength of Warodi's desire to share his knowledge of the world and of the creation with me. Perhaps because of his position within the life cycle, perhaps because he had no sons and I, as his androgynous, foreign, adopted daughter, was more "male-like" than the other women of his household, perhaps because of his attitude toward the dramatic changes the Xavante are currently experiencing as a result of their increasing contact with the outside world and his perception of me as a sympathetic liaison, or perhaps because of a combination of these factors, my understanding of his view of the world became for Warodi a mission.

In an oral culture such as Xavante knowledge passes from one generation to the next through narrative. When there is no one to listen and remember, the knowledge ceases. By passing his knowledge to me, someone who had the ability to commit the oral to writing, it seemed that Warodi could, through the printed medium, continue the life of his words and his memory forever. For Warodi, the tape recordings I made and the translations he anticipated offered a means of preserving his knowledge and memory for future generations. Even though the printed medium, as literary theorist Michael Warner argues, does not in itself entail a natural teleology, it may give the appearance of immutability.[31] Similarly, as reader response criticism and literary critics have shown, neither does it generate fixed or homogeneous interpretations.[32] Yet to Warodi, the written word seemed to offer the promise of perdurability; its material form extended the potential for its content to earn an eternal existence.

My presence appeared to provide Warodi with ideal means for preserving his knowledge. It also offered him opportunities to express himself to the outside world. He hoped that through my work, he, as well as the members of his community, would be recognized by the outside world as the authentic descendants of the first creators. Warodi wished to position his people within a global context. He frequently ended speeches by exhorting me to "take his words across the ocean" so that people there could learn of the Xavante. To become known to the world outside as the descendants of the first creators and to have others know how his people have been neglected were goals I could help Warodi attain by writing down his words and divulging his thoughts. These are, among others, messages situated within the dream performance.

Above all, Warodi believed that, if preserved in the form of written narratives, his knowledge, and thereby some part of himself, could become immortal. If tape-recorded and written, Warodi's tellings of the first creators might remain—indeed, continue to be passed on—as he told them. For Warodi, the written word seemed to offer a way to perpetuate the transmission of his voice long after he was gone. Moreover, through the written word he might communicate with people he would never know. For Warodi, I could become a *griot*, one who tells the tale of another's life and contributes to his memory.[33] Notably, this goal is not unique to Warodi: it is characteristic of Xavante men who belong to the senior age grade. The quest for immortality motivates elders to pass on their memories to the youth; through these tellings they promote the dynamic continuity that enables the Xavante to continue "forever Xavante."

Well after we had completed the dream narrative translation and I had contemplated its wondrous complexities for some time, I began to understand something Warodi told me during my first visit. Sitting on the sleeping mat next to his bed, he whispered to me that he had received a new name from the immortal creators in a dream. That name was *tsiʔutõri õ* (never ending), and he asked me to write it for him. With this name he described himself as one of the *höimanaʔuʔö* (always living).

Warodi's interest in my work helped guide me toward a deeper understanding of his view of the world and the Xavante's place in it. His direction helped shed light on the expressive behaviors by which Xavante construct their worldviews. Because individuals engage in different expressive practices appropriate to their gender and life-cycle phase, these practices vary for individuals and social groups within the society. As we examine the expressive practices of the dream performance in the chapters that follow, it will become clear that Warodi harnessed them in ways appropriate to his position in the life cycle. With them he endeavored to do his best in the interests of the community as well as for himself.

At the end of 1987 Warodi became ill with what we thought was a simple case of pneumonia. Despite his illness he continued to work patiently with me, answering my remaining questions and recounting parts of the creators' tales, *höimanaʔuʔö watsuʔu*, that I had yet to adequately comprehend. Weak and thin voiced, he devoted a good deal of his remaining energy to reaching the end of our collaborative endeavor. During these tellings, perhaps among his last, his wan face became animated. A strong and determined individual, he persisted in his effort to make his dream and part of himself accessible, first to me and ultimately to others. When we completed our work in December 1987, I returned to the United States concerned that Warodi had pneumonia but confident that he was still strong. I looked forward to seeing him soon in another, yet unscheduled visit. But Warodi died the following month, in January 1988. Now, Warodi's memory lives on through the tellings of his life and in tales of the creators' world he inhabits. It is my hope that this book will contribute to Warodi's immortality. Through it his words and memory, and thus Warodi himself, live on.

2

Descendants of the First Creators

Warodi:	I'm not certain
	I'm not certain you know
	I'm not certain you know
	ã
	how
Aiʔrere:	I don't know
Warodi:	how ã
	how
	how ã
	Xavante always
	Xavante always
	for the Xavante
	for the Xavante
	for us to continue living
	for us to continue living
	by what means the Xavante will continue forever Xavante

by that, by that, according to their work
   their work for the Xavante
that [work was] for the Xavante
   for the Xavante they [taught] foods
      first taught foods
      they first taught foods
with this
with this they then
   they then gathered together
      gathered together
for the Xavante,
for the Xavante, they
   they [taught] according to their teaching

ah
then their work
  is the *cara* [root]
    cara
    cara
they
they
they thought carefully about their work
  thought carefully
  ah the Xavante's
    the Xavante's food
    the Xavante's food
they taught the foods according to their wisdom . . .
they united their work
then first they created the dog
then ah they created whatever
ah
ah
ah foods
foods
then they created the *ubdi* roots
then they created the *cara* roots
then

Sibupa: they thought carefully about their work
Warodi: the jaguar
they created the jaguar
then well
ah
then they created *babaçu* nuts [*Orbignya* sp.]
then they created *macauba* nuts
then
yes they created everything
then the bees
well
the bees re[d]
  red bees they also created
then they created [dog]fish
then they created the insects
then they created the ants
then
next they taught the jabiru stork
  they taught [it]

then
    they left off before finishing all they wanted
      the Xavante
      the Xavante
        because the Xavante killed them [1]
ah
well
their work
their work
  I know it well
  I know it well
using this wisdom they worked continuously
it didn't cease, the work for the Xavante
the work for the Xavante didn't cease

Sibupa: that's the word

It is August 1984, and Warodi is telling the elders of his dream, of his meeting with the creators, of learning their songs and their thoughts for the Xavante to continue forever. To continue as Xavante is to continue to inhabit the world the immortals created for the Xavante, a world populated by dogs, jaguars, fish, bees, insects, and jabiru storks. To continue forever Xavante is to continue to abide in a world that abounds with *ubdi* and *cara* roots, the Xavante's food. It is also a world in which Xavante sing and dance to remain fit and healthy. This is the world Warodi and the other elder participants bring to life in their preparations for the dream enactment. In words that recount the immortals' creative innovations, they paint the Xavante world. This is the world in which they will remain forever Xavante.

On November 22, 1981, when I first arrived among the Xavante, I was taken aback to see large tractors and immense harvesters working extensive monocrop fields near the Kuluene villages, the first Xavante villages I set eyes on. I saw small children at play climbing up huge mountains of stacked burlap sacks, each containing sixty kilograms of white rice. At several houses women sat on discarded burlap sacks or tractor tires to avoid contact with the bare ground. Other tires decorated thatched roofs, safeguarding against fierce rainy-season winds that threaten to wrench thatch coverings from their scaffolds. Empty oil cans and discarded truck tires lay about the outside cooking areas and in front of houses.

As I scanned the village I saw young women near many houses bent over hollowed log mortars. They were pounding rice to remove its husks, producing the rhythmic pulsings that I heard resounding throughout the village. At other houses women tended huge pots over cooking fires. As their contents of white rice and water rose to a boil, milky bubbles frothed and overflowed into the fires. Night fell as a tractor rumbled into the village and around the plaza, stopping at about every third house in the horseshoe-shaped arc so that women riding back from their fields in the trailer could dismount and carry their heavy loads of garden produce to homes nearby.

This scene represented quite a departure from that of the seminomadic hunter-gatherers I'd read about in David Maybury-Lewis's accounts of the Xavante as they lived less than thirty years before. With the exception of planting some maize (*Zea mays*), beans (*Phaseolus* sp.), and squash (*Cucurbita* sp.)—which require virtually no tending—those earlier Xavante, according to Maybury-Lewis, abhorred agriculture and thwarted all attempts on the part of the government Indian agents to get them to adopt a sedentary cultivator's life-style.[2] Certainly I had expected change. I knew that ranchers had invaded Xavante lands and deforested huge tracts for agricultural development and cattle grazing. But I thought the ranchers had been removed.

Before me was a staggering view of twentieth-century mechanized agriculture, complete with massive machines and sophisticated technology. The image was different from anything I had imagined. Less than four decades earlier Xavante had been hurling war clubs and shooting bows and arrows at the huge and terrifying mechanical birds that overflew their villages prior to their first peaceful contact. The world I took in clashed head-on with the portrait Warodi later depicted in his narratives. How did his vision of the creation accommodate the tractors, pesticides, fertilizers, oil, and tire changes of the world I saw before me?

"YOU ALL ARE THE DESCENDANTS OF THE FIRST CREATOR"

> here are the descendants of the first chief
> the descendants of the first chief
> the descendants[3]

Over the past two and a half centuries Xavante peoples have endured a series of momentous disruptions which they have confronted with remarkable power. This power is sustained by their formidable sense of cultural integrity and feelings of continuity with the past. Since the mid-eighteenth century Xavante lives have been repeatedly disrupted by invasions of colonists and settlers, capitalist commercial ventures, and, most recently—in the late 1970s and 1980s—by the enormous, government-sponsored agricultural project that took me aback on my first visit to the Xavante. These disruptions have threatened Xavante's claim to land, their economy, and their way of life. Nevertheless, despite the magnitude of these events, Xavante maintain an invincible sense of identity and feeling of control over historical processes. This sense of identity and control has fueled the Xavante's extraordinary resistance to Western domination over the last two and a half centuries. Now, it empowers them to deal with the events they confront as they move forward into the twenty-first century.

The Xavante's remarkable sense of agency in relation to historical processes is localized in expressive practices, and particularly in discursive practices. These practices engender a powerful sense of identity that enables participants to feel their continuity with the past and with the almighty power of the celebrated first creators. By linking themselves to the creators, literally the "always living" (*höimanaʔuʔö: höimana* [to live], -*ʔuʔö* [always]), through expressive media, the Xavante perpetuate a remarkable sense of superiority. After all, the first creators made the world for the Xavante before they worked for any other group.

This sense of self and continuity is kindled and rekindled through expressive performances which, in both form and content, generate feelings of connectedness with the past. In a discussion surrounding the dream narrative, for example, the elder Etẽpa criticizes for their naiveté a group of young men who are uncertain about participating in the rehearsal. Their hesitation, he explains, lies in their ignorance of family history and of their relationship to the creators of Warodi's dream. Had these young men, his sons-in-law, lain down by their fathers' sides "to learn the stories of our lives," Etẽpa explained, they would know that the members of his family are the descendants of the first creators. Had his brothers-in-law told their sons about his family, they would know that here, living in the present in the community of Pimentel Barbosa, are the creators' grandchildren.

> and how?
> and how are you going to know?
> and how are you all going to know?
> do you [lie] by your fathers' sides?
> do you lie down by your fathers' sides?
> of all things!
> you all, my brothers-in-law, you need to learn our family's stories
> you think your fathers don't know anything
> do you lie next to them?
> do you, to learn the stories of our lives?

[you should say:]
"these, all my in-laws, are the descendants of the first creator who are living
all my sons-in-law who are intelligent, they are the creators' grandchildren"
if it were like this you all would know
you all don't know anything

Through their expressive discursive practices—lying by their fathers' sides listening to stories of the past, performing songs and dances, and recounting narratives—Xavante foster an empowering sense of continuity that engenders a feeling of control over historical processes. Yet from an external point of view, a descriptive one focused on events recorded in Western historical documentation, journalistic accounts, and ethnographic writings, the Xavante's past appears chaotic, a series of externally dominated historical processes to which the Xavante have responded with flight, migration, capitulation, and active resistance. Nevertheless, in the community of Pimentel Barbosa at least, the view of historical processes perpetuated through discursive practice is one in which the Xavante, rather than being victims—the recipients of actions over time—are the initiators and controlling agents.

Just as the Xavante ancestors bring things into the world in the agent-centered accounts of the creation, so, too, in narratives of historical time Xavante portray themselves as prime movers who initiate and control the forces of change.[4] Xavante ancestors created the whites and initiated peaceful contact with representatives of Brazilian national society. Xavante translate this agent-centered model of action in the world into their contemporary relationships. In their dealings with FUNAI and its implementation of the rice project in the 1980s, for example, Xavante leaders ingeniously played a corrupt government bureaucracy at its own game, effectively manipulating the system to serve their own ends.

This chapter highlights the voices of Xavante from Pimentel Barbosa who articulate a subjective sense of continuity and control in the midst of what are, from an external point of view, identifiably chaotic historical circumstances. These voices discursively articulate a counterhegemonic interpretation of historical events: they represent their Xavante predecessors as agents, the masters of historical process. Given the sense of power and dignity Xavante express in the face of the changes outsiders have brought to their life-style, we can begin to appreciate the power of their discursive practices. Through these voices of Pimentel Barbosa we can also appreciate how members of this group of Xavante position themselves in relation to other Xavante communities. While subsequent chapters illustrate how this sense of control is engendered through form as well as content, here my objective is to demonstrate how my Xavante interlocutors explain their location in space and time through primarily referential means. By recontextualizing narratives that circulate within communities,[5] they harness a powerful cultural resource to accommodate new historical circumstances. These agent-centered interpretations form part of individuals' conscious understanding of the world and inform the ways they talk and think about their relations with other Xavante communities as well as Brazilian national society.

WHO ARE THE XAVANTE?

The first historical mention of the Xavante is their appearance in colonial documents of the late eighteenth century, which locate them in what is now part of the Brazilian state of Tocantins.[6] Colonial documents refer to them as Chavante or Xavante, a term, Maybury-Lewis notes, that peoples of European descent used to refer indiscriminately to indigenous groups in the Brazilian hinterland, and whose origin remains a mystery.[7]

"Xavante," however, is not the name the people whom it labels use when referring to themselves. Instead, they call themselves *aʔuwẽ*, a term which, like the autodenomination of many indigenous groups, can be glossed as "people." Warodi speaks of his people as *aʔuwẽ*, for example, in this excerpt from his dream-narrative:

> in the [dream] gathering
> I tried to fight
>> [for us] to remain always *aʔuwẽ*
>> [for us] to forever remain always *aʔuwẽ*

When dealing with outsiders, *aʔuwẽ* themselves now adopt the Portuguese name "Xavante." Today there are approximately six thousand Xavante who live on six reserves located between the Araguaia and Batovi rivers (the latter a tributary of the Xingu) in the eastern part of the Brazilian state of Mato Grosso (Map 1). I use the term Xavante following the *aʔuwẽ*'s self-representation to the outside.

The group most closely related to the Xavante, the Xerente, refer to themselves by the cognate term *akwẽ*. Together these two groups make up the central branch of the Gê linguistic family. Early colonial documents place the Xavante and Xerente in a contiguous stretch of territory between the Araguaia and Tocantins rivers in what is now the northern part of the Brazilian state of Tocantins. Historically, the two groups are thought to have been one people, although some debate exists regarding the exact time of their separation. Maybury-Lewis speculates that the separation

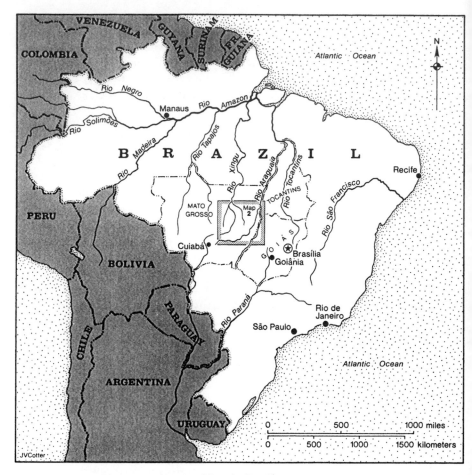

Map 1. Brazil.

occurred in the 1840s.[8] More recent research places it somewhat earlier, perhaps as early as the turn of the century, prior to the first colonial intrusions into the area.[9] It remains unclear whether, at the beginning of the nineteenth century, Xavante/Xerente were one people or maintained two distinct identities while occupying contiguous or a common territory. Whatever the case, their separation appears to have been complete by 1820.[10]

According to colonial documents, it was in this territory which the Xavante occupied either contiguously or in common with the Xerente that they first encountered peoples of European descent. Expeditions of mineral prospectors and *bandeirante* slave hunters entered the region as early as the late sixteenth century and continued their exploits throughout the seventeenth century.[11] *Bandeirantes* took captives to mines in the state of Minas Gerais and to coastal colonies in Rio de Janeiro, Bahia, Pernambuco, and São Paulo. Missionaries also arrived in Goiás from Pará seeking to capture Indians to populate their missions.

Warodi and other Xavante, however, speak of a time when their ancestors resided by the sea, "near Rio de Janeiro," where they first encountered the white people.[12] In fact, according to Xavante of Pimentel Barbosa, their forebear, the "one who made the sea" (*öwawẽ-ʔwa*),[13] created both the sea and the whites. "We are not from here," young Roberto explained. "The *aʔuwẽ* were in the east, where the sun rises. The *aʔuwẽ* created the sea, the planet was small, there was only one small stream."

As Warodi told it, *öwawẽ-ʔwa*, a pre-initiate resident of the bachelors' hut, asked his mother one too many times for cracked *babaçu* coconut to rub in his hair. Irritated by his incessant demands, she cut off her clitoris and put it among the nuts she next gave to him.

Warodi: he chewed his mother's clitoris [substituted for a *babaçu* nut]
   from that his belly swelled TUUUU
   enormous!
   wow! it was huge, heavy

   he fell in the water
   there wasn't to be a sea
   there was only a small lake, or a river

   the water began to flow, KUUUU
   he was beneath a waterfall
    bent over on his knees
   [the noise] was like this, KWUUUU
   he was dragging himself along the path to the river

When his relatives came back to look for him, *öwawẽ-ʔwa* promised to make long hair as a remembrance only for them, since he was now going to live far away across the ocean. He made long hair for his relatives, giving the Xavante their long, brilliant black hair, but not for his selfish agemate companion, whom he fooled and turned into a toad. The next time his relatives returned to look for him the water was enormous, impassable. Far away, across the water were many whites, *öwawẽ-ʔwa*'s wife and children, and their clothes drying on a clothesline.

Warodi: it was then that the water grew
             that one, that one made the whites
             it was then that the whites began
             he created the unknown whites
             his name was Sereñi?ru

In the years following the 1722 discovery of mineral deposits in Goiás, prospectors arrived, mines were established, and *bandeirantes* stepped up their efforts to take captives. These intrusions prompted the Xavante to seek refuge in the hinterland. Eventually, in the 1770s, with the discovery of more rich deposits of minerals and ores, official policy opened the Araguaia to navigation, thereby promoting agricultural development in the area and necessitating a new government policy for dealing with Indians.[14] Accordingly, in 1774 the government instituted a system of *aldeamentos*, or controlled indigenous settlements, which affected thousands of Indians including the Javaé, Karajá, Acroá, Xacriabá, Kayapó, and eventually some Xavante. Xavante generally resisted government overtures to corral indigenous peoples into the *aldeamentos*. However, following violent clashes with settlers, some two thousand assented to living in the *aldeamento* Pedro III, known as Carretão, in exchange for subsistence. In Carretão, the *aldeamento* with the greatest concentration of Xavante, the population suffered a devastating epidemic of measles.[15]

By no means did all Xavante submit to the *aldeamento* system. According to Aracy Lopes da Silva, several groups maintained settlements near *aldeamentos* and provided safe haven for refugees who, beginning in the 1830s, fled forced labor, epidemics, and ill treatment.[16] In 1842, having completely abandoned the *aldeamentos*, Xavante groups launched attacks on settlers in the northern part of Goiás province, which they continued until the end of the nineteenth century. Throughout this period they maintained significant interrelations and formed military alliances with the Xerente against the colonial intruders.

Then, sometime in the mid-nineteenth century, as the number of settlers grew and commercial activity continued to increase, the Xavante began to move from their homeland in the province of Goiás. Fleeing the whites' intrusions, they migrated south and westward toward what is now the state of Mato Grosso. Meanwhile, the Xerente, acquiescing to colonial domination, remained in the east, where their descendants continue to live. As Lopes da Silva observes, "the Xavante constituted the group which rejected life with the whites" and, seeking self-determination, once again sought refuge from colonial domination.[17]

Amusedly, Warodi recalled what may have been the definitive separation between the Xavante and Xerente—the crossing of the Araguaia

River—in a story in which a fresh-water dolphin grew to enormous proportions.[18] The dolphin grew so large that it separated the group that had traversed the river from the group that had not yet made it across. Notably, unlike their telling of tales of the creation—the origin of Xavante foods or the white people—Warodi and others recounted this story of the separation from the Xerente only when I asked to hear it. Indeed, during the time I worked in Pimentel Barbosa, no one spontaneously recalled the separation from the Xerente as part of an interpretation of the group's present circumstances. In contrast, individuals such as Warodi frequently blended accounts of the creation into conversation about contemporary or recent historical events, blurring the distinction between what may be called mythic and historical forms of consciousness.[19] This suggests that the people of Pimentel Barbosa discursively situate themselves not in relation to their more distant relatives, the Xerente, but in relation to a "mythic" past as well as in relation to other contemporary Xavante groups. For people in Pimentel Barbosa, their historical relationship with the Xerente is not a focus of current identity.

Today, both men and women of Pimentel Barbosa legitimize themselves vis-à-vis other Xavante groups through references to the mythic past. Specifically they recall *their* descent from the first creators and *their* creation of the whites. Speakers deploy these attributes as markers of legitimacy to which, they point out, other Xavante groups have no claim. Significantly, their discourse focuses on their relationship to other Xavante groups with whom they compete for government resources. In Pimentel Barbosa, speakers bolster their claims to material resources through their agent-centered self-representations: as the creators of the whites, as the descendants of the first creators, and as the continuous occupants of the land in the area of the large historic village Tsõreprɛ, they are the true aʔuwẽ.

THE DIFFERENT XAVANTE: DESCENDANTS OF THE FIRST CREATORS VERSUS DESCENDANTS OF BEASTS

The Xavante group that crossed the Araguaia River some time in the second half of the nineteenth century consisted of a number of disparate factions united momentarily, as Ravagnani speculates, to increase their chances of conquering a new territory.[20] They settled in the area of the Rio das Mortes (Map 2), the region of the Serra do Roncador, and thus intruded on lands previously occupied by the Bororo and the Karajá. In this area they appear to have moved through a series of settlements, relocating after internal fighting and accusations of sorcery and finally settling in a large village known as Tsõreprɛ.[21] Lopes da Silva provisionally dates its occupation from the end of the nineteenth century to the end of the 1920s.

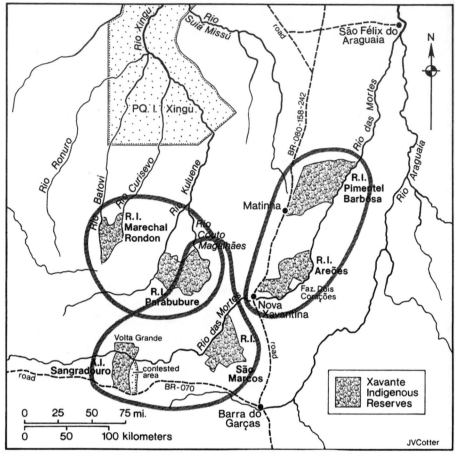

After Lopes da Silva (1986). Encircled areas indicate groupings of communities
in contemporary reserves.

Map 2. Area of Xavante Reserves.

Although individuals from other contemporary villages identify names of
villages prior to the occupation of Tsõreprε,[22] residents of Pimentel Barbosa focus on Tsõreprε as the original village of their predecessors who
traversed the Araguaia. Pimentel Barbosa's elder men situate Tsõreprε to
the north of Pimentel Barbosa on land now owned by ranchers.

According to Warodi, five age-sets were initiated in Tsõreprε before
"there was a great deal of killing with arrows and *uibrɔ* clubs."[23] From
there, various factions splintered off and the Xavante began to populate a
broad area between the Rio das Mortes on the east and the Kuluene River
on the west. Data I gathered in Pimentel Barbosa concerning the break-up

of Tsõrepre confirm Lopes da Silva's hypothesis that various Xavante groups have different versions of this epoch.[24] Warodi's account of Xavante movements and village locations in the immediate precontact period is, for example, most elaborate for the group that remained in the Rio das Mortes region. Lopes da Silva, on the other hand, recorded detailed accounts concerning the movements and settlements of Xavante groups who moved farther west. Warodi appears to collapse time and movements of groups distantly related to his own in the same way that Lopes da Silva's consultants appear to collapse the movements of those who remained in the Rio das Mortes vicinity.

In Warodi's version, three groups separated out from Tsõrepre. One group moved north and west toward the Suiá Missú River area. Another also moved westward into territory near the headwaters of the Couto Magalhães River, where they founded the village Parabubure. A third group, the forebears of those currently in Pimentel Barbosa, remained in the general area of Tsõrepre near the banks of the Rio das Mortes. Subsequent to their departure from Tsõrepre they moved between several village sites within the area. In contrast, Lopes da Silva's sketch of Xavante movements from Tsõrepre, based on sources from groups that moved farther west, indicates that the village of Tsõrepre fissioned in two stages. In any case, despite the variation in these accounts, it appears that all contemporary Xavante identify Tsõrepre as the focal ancestral village. From it groups departed to the west and northwest, eventually ending up in the region of the Couto Magalhães and Suyá Missú rivers, while another group remained in the area of the Rio das Mortes.

While all Xavante groups appear to identify Tsõrepre as the source from which contemporary villages originated, those of Pimentel Barbosa take great pride in the fact that they have continued to occupy this ancestral region up to the present time. They cite this fact to legitimate their claims to being the most powerful of all Xavante groups, descendants of the first chiefs, and descendants of the immortal "always living" creators. Roberto states, "Here we are the strongest. We are the descendants of the always living. Those others, in São Marcos, are descendants of beasts. *Here* was the biggest village, Tsõrepre."

The migrations from Tsõrepre, which took place throughout the 1930s and early 1940s, spread the Xavante across a broad region in what is now the eastern part of Mato Grosso state. As in the past two centuries, they remained hostile toward outsiders and resisted attempts to establish peaceful contact with them. However, by the mid-1940s, hemmed in by other indigenous groups on one side while the expanding Brazilian frontier pressed farther west on the other, the Xavante were without possibilities for further flight and migration.

"SAVING THE WHITES": THE RIO DAS MORTES CONTACT

On November 1, 1934, Fathers Pedro Sacilotti and João Baptista Fuchs, who had insistently sought to attract and convert the Indians from their mission post at Santa Terezinha, were attacked and killed by a group of Xavante.[25] A year later an entire Xavante village was massacred by what was originally a government-sanctioned expedition to retaliate for the death of a twelve-year-old boy, which had been attributed to the Xavante.[26]

Pressures on the Xavante increased during the 1940s as settlers arrived in growing numbers and the Brazilian government pressed ahead with its plan to pass a transnational telegraph line through the area. Xavante responded to settlers' intrusions by raiding squatter settlements. As hostilities mounted, the Xavante's fierceness became well known throughout Brazil; press reports of Xavante attacks raised fear among potential settlers. The Xavante's aggressive attempts to hold out against Western domination were delaying settlement and impeding the government's efforts to colonize the area.

Consequently, in the 1940s the government stepped up its efforts to "pacify" these resistant Indians according to nonaggressive techniques developed by General Cândido M. Rondon, founder of the Indian Protection Service (SPI). These pacification efforts—consisting of patient waiting and leaving gifts in areas frequented by Indians—were designed to convince the "target group" that, within the local sea of violence and unrest, the government Indian agents were their allies.

In 1941 Genésio Pimentel Barbosa led the SPI's first Rio das Mortes "attraction front" to pacify those Xavante who had remained in the vicinity. Members of the attraction front set up camp in the vicinity of the target group, the Xavante who had remained in the Rio das Mortes area following the break-up of Tsõrepre. Under the leadership of the renowned Apöwẽ, about whom Maybury-Lewis wrote, this group had eventually relocated to a new village called Aroboñipɔpa on a tributary to the Rio das Mortes known as the Corixão River (Map 3). Apöwẽ, Warodi's father and a man beloved by those in Pimentel Barbosa, was fondly remembered during my visit.

> Apöwẽ was not in the village when the Xavante killed the whites. Someone now in Areões [a community founded after contact] killed them. Tɛbɛ came and told him [Apöwẽ] and he wept a ʔri-ñoʔre [lament.] He had had a dream and the "always living" höimanaʔuʔö creators had told him "be kind to the whites, they are not our enemies." The "always living" explained to Apöwẽ that he had created the whites as our relatives. Then Apöwẽ told the Xavante not to kill them, our relatives, anymore.[27]

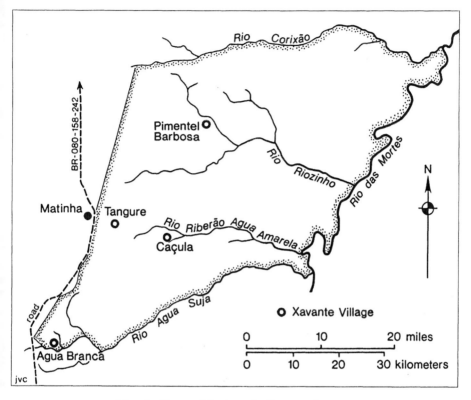

Map 3. Pimentel Barbosa Indigenous Reserve.

After encountering a group of Xavante, a meeting in which the Indians did not signal their intent to enter into peaceful communication, Pimentel Barbosa had disarmed his men. He feared that, in their nervousness, one of his men might get trigger-happy and violate the SPI motto, "Die if necessary, kill never!" The next day, the attraction front suffered a surprise attack by a party of Xavante. With the exception of a few who had briefly left the encampment, all were killed, including Pimentel Barbosa.

Determined to pacify the hostile Xavante, in 1944 the SPI installed a new team in the Rio das Mortes area. Headed by Francisco Meireles, the new attraction front deliberately made its base in the location where Pimentel Barbosa had made camp, a place known as São Domingos on the eastern bank of the Rio das Mortes. On June 6, 1946, after two years of patient waiting, the first peaceful contact was made with members of Apöwẽ's group (Fig. 3). In Warodi's telling, his father, Apöwẽ, initiated and controlled the contact.

3. "Saving the Whites," Rio das Mortes, during one of the first peaceful contacts with members of the Indian Protection Service Attraction Front led by Francisco Meireles. (Photo courtesy of the Museu do Indio, Rio de Janeiro, RJ.)

Apöwẽ called the white man back and Chico Meireles came. Apöwẽ saw him in a boat and called out, "Wɛ pedzɛ di (Come, I miss you)!" Chico Meireles then came with horses. Frightened, the aʔuwẽ killed one. Apöwẽ said, "Mare di (No more)!"

He met Meireles, who brought many knives. Then he said, "Tso ai-morĩ, tsɛtẽ (Hurry, you must leave)!" "Other Xavante are still angry." To help him, Apöwẽ told him to leave. Apöwẽ saved Meireles from the other Xavante who were angry. They [the whites] set up a post at São Domingos so the aʔuwẽ could look after them. The aʔuwẽ saved the white men.[28]

From Aroboñipɔpa on the Corixão River, Apöwẽ's group moved to Etɛñitɛpa (Pimentel Barbosa), site of the present-day village. There, internal factionalism and accusations of sorcery prompted another split, and a group left and moved southward into the area of the present-day indigenous reserve of Areões. Then, in 1953, Apöwẽ's group decided to move to the SPI post at São Domingos, where they settled in a new village they called Wededze. This was the location in which David and Pia Maybury-Lewis did the first anthropological fieldwork among the Xavante beginning in 1958.

In the 1960s the SPI decided to accept an offer from a ranch owner to exchange the post at São Domingos for a location near the Xavante's former village, Pimentel Barbosa [Eteñitepa]. As part of the deal the SPI got the ranch's infrastructure, a house and several outbuildings which the rancher had installed after the Xavante's departure for São Domingos/ Wededze. This new post became known as Pimentel Barbosa in memory of the leader of the ill-fated SPI attraction front.[29] Eventually, to obtain material goods and medication, the Xavante relocated to Pimentel Barbosa, where the SPI had an elaborate cattle ranching operation as part of its facility.[30] The post was staffed by the post chief and his wife as well as a cattle rancher and his family, and was supplied by weekly flights by the Brazilian Air Force.

The 1946 Rio das Mortes contact constituted the first peaceful contact between representatives of Brazilian national society and one of the many disparate Xavante groups in eastern Mato Grosso state. Indeed, the Xavante did not present a unified front against attempts to contact and "pacify" them. As politically autonomous communities, the groups that fissioned from Tsõrepre differed in their strategies for dealing with mounting pressures from the outside. In at least several cases, differences of opinion about how to deal with settlers aggravated the Xavante's political system of internal factionalism, and village fissioning resulted.[31] Weakened by diseases to which they had no resistance, worn from their confrontations with settlers, and in some cases terrorized by overflights of Brazilian Air Force planes, each Xavante group entered into peaceful relations with different representatives of Brazilian national society during the 1940s and 1950s. In the mid-1960s, at the time the contact was complete, the Xavante population is estimated to have been somewhere between 1,500 and 2,500.[32] This estimate represents a dramatic decrease from precontact figures, perhaps as little as half the estimated precontact size.

The first group to make peaceful contact with the whites, the one that "saved the white men," now lives in the community of Pimentel Barbosa in the present-day Pimentel Barbosa Indigenous Reserve. As a young man named Paulo phrased it, "Here the whites were created, by us not by the other Xavante. Here we are strong. Here we are privileged." As Paulo's comment demonstrates, individuals in Pimentel Barbosa use tellings about the past to construct a superior image of themselves vis-à-vis other contemporary Xavante communities.

Although it is still possible to think of the Xavante as forming a more or less integral group of politically autonomous communities whose members share similar cultural and linguistic patterns, today—as Lopes da Silva points out—it is most useful to think of the Xavante in terms of three basic groupings.[33] These three groupings distinguish the Xavante according to their distinct historical experiences during contact, their relation-

ship to the lands they now occupy, and the unique identity each group has
acquired as a result of its experiences with Brazilian national society as
mediated through different agents of contact. The three groups can be
identified as the following aggregates of communities in the present-day
indigenous reserves shown on Map 2: (1) Pimentel Barbosa (except Agua
Branca village) and Areões; (2) São Marcos, Sangradouro, and villages
situated near the Couto Magalhães River in what is now the Parabubure
Reserve; and (3) Marechal Rondon and villages located near the Kuluene
River, which is now in the Parabubure Reserve, and marginally those from
the Couto Magalhães River area. I briefly summarize the history and characteristics of the second and third groups before returning to the first, the
group to which Warodi belongs.[34]

The second group of Xavante consists of a composite of refugees—
some from the Suiá Missú area—who, during the contact period, sought
safety from epidemics and conflicts with settlers and ranchers at the Salesian mission of Merure. Because of the Xavante's hostile relations with the
mission's Bororo occupants, the Salesians moved some of the Xavante to
São Marcos, where they established a new mission; the area is now a distinct Xavante reserve (area 188,478 ha). The Salesians also moved some
Xavante from Merure to Sangradouro, where another Xavante reserve
was created (area 100,280 ha).

This second group continues to inhabit territory that was not traditionally Xavante. FUNAI did not begin to intervene actively in these areas
until 1977, when it implemented its mechanized agricultural projects.
Catholic mission influence prevails, and most Xavante from São Marcos
and Sangradouro consider themselves to be Catholics as well as upholders
of Xavante tradition.[35]

The third group consists of people whose ancestors splintered from the
precontact village of Parabubu on the Couto Magalhães River. Destitute
from disease and conflicts with settlers in the 1940s and 1950s, they fled
their ancestral lands; most took refuge with SPI representatives farther
west, where they were considerably influenced by Protestant missionaries
from the South American Indian Mission and the Summer Institute of Linguistics (Wycliff Bible Translators). Other descendants of the Parabubu
Xavante took refuge with the Salesians.

In the mid to late 1970s, many of these Xavante began returning to their
ancestral territories, which they found occupied by settlers and agribusi-
nesses who, since the government had repossessed the lands, had legal title
to them. After a period of extreme tension, the Xavante recouped this
land; in 1979 the Parabubure Reserve (224,447 ha) was created, uniting
separate pieces known as the Kuluene and Couto Magalhães areas into
one continuous reserve. Other refugees remained in the east in what is
now the Xavante reserve of Marechal Rondon (area 98,500 ha). Many of

this third group now consider themselves to be *crentes*, or believers, and regularly attend evangelical church services in their villages. Those descendants of Parabubu who returned to this area from the Catholic missions can be grouped together with this mostly Protestant third group because, although they consider themselves Catholic, they have been able to reestablish themselves on territory their ancestors traditionally inhabited prior to contact.

The first group, to which Warodi's people belong, consists of Xavante who remained in the Rio das Mortes area and who responded to SPI overtures to establish peaceful relations in the mid-1940s. Following the first peaceful contacts with members of the SPI attraction front, this group divided as a result of internal hostilities into the groups that presently live in the indigenous reserves of Pimentel Barbosa (area 328,996 ha) and Areões (area 218,515 ha). These Xavante continue to occupy lands they inhabited prior to contact. Their relationship with members of Brazilian national society has, since contact and up until recently, been mediated by agents of either the SPI or FUNAI. They have experienced very little influence from missionaries; no permanent religious mission has been established in either of these areas, although the Indians (particularly in Areões) have received intermittent assistance from Salesians in the region. These Xavante can be characterized as the most traditional of the contemporary Xavante communities and as those who have remained, through efforts of their own (including force), on lands they occupied in precontact times.

LAND: A SOURCE OF PERSISTENT TENSIONS

The Indians of the Pimentel Barbosa Reserve lived through an intense period of conflict with Brazilians concerning disputes over land during the 1970s. Settlers and ranchers, responding to government fiscal incentives designed to encourage settlement and economic development of the area, invaded their territory in the 1960s and 1970s. Government officials allegedly engaged in fraudulent activities such as altering maps, which enabled squatters and corporate ranchers to acquire legal title to these lands.[36] According to several functionaries, in 1975 local FUNAI officials arranged a fraudulent demarcation of the Pimentel Barbosa Reserve: the Xavante exchanged land for twenty-five head of cattle and six treadle sewing machines. Lots were signed over to large corporations as well as to individual settler families.

The intrusion of commercial activity significantly disrupted the Xavante's traditional life-style and economy. Ranchers implemented large-scale monoculture agriculture (primarily upland rice) and deforested large tracts of savannah forest for cattle ranching. A number of corporate ranches were equipped with landing strips for small aircraft, and many, such as the Fazenda AUTA (United Association of Air Taxis), located seven kilometers from Pimentel Barbosa, installed sawmills whose operation could be heard in the village. So close were the encroaching ranch activities that the Xavante experienced difficulty maintaining adequate subsistence activities. In the early 1970s many were abandoning their swidden gardens and men were beginning to hire themselves out as laborers to nearby ranches, whose managers promoted peaceful relations by doling out sugar, coffee, and other small gifts to placate the Xavante.

Today, little of the ranches' infrastructure remains. Throughout the reserve, dilapidated houses, corrals, work sheds, and scattered metal equipment have deteriorated from disuse and weather. This detritus of the abandoned ranches provides eerie testimony to the previous decade's intensive commercial activities. Whatever could be taken by ranch occupants was carried away when, in their efforts to reclaim their territory, Xavante attacked the ranches that operated on lands they sought to reclaim.

Devino, a young ranch hand who was present at the time the Xavante made their last attack on Fazenda AUTA and expelled its occupants, witnessed the entire community of Xavante men from Pimentel Barbosa, armed with war clubs, bows, and arrows, surround the main ranch house before dawn. For Devino, the number of armed men and their impressive appearance left no room for mistaking the seriousness of the Xavante's threat.

> At dawn the house was surrounded. One of them [Xavante] summoned the foreman to inform him that we had until noon to be gone. Then he gave a signal, a call, and several Xavante men immediately stormed the house. They headed first for the shortwave radio and destroyed it to prevent us from calling in for air support assistance. Then they helped us pack the pickup with all we could carry. Just before noon they sent us on our way. They'd always been friendly to us, but Jesus, they were angry then! We didn't even try to resist. As we were leaving we saw the women arriving with their baskets, to carry off whatever they could manage.

None of the attacks in the Pimentel Barbosa Reserve involved personal violence; there were, in fact, no injuries. The Xavante were as considerate of the ranch occupants' personal property as they were of their personal safety: the Xavante helped the ranchers pack their belongings into their vehicles and whatever did not fit, the Xavante carried back to the village. This explains the mysterious presence of several "luxury" items in Pimentel Barbosa. During the first years I lived in his house, Warodi and his wife slept in a four-poster bed (see Fig. 8). He also owned a beautiful golden Labrador retriever that stood out against the village's pack of mangy canines.

In 1979, according to Fernando Schiavinni, post chief at the time, after a series of further clashes with settlers, failed promises by FUNAI, and extreme tension over land, the Xavante of Pimentel Barbosa held a long, serious meeting: "Warodi spoke for over an hour and the elders decided it was time to expel all ranchers" and show FUNAI the limits of their reserve, according to their terms. Following this decision Warodi summoned leaders from all Xavante communities to assist the people of the Pimentel Barbosa Reserve in the demarcation. "Leaders came to Pimentel Barbosa from all areas except Sangradouro. It was an emotional reunion for the members of Warodi's age-set, and in preparation they held a *waiʔa* ceremony to strengthen and empower themselves."[37]

Armed with axes and machetes, as Brazilian Air Force planes overflew the operation, this group began to cut trees and brush to mark the reserve's border according to Xavante demands. Through their action they demonstrated to FUNAI the seriousness of their intent. This action differed from efforts to reclaim land in other Xavante areas in that the leadership of Pimentel Barbosa organized their struggle in a way that involved Xavante from nearly all reserves. For this reason, it alarmed FUNAI. "From then on FUNAI began to divide them. It feared the Xavante's collective strength."[38]

Finally, at the end of the 1970s, FUNAI expelled the ranchers and squatter settlers and officially demarcated the Pimentel Barbosa Reserve according to its present boundaries. Nevertheless, intense hostilities persisted into the early 1980s as local FUNAI officials continued to generate revenue by leasing Xavante land to ranchers for cattle pasture. By 1982, bending to Xavante demands, the last rancher removed his cattle from Xavante land. Now one family of settlers, the Arcanjos, remains in the reserve. Their homestead is located at the northeasternmost corner of the reserve, where, according to a mutual agreement between the Xavante and Mr. Arcanjo, the settler and his family maintain a vigilant outpost against intruders.

The Xavante have found utility in some of the abandoned ranch sites despite their neglected condition. Today trekking groups stop to harvest fruits such as oranges and mangoes that ranchers planted during their occupation. Old buildings are also used for shelter and have even provided temporary housing for groups that splintered from Pimentel Barbosa, the reserve's original settlement. For example, a group that split from Pimentel Barbosa in 1980 chose the abandoned Fazenda Real (previously owned by the Real Expresso transport corporation) as the site for its new settlement, in part because of its rich orchards. In July 1991 the inhabitants were in the process of completing some twenty thatched dwellings to house a new set of immigrants who had arrived in April. Similar occupations of abandoned ranch buildings have taken place in other Xavante reserves. In the Parabubure Reserve, for instance, families moved into abandoned houses and buildings left from the old Fazenda Xavantina. Having actively resisted the ranchers' occupation, these Xavante recuperated lands that they had lost. However, in both reserves contention persists over territory that lies outside the reserves' boundaries. In both cases, Xavante have engaged in some active resistance to the reserves' present borders (for instance, the roadblocks, described below, that the Areões constructed on the highway that runs parallel to the reserve's border), but generally the mood is one of acquiescence to the status quo.

By the end of 1980, all the squatters and commercial ranches had been removed from the Xavante's land. Nevertheless, the land situation continued to be extremely tense, as I discovered during my first days in Pimentel Barbosa in December 1981. Whereas FUNAI representatives in the area had arranged to lease portions of the Pimentel Barbosa Reserve to local ranchers for cattle pasture—a "small gratuity" for the ranchers' uncontested relinquishment of title, according to the post chief, Boanergis— Xavante demanded *full* control of their lands. They refused to tolerate any deals with the ranchers. Concessions had no place in the Xavante's interpretation of their rights to the land; the cattle "are eating *our* rice," Sõrupredu exclaimed.

Through FUNAI negotiators, Xavante leaders informed the two ranchers whose more than one thousand head of cattle remained on Pimentel Barbosa land that they had until January 30, 1982, to get them off. If they didn't, the Xavante would attack their ranches. Because tensions were so high over this particular situation, and evidently because FUNAI representatives perceived me as a potential threat to their control, I was expelled from the reserve. By the time I was readmitted in early March, the issue had been resolved—without violence. However, even today tensions persist over rights to land and boundaries in the Pimentel Barbosa Reserve, as in most other Xavante reserves, despite the Xavante's in all six reserves having secured legal rights to the lands they now occupy.

For example, stress over a disputed piece of land near the Kuluene River, within the Parabubure Reserve, escalated to near violence in 1987. In this area Xavante are attempting to gain rights to a piece of land they voluntarily ceded to a family at the time of the initial Kuluene land settlement in 1977. The Xavante, who had befriended the Machado family prior to the settlement, agreed to leave the Machados' piece (between 9,000 and 11,000 ha) outside their reserve. In 1987, news that the Machados had sold their property to a consortium which had begun deforestation and fence construction reached the Xavante. In response to these rumors, the Xavante sent out a group of men on a reconnaissance mission to investigate. En route they met with armed gunmen, allegedly hired by the manager to keep the Xavante off the property. Angered by this, the

Xavante kidnapped four of the gunmen, whom they held captive for four days before they escaped. The Xavante then raided the ranch, burned wooden houses, and stole a F4000 Chevrolet pickup.

Xavante of the Sangradouro Reserve are attempting to retake an area they traditionally exploited for hunting (and where they continue to hunt). This piece of land, known as Volta Grande (14,680 ha), is partially separated from the reserve by the BR-070 highway (now almost completely paved) that links the cities of Barra do Garças and Cuiabá (see Map 2). In October 1987 the government recognized Xavante claims to the area north of the road only (11,640 ha).

Similar situations existed in Pimentel Barbosa and Areões as of 1994. In Pimentel Barbosa, the Xavante contest the northern border and wish to enlarge the reserve to include the site of the ancestral village Tsõreprε and the surrounding area where they procure raw materials used to make hunting implements and ceremonial paraphernalia. The materials obtained in this area are not available elsewhere in the Xavante domain. In Areões, a piece of land that actually lies within the natural boundaries of the reserve is now the Fazenda Dois Corações. According to a former FUNAI official, this area was fraudulently excluded from the initial Areões land settlement. The Areões Xavante currently demand its return. Rumors also circulate that the Xavante entertain plans to recover territory in the Suiá Missú area, although it is unlikely that this will be possible. In São Marcos, intermittent conflicts continue with neighboring ranchers on whose land Xavante trespass when hunting. Several lawsuits, initiated by ranchers who lost their claim to land when Xavante reserves were officially fixed, were pending in state courts in 1994.[39]

Over the last decade Xavante territories have been invaded by mineral prospectors. In 1985 the federal police were called upon to remove prospectors from the Pimentel Barbosa Reserve. Renewed invasions, principally near the village of Agua Branca, were again reported in 1989.[40] Toxic chemicals, indiscriminately used in the soybean plantations of an upstream ranch (and possibly on Indian lands as well), caused pollution in a stream on the Sangradouro Reserve.[41]

Where state highways cross their reserves, or territory they consider to be theirs, Xavante have demanded indemnities for public use of their land. In 1986, the São Marcos Xavante, together with Bororo Indians, held up work on a stretch of BR-070 that cuts through their land. For several days they effectively stopped all traffic along this road. In 1986, Nova Xavante from Areões constructed roadblocks on the BR-080 that connects Xavantina with São Félix. Decorated with body paint and carrying bows, arrows, and their menacing *borduna* clubs, Xavante men halted private cars, transport trucks, and buses, demanding payment before allowing traffic to pass. This road skirts the perimeters of both the Pimentel Barbosa and Areões reserves. Although it actually enters neither reserve, it cuts into territory Xavante regularly pass through on trek. As these examples illustrate, Xavante continue to discover ways, appropriate to new historical circumstances, to assert themselves and their interests.

ECONOMY

The invasion of their lands by settlers and ranchers in the 1960s and 1970s forced the Xavante, traditionally seminomadic hunter-gatherers, to remain close to their villages and, despite their traditional aversion to agricultural work, to increase their reliance on cultivated crops. This change accommodated FUNAI's vision of the indigenous economy for, since contact, indigenous policy had endeavored to promote sedentarism and intensive agriculture. These policies were designed to encourage the Indians to conform to Western ways, to incorporate them into the capitalist economies of their regions, and, by extension, to make them more manageable.

Traditionally, agriculture—principally the cultivation of maize, beans, and squash—had played only a minor role in the Xavante economy. Wild roots, nuts, fruits, and vegetables supplemented fresh game and smoked meats, the most coveted foods in their diet. Xavante procured these "tasty things" given to the Xavante by the creator figures—as Etẽpa states in the dream narrative—while on trek, lengthy trips of up to several months at a time in which extended family groups harvested the natural resources of their land. In the dry season, the trekking groups reunited in large, semipermanent villages which housed up to a thousand inhabitants, in order to participate in ceremonial activities. Because of this trekking pattern, the territory the Xavante required for subsistence spanned the area each group could exploit in a year.

Today, the traditional trekking pattern has all but disappeared owing to the significant reduction of lands available to the Xavante for exploitation and to the reduced supply of game within the reserve lands. Extended family trekking is still in place only in the larger Xavante reserves such as Pimentel Barbosa and Areões, where there is sufficient territory to support it. Even in these areas Xavante practice trekking with diminishing frequency. In smaller reserves such as São Marcos, groups of men make extended hunts for special ceremonial occasions such as the *da-batsa* bridal hunt, which requires that the groom give large quantities of meat to his bride's mother. To find sufficient game, hunting parties from smaller reserves often must trespass onto private lands beyond the reserve's boundaries. This trespassing has, in some cases, led to clashes with neighboring landholders. Although the pattern of extended trekking is now nearly defunct, groups in all villages often take short hunting or fishing trips and stay out for one or two nights.

Despite the Xavante's switch from seminomadism to a more sedentary life-style, meat continues to occupy a prominent position in the diet and in social life. For men, hunting is an important economic task as well as a marker of male prowess. Finding game, however, has become increasingly difficult because of the size of the reserves and damage to their ecosystems, as well as destruction of ecozones adjacent to reserve lands. The present-day reserves represent but small patches of the total area in which the Xavante once hunted for subsistence. In parts of the reserves, significant portions of the natural habitat were destroyed by the ranching activities of the 1970s. Large areas were deforested either for cattle pasture or for monocrop cultivation of soybeans or upland rice. Ranchers also introduced several species of exotic feed-grasses such as *Brachiaria* spp., and *Rhynchelytrum repens, Andropogon* spp., and *Panicum maximum,* which are extremely aggressive and are displacing natural flora.[42] Commercial activities on lands adjacent to Xavante reserves, in addition to intrusions for timber or mineral extraction, have also seriously disrupted the demographics of game populations within Xavante territory.

Owing to their reliance on subsistence crops which require that Xavante remain in the vicinity of their gardens, Xavante are reluctant to leave their villages for the prolonged periods characteristic of the traditional trekking pattern. They have adapted to the need to stay close to home by hunting in areas near their villages. This shift has led to overexploitation in areas where Xavante continue to hunt. Frans Leeuwenberg, a research ecologist who has worked in Pimentel Barbosa since 1990, finds that Xavante hunt only some 65,000 hectares of the reserve's total 329,000 hectares. An area of some twenty-five kilometers around the village suffers from intensive overhunting: "From February to October [1991], the Xavante had 82 hunting days, of which 85% [took place] in this area."[43] From the results of his preliminary two-year study, Leeuwenberg concludes that this regular overhunting is having a deleterious effect on several species, including tapir, giant anteater, and marsh and pampa deer. Within this area, a number of species that are basic to the Xavante diet risk extinction.[44]

As in the immediate postcontact period, and presumably during the precontact era too, women's work supplies the basis of the Xavante diet. Even in the smaller reserves women continue to set off in groups to gather forest products such as *buriti* palm fruit, *piqui, babaçu* and *macauba* coconuts, honey, palm hearts, and various roots near the village according to season. While these collected forest products add some variety to the diet, each woman now sustains her family with produce from her gardens. Today Xavante grow a variety of cultivated crops such as manioc, rice, squash, maize, potatoes, bananas, and papayas. They also plant watermelons, beans, and occasionally peanuts in their swidden gardens.

Each adult woman has one or more of her own gardens, which are cleared by her husband and are located adjacent to those of her sisters and mother. Often accompanied by her small children, she makes several trips to the gardens per week. During the clearing and planting seasons, families frequently stay overnight in their gardens, sleeping in small, thatched, beehive-shaped domes like those constructed on trek, which they build for shade and shelter.

In addition to collecting and cultivating, women are also in charge of food processing, preparation, and distribution. When a man returns from a hunting trip, he turns his share of the meat over to his wives or, if he is unmarried, to his mother, who distributes it to the appropriate relations.[45] Although women control this distribution, if a man feels that one of his relations has been slighted, he may prevail upon his wife to give a larger share.

Since the mid-1970s, when FUNAI implemented the colossal project of mechanized rice cultivation throughout the Xavante reserves, rice has supplanted the variety of nutritious root crops that once formed the staple diet. Rice now constitutes the principal subsistence food. The tiring and redundant task of pounding to remove its husks typically falls to a household's youngest female members. Young girls often spend hours bent over hollowed troughs in this boring and tedious work.

Even with the addition of copious amounts of rice it is difficult to speak of an abundant Xavante diet. Each year there is a lean period accompanied by parents' angst that there will be insufficient food to feed their hungry children. With rice often eaten twice a day, frequently unaccompanied by other foods and often without salt to bring out a taste, there is truly neither much variety nor much nutrition in the current diet. It is no wonder that Warodi comments of the creation in the dream narrative, "For the whites, they taught nothing but rice!"

THE INTEGRATED DEVELOPMENT PLAN FOR THE XAVANTE NATION: THE XAVANTE PROJECT

In the evening men's council of April 13, 1982, it was decided that a group of senior men would depart the next Sunday for a field initially cleared by ranchers some sixty kilometers from Pimentel Barbosa, to relieve another group, mostly young men, who had begun work on the harvest during the previous week. Warodi and I went along to see the encampment. When we arrived we saw that the novitiates were sleeping together as a group, set off from their seniors. In this way they replicated the pattern of the traditional trek. As Warodi and I entered their camp, he launched into a speech reiterating for the youths the elders' proud sentiment that crops harvested from the Xavante's own land represented hope for their future. Their work today constituted an investment in tomorrow.

Warodi startled me by beginning his speech, "Bom dia rapazes!"—a Portuguese greeting meaning, "Good day, young men." He continued:

ro wẽ di	all is well
ro wẽ di	all is well
romhuri wẽ di	the work is well done
trabali wẽ di	the work (Portuguese *trabalho*) is well done

Following these opening statements Warodi, a monolingual Xavante speaker, went on to deliver the body of his speech in Xavante. Then, after ten minutes of melodically intoned elders' speech, he abruptly ended with a Portuguese expression, *pronto* (done, it is finished), that again surprised me. Although he and most others had incorporated a few Portuguese words such as "tractor" (*tratore*) and "money" (*ñiñɛru*; Portuguese *dinheiro*) into their discourse, I had never heard him use these colloquial expressions in speeches to Xavante audiences. With *bom dia*, *trabali*, and *pronto*, Warodi underscored his enthusiasm for the rice project, for Brazilian national society, and for the Portuguese language. With these few words he took a step away from the antagonisms of the previous decade and the ardent fight to reclaim Xavante lands, to linguistically represent the move toward reconciliation. In his speech, specifically through these words, Warodi expressed a sentiment he shared with most other Xavante at that time: the rice project offered a promise for the Xavante, an indigenous people, to have a dignified place as both producing and consuming members of the larger Brazilian national society.

As Warodi's speech indicates, the Xavante were initially enthusiastic about the rice project. During the 1982 harvest in Pimentel Barbosa, for example, nearly the entire village willingly relocated to assist with the harvest. It seemed that rice cultivation, rather than trekking, was the major activity that ordered their lives. As the FUNAI post chief Boanergis perceived it: "The Xavante have adapted exceptionally well to the rice project. In many ways it is filling in the gap for hunting."

The Xavante took great pride in their work and the large harvests they reaped at the outset. In Pimentel Barbosa, according to Fernando Schiavinni, another FUNAI post chief, the Xavante reaped 1,500 sixty-kilogram sacks of rice in 1979, the project's first year. For the 1981–1982 harvest, the first Xavante harvest I witnessed, FUNAI budgeted Cr$2,471,042.00 (U.S. $19,159.08) for the 110-hectare plantation on the Pimentel Barbosa Reserve.[46] It anticipated a yield of approximately 2,310 sixty-kilogram sacks. For the same year, the communities of the Kuluene River area within the Parabubure Reserve were expected to reap some 4,200 sixty-kilogram sacks of upland rice from their 200-hectare mechanized plantation. Ministry of the Interior documents for the communities of Kuluene indicate that for the 1981–1982 fiscal year, FUNAI projected expenditures to total Cr$4,571,768.00 (U.S. $35,446.93), including the cost of diesel fuel, fertilizer, and pesticides; it anticipated a profit of Cr$1,035,665 (U.S. $8,029.97).[47] To the Xavante, witnesses to the fantastic machinery FUNAI imported to their reserves, the huge expenditures, and the awe-inspiring harvests, it appeared that the project would afford them the material status they had seen in the prosperous local ranches.

The mechanized rice cultivation project, which came to be known as the Xavante Project, was conceptualized within an overall plan entitled "The Integrated Development Plan for the Xavante Nation." The plan combined indigenous policy with the economic ideology of the post-1964 military government.[48] Its official objectives were to expedite special attention to the Indians in the areas of health and formal education and, most importantly—because they could no longer support themselves with their traditional hunter-gatherer economy—to provide the means for their eventual economic self-sufficiency.

The project was adopted in part to justify the decision to honor Xavante claims, on the basis of their potential to contribute to the national economy, to the relatively large reserves that were then in the process of being demarcated. Because their lands fell within an area that the military government had targeted for economic development, the Xavante were considered relevant to national security interests. Central Brazil fit within the government's overall plan to develop Amazonia and the interior through road building, colonization, and the development of agribusiness. From the point of view of Brazil's "economic miracle," the Xavante's large reserves were situated in the midst of prime real estate. FUNAI, under the auspices of the Ministry of the Interior, hoped to integrate the Xavante into the capitalist economy of the region. The location of their reserves explains, at least to some degree, the considerable attention lavished upon the Xavante at the time.

In addition to its economic objective of inserting the Xavante into the region's economy, FUNAI clearly had a strong political agenda. The plan's engineers sought to alleviate the terrific pressure Xavante leaders were exerting on FUNAI in their efforts to reclaim their lands. Of these, the efforts of Mario Juruna, a young leader from the São Marcos Reserve, brought popular attention to the Xavante's cause. Through an ingenious understanding of the media and its ability to manipulate popular sentiment, Juruna involved the press in the Xavante's struggle. On trips to Brasília to negotiate with government officials, he tape-recorded officials' speeches and promises to the Xavante. Then, when these promises were broken,

Juruna—this time accompanied by Xavante men and members of the press—returned to confront the government officials with his tape recordings of false promises in hand. Juruna thus publicly revealed the blatant corruption of FUNAI and the Ministry of the Interior and exposed government officials' all too common practice of public deception, making it impossible to overlook.[49] Spearheaded by Juruna's leadership, the Xavante's fight against big business in the face of government corruption captured national and even international attention. The Xavante as a people came to stand for oppressed groups throughout Brazil: their struggle represented the cause of all who struggled to gain a voice in government. Juruna, catapulted to the status of a national hero, was elected in 1982 to the national chamber of deputies from the state of Rio de Janeiro.

Through their campaign the Xavante achieved a prominence which threatened to tarnish FUNAI's public image as the guardian of indigenous peoples. FUNAI officials hoped that the rice project would placate the Xavante as well as publicly demonstrate its goodwill toward them and, by extension, its benevolence toward all indigenous peoples. However, as Lopes da Silva points out, the FUNAI plan involved indigenous peoples in government-sponsored economic development projects precisely at the time when governmental decisions were being implemented from the top down.[50] No Xavante representatives, for instance, were involved in planning for the project. Clearly an unstated objective of the project was to develop a means for gaining political control over the Xavante.[51] Bureaucrats hoped that the project would keep Xavante leaders occupied with business on their reserves, away from Brasília and far from access to the media. FUNAI officials hoped to gain control over a group whose leaders, in the fight for their land, had demonstrated not only their strong will but also impressive political acumen in the national arena.

RICE AND RESISTANCE: BEATING A CORRUPT GOVERNMENT AT ITS OWN GAME

> ah
> ah the Xavante
> the Xavante's foods
> the Xavante's foods
> they taught the food according to their wisdom . . .
> for the whites they taught nothing but rice

Often to the chagrin of other Indians and eventually of FUNAI itself, with the advent of the Xavante Project the Xavante again came to dominate attention within FUNAI. As FUNAI increased its vast spending in Xavante areas, Xavante leaders increasingly demanded bureaucrats' time and attention. Indeed, the project actively cultivated the Xavante's sense of importance, which was, after all, demonstrated by the agricultural technicians, the experts who mixed potions of fertilizers and pesticides, and the mechanics who repaired and operated complex equipment—all of whom regularly visited *their* reserves. Undoubtedly Xavante leaders still tasted the power they had wielded during the land crises. They grew to be extremely aggressive in their relations with FUNAI administrators. At the same time, their demands expanded to increasingly unrealistic proportions.

The Xavante aspired to emulate the ranchers' model of agribusiness, while the considerable resources which flooded into their reserves as a result of FUNAI's project nourished their aspirations. Tractors and trucks became prized objects and indicators of community status. Leaders sought to gain independent title to their own trucks and thereby to promote their community's status vis-à-vis other Xavante communities.

In November 1981, under the leadership of *cacique* Tomás and with generous assistance from FUNAI, the Kuluene village of Aldeinha became the first Xavante community to acquire its own truck. The occasion was marked by an enormous celebration and great fanfare. The proud driver roared the truck into the central plaza where Tomás, orating from the truck's platform as community members admired the shining paint glistening in the afternoon sun, gave voice to the feelings of superiority that ran high in the village that day. Marino, another prominent figure, summarized their attitude this way: "We bought this truck with our own money from the sale of our rice. It is good. The FUNAI president commends us and helped us to purchase our truck. If other villages want to spend money on other frivolous things, that is their affair."

Word of this and subsequent acquisitions spread quickly among Xavante communities. FUNAI's acquiescence to the demands of one community soon invited similar or even greater demands from other leaders. With each new act of beneficence, FUNAI raised the stakes for Xavante leaders. Aniceto of São Marcos, for example, collected enough to install an enviable stereo system in his Chevy pickup. By acceding to Xavante demands, FUNAI successfully cemented their dependence. In the process, however, it created an insatiable appetite for material goods. The project had not, after all, alleviated the constant pressure Xavante leaders exerted in Brasília. If anything, it had exacerbated the situation and the pressure had grown.

After its first decade, the deleterious effects of the Xavante Project became unmistakable. The Xavante's dependence on FUNAI, particularly their need for technical assistance and material goods, had increased dramatically. For example, since soil conditions in the central Brazilian Plateau require intensive fertilization, and monocrop agriculture demands pesticides if it is to produce cost-effective yields, maintenance of large-scale cultivation such as that implemented in the Xavante areas demanded the constant attention of specially trained agronomists. The project, however, provided no training for Xavante; communities depended entirely on FUNAI to supply the experts. Similarly, although some young men learned to operate machinery such as tractors and trucks, none acquired the technical skills needed for long-term maintenance or repairs. Communities depended on FUNAI mechanics. Additionally, FUNAI's policy of contracting a few individuals such as truck and tractor drivers and paying regular salaries for their services exacerbated disruptions to the traditional economy. Since salaried positions invariably fell prey to power politics, appointments aggravated factional rivalries. Moreover, a young man could not simultaneously perform service for the community and perform his domestic duties; his work for "the project" placed an extra burden on his household. But, in compensation, with his salary he could supply his household with luxury items such as coffee, sugar, cooking oil, a radio, and batteries.

Serious health and nutritional problems began to arise as rice became widely substituted for the nutritious root crops that once formed the basis of the Xavante diet.[52] Tuberculosis, for example, plagues the Xavante and is aggravated by poor diet. The remarkable increase in sugar consumption that accompanied the Xavante's initial moves into a money-based economy dramatically affected dental hygiene. Dental diseases are now among the most serious health problems confronting Xavante communities. And a recent study conducted by a University of Brasília medical team found that the Xavante may have the world's highest per capita incidence of endemic pemphigus foliaceus, a treatable but potentially fatal skin disease.[53]

Although all FUNAI posts are ideally staffed by trained nurses and Xavante attendants, medical attention in most areas has been (and continues to be) sporadic. FUNAI infirmaries are often understocked, and what medications there may be are often out of date. Nor are the infirmaries equipped to deal with the host of maladies that have accompanied the transition to a more sedentary life-style and the use of clothing. Scabies, for instance, are endemic in the Pimentel Barbosa Reserve; although this is an easily treatable malady, FUNAI provides no medication for its eradication. Poor medical attention has, in fact, been one of the principal factors that motivate leaders like Tomás to seek independent means of transportation. In the absence of adequate local health care, communities require vehicles to transport the sick to regional health posts, which in many cases are located at distances of over two hundred kilometers from Xavante villages.

VILLAGE FISSIONING AND THE XAVANTE PROJECT

In the 1980s, with health care deteriorating, demands for salaried positions and trucks on the rise, and appetites growing for consumer goods such as clothing, coffee, oil, and salt, established leaders as well as aspiring ones began to exert pressure on FUNAI to accede to their demands for material goods and benefits to distribute among family members. Competition for resources exacerbated tensions within and between communities, and the desire for material goods gave new impetus to the traditional Xavante pattern of village fissioning.

In Pimentel Barbosa, for example, Warodi was recognized by FUNAI as *cacique*, "chief," until mid-1985. As an incumbent of this officially recognized leadership position he received a salary from FUNAI, as did his officially recognized assistant, or "secretary." Sõrupredu, who held the secretary's position in 1981 during my first visit, regularly accompanied Warodi, primarily to act as translator, on community business trips to FUNAI's regional office in Barra do Garças or to its Brasília headquarters. Sõrupredu's ability to speak some Portuguese was a principal reason for his occupation of this post.

Then, in 1983, accompanied by a few families—not more than twenty individuals—Sõrupredu left the main village to form a new community, Tangure, close to the highway BR-080. While tension between Sõrupredu's faction and Warodi's supporters had been simmering for some time, in Pimentel Barbosa the stated reason for the exodus was an alleged unsanctioned sale of a number of the community's collectively owned cattle, as well as accusations of theft and sorcery. "Sõrupredu stole money and tried to kill Warodi with *abdze* [a sorcerer's potion]." It was quite clear that Sõrupredu coveted more benefits than his secretarial post could offer.

By establishing his own village, thereby promoting himself from secretary to *cacique*, Sõrupredu could demand a higher salary from FUNAI. Moreover, with independence from the principal village, his community would become eligible for its own "project," including, among other benefits, an independent rice plantation, cattle, a tractor and a salaried position for its driver (Sõrupredu's son), a Toyota jeep, a nurse attendant, a schoolteacher, and a shortwave radio. All these material acquisitions formed part of "a project" and represented status among Xavante communities.

By establishing himself as the leader of an independent community, Sõrupredu conformed to a pattern of political strategizing practiced by many individuals throughout Xavante reserves during the 1980s. Scores of new leaders emerged, each forming a new settlement in order to gain access to FUNAI's resources. Structurally, the emergence of new settlements conformed to the traditional pattern of Xavante factionalism and village fissioning in which, typically, the leader of a weaker faction breaks from an established community.[54] In the early 1980s, the possibility of obtaining "a project" offered leaders of minority factions, like Sõrupredu, the potential to increase both their prestige and their generosity toward the members of their factions. Both qualities, important in Xavante leadership, could be serviced by founding a new village, with—of course—financing from FUNAI.

In this respect the motive for forming new settlements in the 1980s differed from the motives Xavante stated in the late 1970s, when several new communities were established. At that time the Xavante formed new villages in order to fortify their claims to land and maintain surveillance over unoccupied parts of their territory. Whereas in 1974 there was one village per Xavante reserve, by 1980 four of the reserves had two or more villages: the population in Kuluene had divided into three villages; the Sangradouro mission village fissioned into two settlements; the Couto Magalhães community (established in 1979) had fissioned into three separate villages; and four new settlements had formed in São Marcos. As Lopes da Silva has observed of the 1970s, the Xavante "aligned factionalism, as a characteristic of their political system, with a pragmatic strategy to defend their territory."[55]

During the 1980s, in contrast, the Xavante were aligning this same tendency toward village fissioning with a pragmatic strategy to obtain financial resources and material goods. Currently, with the exception of Marechal Rondon, each reserve has multiple communities (Table 1). The number of Xavante settlements FUNAI officially recognized in 1980 had more than doubled by December 1985; the total jumped from sixteen to thirty-five (Table 2). Kuluene, which had a total of three villages in 1980, had seven settlements in 1985. By late 1987 the number had grown to eleven. Driving through the area, one now comes across settlement after settlement, many consisting of only one or a few families. Between 1980 and 1985 in the Couto Magalhães area, the number of villages jumped from three to nine. This particular increase can be partially explained by the influx of Xavante from São Marcos and Sangradouro, who came to resettle in their ancestral territory and gain autonomy from the Catholic missions. Nevertheless, rather than augmenting the population of the existing settlements, many leaders opted for forming new villages and sought projects from FUNAI. Xavante actively responded to FUNAI's development policy in ways they perceived to be to their own advantage; the formation of new villages constituted a form of resistance to the dependency FUNAI sought to establish.

By 1985 there were six villages in Areões and four in Pimentel Barbosa. Within the latter reserve, the principal village, Pimentel Barbosa itself, split in 1980 when Warodi's brother Pahöri and the members of his faction left for the abandoned Fazenda Real and established the village

TABLE 1. XAVANTE VILLAGES AND POPULATION (1984)

Indigenous Reserve	Villages	Population
Marechal Rondon	Batovi	215
Parabubure (Kuluene area)	Aldeona	224
	Aldeinha	329
	Patrimonio	176
	Buritizal	103
	Sta. Cruz	123
	Caçula	104
	Nova Campinas	105*
		Total: 1,164
Parabubure (Couto Magalhães area)	Couto Magalhães	106
	São Domingos	145
	São José	108
	Pizzato	90
	Estrella	115
	N. Sra. Auxiliadora Padroeira do Brasil	140*
	São João Batista	19
	São Pedro	105
	Parabubure	112
		Total: 940
Sangradouro	Mission	320
	Dom Bosco	126
		Total: 446
Xavante (São Marcos)	Mission São Marcos	350*
	Namukura	n.a.
	Auxiliadora	600*
	Aparecida	n.a.
	Buriti Alegre	n.a.
	São José	82
		Total: 1,032
Areões	P.I. Areões	337
	Dois Galhos	66
	Joacita/Tritopa	17

TABLE 1. (*continued*)

Indigenous Reserve	Villages	Population
Areões	Fazenda Mutum	27
	Buritizal	59
	Novo Xavante/Bosocu	5
	Total:	511
Pimentel Barbosa	Pimentel Barbosa	304
	Caçula	24
	Tangure	41
	Agua Branca	157
	Total:	526
	Total Villages:	35
	Total Population:	4,834

Source: FUNAI Health Sector, 7th Regional Delagacia (1984 data)
* estimated population

known as Caçula. Sõrupredu made his exit in 1983. The fourth village, Agua Branca, is made up of the exiles from Couto Magalhães.

The populations of Sangradouro and Marechal Rondon remained stable through the early 1980s. São Marcos underwent a considerable process of fissioning in the mid-1970s but has remained relatively stable since then. The one new village that formed in 1982, Buriti Alegre, consists of a single family. The proliferation of new villages continued throughout the latter half of the decade. By December 1987, FUNAI employees estimated that there were as many as fifty Xavante villages.[56]

In the 1980s, the Xavante experienced a significant population increase. However, it is doubtful that the rapid fissioning process can be attributed to demographics alone. The quest for material goods and their associated prestige provided the greatest incentive for the formation of new villages during the Xavante Project years. According to the 1980 FUNAI census, the Xavante numbered 3,405. By 1984, a period of rapid proliferation of villages, the population had grown to 4,834. Today, estimates place the number of Xavante near 6,000. This increase has resulted, in part, from the medical assistance that has been provided (despite serious deficiencies in some areas) by missionaries and FUNAI.[57] Population expansion certainly must be considered as a factor in the remarkable proliferation of

TABLE 2. INCREASE IN NUMBER OF XAVANTE VILLAGES

Indigenous Reserve	Number of Villages					Population			
	1974	1980	1985	1987	1990	1977	1980	1984	1987
Marechal Rondon	1	1	1	1		111	120	215	
Parabubure (Kuluene area)	1	3	7	11+*		710	808	1,164	
Parabubure (Couto Magalhães area)	–	3	9	n.a.		356	371	940	
Sangradouro	1	2	2	n.a.		548	497	446	
Xavante (São Marcos)	1	5	6	n.a.		1,010	993	1,032	
Areões	1	1	6	n.a.		303	347	511	
Pimentel Barbosa	1	1	4	4		266	269	526	
Total	6	16	35	50*	78	3,340	3,405	4,834	6,000*

Sources: 1977/1980 Lopes da Silva (1980)
1984/1985 FUNAI Health Sector, 7th Regional Delegacia
1987 FUNAI employee estimates
1990 Benjamin Xavante, in Miamoto (1990)
* estimated figures

Xavante villages that occurred during the 1980s, but the prospect of gaining a project from FUNAI clearly provided the greatest incentive.[58]

WHO CONTROLS WHOM? FUNAI VERSUS THE XAVANTE REVISITED

While a "divide and conquer" strategy may not have been part of the project engineers' original plan, the rapid proliferation of Xavante villages during the 1980s certainly assisted FUNAI in gaining control over the Xavante by creating a dependency situation, at least at the outset. A number of the plan's coordinators were undoubtedly aware of the Xavante's characteristic pattern of village fissioning and might have anticipated this effect. However, rather than gaining lasting dominance over docile dependents, FUNAI confronted a people accustomed to taking charge of their historical circumstances. Armed with their firm sense of self, the indomitable Xavante again demonstrated political savvy in playing a corrupt government at its own game. As the number of settlements dramatically increased, so did new demands—taxing FUNAI's budget and administration to their limits. The Xavante Project eventually devolved into an administrative quagmire. And once again the Xavante managed to place FUNAI in an embarrassing light by publicly highlighting the bureau's administrative incompetence.

The proliferation of new villages in the 1980s instigated a flood of Xavante men who descended on FUNAI's administrative centers in Barra do Garças and Brasília (Fig. 4). Leaders had quickly caught on to the fact that FUNAI representatives in the indigenous reserves were ineffective bureaucrats without power. They realized that to resolve anything they needed to travel to FUNAI headquarters. Naturally, they preferred hotels and pensions there to the less desirable FUNAI-run "casas do Indio," which, dirty and overcrowded with the infirm, offered inhospitable accommodation.

Growing numbers of Xavante leaders flooded into administrative offices and intimidated FUNAI officials. Fearing their political ingenuity, FUNAI placated these leaders by willingly paying travel expenses. With time, Xavante leaders grew to expect FUNAI to pick up the tab for all their expenditures. As the number of leaders increased, so did the demands and the bills. Xavante leaders came to cities with their own money, then threatened to stay until FUNAI met their demands (for example, a Toyota jeep or truck), claiming they had no money to finance the return to their villages. Overwhelmed by the numbers that swelled its halls as leaders waited for an audience, FUNAI was hard-pressed to develop a strategy for sending them back to their reserves. The strategy they came up with was a system of bribes known as "supplements." These consisted of, for each

4. Xavante leader Celestino en route to a federal ministry building in Brasília, 1980. (Photo courtesy of *O Globo*.)

leader, a travel stipend for a return trip, plus spending monies. Men used these monies to buy gifts for their families.

When the day grew near for Warodi's return from a trip to Barra do Garças or Brasília, for example, members of his household eagerly anticipated his return. At the first distant rumblings of the Toyota engine after dark, the small children shouted "Toyota! Toyota!" barely able to contain their excitement over the inevitable delicacies Warodi would bring: oranges, sweet bread, cloth for the women, flashlight batteries for hunting, sugar, cookies, and hard candy. Once these had been distributed, as mutual news was exchanged, members of his household and others who had gathered for a share of the booty smacked their lips, finally enjoying the awaited delicacies in the darkness. The appetite for such treats expanded with each homecoming, and Warodi confided to me his fears of humiliation should he ever return empty-handed.

In June 1987, FUNAI paid "supplements" to thirty-three leaders in amounts that averaged about Cr$60,000 (U.S. $1,260). The amount varied according to the status of the recipient and the degree of pressure he exerted on FUNAI officials. While FUNAI officials were literally paying Xavante to get them to leave the cities, among Xavante, obtaining a supplement eventually developed into a motive for travel itself. Men who did not occupy positions of leadership gradually began to swell the ranks of travelers in order to collect supplements of their own. As men went in search of supplements, satisfying the wanderlust of seminomadic hunter-gatherers, villages remained occupied primarily by women.

As Xavante leaders became increasingly aware of their political clout, they began to threaten to remove FUNAI officials from office should they fail to acquiesce to Xavante demands. In June 1985, for example, leaders from São Marcos attempted to expel the FUNAI delegate from the regional headquarters in Barra do Garças. The Xavante as a whole were not of a single mind over this issue, however. According to men from Pimentel Barbosa, leaders from São Marcos wanted a more manipulable FUNAI representative: the present delegate did not conform to the established pattern of paying disproportionately large supplements to leaders of São Marcos, the reserve closest to the regional office and therefore the reserve whose leaders were most often present at FUNAI to receive cash supplements. With jealousy and antagonisms elevated, Xavante men from all reserves converged on Barra do Garças to debate this issue. Angrily, a man named Waldo recounted the prevailing sentiment in Pimentel Barbosa regarding the Xavante from São Marcos:

> The problem is [Mario] Juruna. He claims his father was the first to make contact with the whites and that therefore he has the right to command and make decisions in FUNAI. Here we know it's just not true. The families of Juruna and Aniceto [another leader from São Marcos] wanted to kill the white man, in fact they killed the first whites, and threw clubs at their airplanes. Apöwẽ forced them to leave the village. He wasn't afraid because his family created the whites.

Waldo's statement illustrates that distinctions between myth, history, and politics are not always neat.[59] Like others from Pimentel Barbosa, he merges all three into his interpretation of current affairs: as descendants of those who created the whites, the people of Pimentel Barbosa are superior to all other Xavante. Even though individuals from this group have not, in fact, been the principal leaders in dealings with Brazilian national society since contact, they use their historical relationship to the whites to assert their right to be the lead brokers in external relations and to undermine the position of others.

In the final months of 1986 the situation between FUNAI and the Xavante reached crisis proportions. Contingents of Xavante men, often nearly the entire male population of a given village, accompanied leaders to Brazilian cities (Fig. 5). Many established semipermanent residency at boarding houses and passed their bills on to FUNAI. Predictably, disputes over payment of room and board expenses erupted.

Once again, in late 1987, the Xavante capped the headlines of major Brazilian newspapers: "Indian Fight Costs FUNAI Dearly: Xavante depart but leave bills to be investigated by Federal Police." Their tab for 1,496 cookies, 892 steaks, 2,912 slices of cake, 322 smoothies, 2,690 large shots of *pinga* (a local rum), 786 orange juices, 646 liter-size soft drinks, 1,184 single servings of soft drinks, 690 bottles of mineral water, and 832 cup servings of mineral water reached a total of Cr$418,380 (U.S. $6,969). This bill wound up on the desk of FUNAI's president.[60]

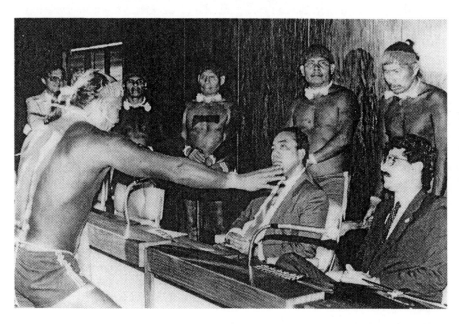

5. Sõrupredu haranguing FUNAI president Romero Jucá Filho, 1987. (Photo by José Varella, courtesy of *Jornal do Brasil*.)

For FUNAI, the Xavante, a continuous insupportable nuisance, were now also a substantial financial burden. In addition to their considerable bills for room and board, in order to pressure FUNAI to meet their demands they engaged in other acts of civil disobedience. For example, in 1987 Xavante leaders invaded the office of the special advisor to FUNAI's president and were subsequently expelled from Brasília by the military police. The next day, MPs formed a menacing guard at FUNAI headquarters. Only unarmed Indians, without clubs or bows and arrows, were allowed access to the building, and then only according to a series of restrictions. Xavante were barred from the hall where the president's office is located.[61] Later, ten *caciques* attempted to kidnap a FUNAI functionary, demanding Cr$60,000 (U.S. $1,000) for each of the thirty-three Xavante leaders who were in Brasília at the time. Refusing to pay, FUNAI claimed it had already sent Cr$27,000,000 (U.S. $449,742) to Xavante communities. The number of demanding Xavante leaders was staggering, the expenditures unsustainable.

It took an administrative overhaul within FUNAI (Presidential decree 92, March 18, 1986), effectively dispersing administrative responsibilities away from Brasília, to alleviate the situation. The Xavante and the pressure they exerted on FUNAI may well have been one factor in FUNAI's decision to reconfigure its administration. Similarly, the enormity of their demands undoubtedly played a role in the demise of the Xavante Project.

By the mid-1980s FUNAI was beginning to taper off its investments in the Xavante agribusiness venture. Over successive years the size of plantations diminished. Simultaneously, conforming to the trend in local agricultural practice, FUNAI began to encourage diversification of the large-scale rice plantations, and the Xavante began to plant soybeans in addition to rice. FUNAI also encouraged Xavante to expand their cattle holdings, despite the fact that, for the most part, Xavante do not manage the herds themselves but prefer to hire ranch hands instead. During the 1980s, on their own the Xavante began to devote more attention to the traditional swidden gardens which they had all but abandoned in the late 1970s.

By early 1987 it became clear to administrators that FUNAI could no longer sustain the high cost of maintaining the Xavante Project nor meet the appetites it had engendered among the Xavante. At that time the Xavante had no idea that the future of their projects was in jeopardy. FUNAI appointed an administrator in Brasília whose specific task was to "evaluate" (a euphemism for phase out) the Xavante Project. During the October–November planting season of 1986, crop sowing proceeded according to the normal schedule (chronically late). The area planted in Pimentel Barbosa was scaled back to a comparatively small 35 hectares, from 110 hectares in 1981. FUNAI released only half the expected funds for the tractors' diesel fuel.

Although smaller areas were planted than in previous years, Xavante in all reserves anticipated abundant harvests and expected continued assistance from FUNAI. When the time came to prepare for the harvest, however, FUNAI failed to disperse funds for diesel fuel to run machinery. Even more discouraging for the Xavante was the fact that FUNAI made no attempt to restore the harvesters that remained in derelict condition from the previous year's mechanical debacles. So dependent were they on FUNAI that they could not even reap their crop.

The previous harvest (spring 1986) should have served as a warning of FUNAI's eventual withdrawal from the project, although the Xavante interpreted the disorganization as just another example of FUNAI's administrative inefficiency. Events in Pimentel Barbosa are representative. FUNAI sent two mechanics, in December 1985, to repair a harvester to be used in the spring. They spent three weeks hard at work dismantling the harvester. Before putting it back together, however, FUNAI called the mechanics to another job. They left the harvester in pieces, exposed to the weather. The machine was not serviceable for the 1986 harvest, nor was it repaired for the 1987 crop.

So as not to lose their crop, members of the community contracted with a local rancher to complete the service in exchange for over half the harvest. This drained the village of its source of liquid income for the year. No one went hungry, but there was a shortage of rice that year. Few individuals, apart from the small number of salaried FUNAI employees and those who received a pittance in social security payments, had money to purchase items such as sugar, coffee, cooking oil, or clothing, for which the Xavante had acquired a taste in recent years. Similar stories circulated from other reserves.

Again in 1987, FUNAI released funds for planting but none for the harvest. Xavante themselves were hard-pressed to underwrite the cost; they could not afford to repeat payment for outside assistance. Again, as in their response to the contact with representatives of Brazilian national society some thirty years before, leadership in different communities responded in different ways to the crisis. In some areas, such as Sangradouro, where they had planted six hundred hectares of rice, men, women, and children went to the fields to cut the crop by hand. When it became evident that they could not possibly accomplish the monumental task and that a sizeable portion of their crop risked rotting in the fields, Sangradouro's leaders, with the help of Ailton Krenak (organizer of União das Nações Indigenas, Union of Indigenous Nations), were able to schedule a meeting with a senator from Mato Grosso state. In an audience with the Xavante, he arranged for a harvester from the state agricultural co-op to harvest their crop free of charge. The Pimentel Barbosa Xavante traded precious cattle for their harvest.

From these experiences it became apparent to the Xavante that they could no longer rely on FUNAI's financial assistance. In July 1987 FUNAI dispensed Cr$300,000 (U.S. $6,676) to each leader to buy miscellaneous items such as soap, cloth, and cooking oil. There would, however, be no "project" in 1988.

By this time Warodi and other Xavante leaders had begun to express their desire to become independent of FUNAI. Jé Paulo, a young man from Pimentel Barbosa, put it to me this way: "We need to develop our own projects, to be free of FUNAI." Given that the frontier of capitalist expansion had moved farther west, at the end of the decade the Xavante were no longer within a zone considered vital to Brazil's national security interests. Their treatment conformed to the general pattern in Brazil: once an area's strategic importance has diminished, its indigenous peoples cease to be a priority and their needs for basic services in such areas as health care and education are neglected. Lack of FUNAI assistance can also be attributed, in part, to implementation of structural adjustment policies, which involved massive cuts in public sector expenditures.

By the end of the 1980s, Xavante communities, particularly non-mission communities, were essentially on their own to discover ways to develop an income to meet their new material needs as well as to provide basic health services and education to community members. In Pimentel Barbosa, where for years Warodi had pleaded for a truck to transport the infirm to Nova Xavantina for medical assistance, the community elected to apply 150 head of cattle toward the purchase of a truck. Having finally given up, they completed this transaction wholly independent of FUNAI.

THE 1990S: BEYOND FUNAI AND INTO THE INTERNATIONAL ARENA

Accepting neither defeat nor a subservient position, in the late 1980s Xavante leadership began to seek contacts with potential funding sources outside FUNAI to assist them with development projects. Those from the mission villages, who had had considerable experience dealing with Brazilian national society, began to procure funds for their agricultural projects at foreign embassies in Brasília. From Pimentel Barbosa, Warodi's nephew Cipassé, who studied in Goiânia, stepped in to continue the line of his family's leadership, for which he had been groomed. On his trips to the village, and when Warodi stopped in Goiânia on his trips to Brasília, Cipassé had spent many hours lying by his fathers' sides learning the stories of his ancestors. From them he knew that he was a descendant of the first chief and descended from the first creators.

Cipassé pursued contacts with Ailton Krenak, the charismatic leader of Brazil's Union of Indigenous Nations (UNI), and through UNI he developed contacts with nongovernmental organizations (NGOs) such as IWGIA (International Work Group for Indigenous Affairs) and the World Wildlife Fund (WWF). Inspired by Krenak and other indigenous activists, Cipassé began to develop a new vision for Pimentel Barbosa's future. Rather than seeking to integrate the Xavante into the local region's capitalist economy, as FUNAI had attempted, Cipassé envisions developing the reserve's natural resources for sustainable exploitation and modest long-term returns.

Following Cipassé's lead, together with UNI the community of Pimentel Barbosa developed a plan to export savannah fruits in the hope of earning a steady but modest income without further destroying the reserve's natural ecosystem. According to the plan, some food processing is to be carried out in the village as well as at a small-scale production center in Nova Xavantina. Funds obtained from the Inter-American Foundation (IAF) have been used to remodel the abandoned Fazenda AUTA for food processing and for sowing harvestable indigenous plants such as *urucum*, for which there is an international market. IAF funds have also made it possible for the community to open and maintain a small office, with a telephone, in Nova Xavantina. The Body Shop, Gaya Foundation, Eisher, and other enterprises that distribute natural products are slated to handle marketing of the harvested forest products, which will be primarily in Europe. Assistance from the World Wildlife Fund has supported research into the reserve's wildlife demographics. Cipassé and community members hope that this will provide a basis for a future plan to restore, insofar as possible, the reserve's ecosystem and its faunal population to their natural balance.

Cipassé's ideas and contacts with NGOs in the national and international arenas have transformed Pimentel Barbosa from one of the Xavante communities least connected with the outside into the avant garde of Xavante communities. News of Pimentel Barbosa's innovative plans have been reported in major Brazilian newspapers.[62] Cipassé has traveled to West Germany and Japan, seeking assistance and markets for the forest products the community plans to harvest.[63] He and his wife, Severiá Karajá, both members of the Forest's People Alliance, accompanied the internationally known musician Milton Nacimiento on his 1990 tour of the United States. In the U.S. they met with representatives of various North American indigenous groups as well as NGOs including Cultural Survival and Rainforest Action Network.

Cipassé's innovative ideas and his involvement in community affairs after so many years away were not, however, unanimously embraced by all members of the community. Differences of opinion over community projects exacerbated factional rifts. The fissure between two opposed factional groups widened until the chasm became unbridgeable. In April 1991, Milton (Warodi's immediate successor to the position of *cacique*) led some eighty people to join the group at the abandoned Fazenda Real, now known as Aldeia Caçula.

The Xavante, like other Brazilian Indians such as the Kayapó, are now beginning to broaden their contacts beyond FUNAI and move within national and international arenas. In this process, local politics influence the relationships they develop with outsiders as well as the nature of their potential collaborative work. It remains unclear, for example, whether and in what ways the various groups originally from Pimentel Barbosa will be able to collaborate in the projects implemented on territory they own in common. Once again, the Xavante embark on uncharted terrain, this time to navigate the interface between local factional and global systems.

Throughout their history Xavante groups have differed in their strategies for dealing with novel circumstances—the intrusion of the whites and the traumas of the commercialization of their land. Now, as throughout their past, Xavante continue to respond in various ways to new challenges. The greatest resource Xavante have with which to confront their new historical circumstances is their feeling of connectedness with the past, the connectedness that underlies their sense of self as empowered peoples. This continuity and sense of identity is perpetuated, in the midst of such dramatic historical circumstances as those I have recounted here, through the discursive practices and expressive performances that circulate within communities. Warodi and the other elders who staged the dream performance endeavored to bring these narratives to life, giving the youths who participated that day in August 1984 the means by which they might remain forever Xavante. The dream-narrative performance is Warodi's gift to future generations of Xavante, a gift—as Etẽpa says in the dream narrative—for them to draw upon in their effort "to remain forever aʔuwẽ."

> now, for this, [to remain forever aʔuwẽ]
> if I live longer than you [Warodi]
> I will tell the Xavante
> passing on your story

3

Sounds of Time, the Time of Sounds

In March 1982, after my expulsion the preceding January, FUNAI allowed me to return to Pimentel Barbosa. When I did, Warodi invited me to live in his home, as a member of his family. He adopted me as his daughter and began to refer to me as *ĩ-ʔra* (my child). From then on I called him *ĩ-mama* (my father). As a resident in Warodi's household I became familiar with the ways in which members of the community arranged the production of vocal sounds in their daily lives and according to the seasons. These cycles of sound promote an acoustic continuity to life in Pimentel Barbosa. Imposing an order onto their acoustic environment through repeated patterns of familiar sounds, members of a community constitute a sense of perpetuity and enduringness.

When imagining life in a savannah community, many urban dwellers may conjure up images of silence and tranquility. The bustle and din of modern cities opposes the imagined serenity, tranquility, and, above all, quiet of village life. The truth is that wherever there are people, there is noise. Decibel levels may differ in orders of magnitude between industrial and nonindustrial societies, but the fact remains that humans are noisy. The Xavante soundscape is no exception.

Step outside the perimeter of a Xavante village and walk behind the semicircular row of houses into the outlying strip of manioc gardens. If you stop to listen, you hear the din of dogs barking, chickens clucking, babies crying, the thump of wooden mortars as women pound the husks from rice, children's laughter, and voices: above all you hear voices, the murmur of people talking, conversing inside and outside houses. Voices travel between houses, for the thatched dwellings are close enough to permit conversation between adjacent homes. Sometimes people shout from one house to another across the central plaza. And, depending on the time of day or night, you hear the soft murmur of the men's council, young men singing, or someone expressing grief in a plaintive, tuneful lament.

You might at first, as I was, be surprised by all the noise. In Pimentel Barbosa, as in many lowland South American villages, sound travels well within the semicircular arrangement of houses.[1] Indeed, from where you stand amongst the manioc stalks it might seem that the village emits a cacophonous symphony of sound. But, in the apparent clamor of human voices, there is order. The Xavante, like all people, organize human sounds in meaningful ways. They draw upon distinct expressive resources and configure them differently in their expressive vocal styles to achieve distinct social ends. This socially organized sound occurs at all times of day and night. The Xavante soundscape is a twenty-four-hour affair.[2] In fact, certain types of vocalizations are appropriately performed only at certain times of day. Xavante classify types of song and dance, for instance, according to when they are appropriately performed within a full cycle of the sun: some songs are "for midday," others are "for evening," and still others are "for early morning" and "just before dawn." Since people often rest or nap during afternoon hours when the sun is strongest, many remain awake for periods of the night. Indeed, a great deal of activity goes on in and outside Xavante dwellings from dusk to dawn.

THE TWENTY-FOUR-HOUR CYCLE OF SOUND

By the time the Toyota jeep rumbled into the village on the night of March 3, 1982, when I returned to Pimentel Barbosa with Warodi, nearly everyone had gone to bed. But as the jeep pulled to a stop outside Warodi's house, his wife, daughters, and son-in-law emerged to greet us and help collect our baggage. A touch on the chest, a brush of the hand served as a silent welcome for Warodi. As I stepped out of the cab, Warodi's son-in-law Agostim intoned a merry "*Pra! ma we mo!* (Well! She *did* come back!)" Word of FUNAI's radio communication concerning my return, like news of any novel event, had swept like wildfire through the twenty Xavante dwellings that day. Members of Warodi's family knew I was coming. They didn't know, however, that I was to become a member of their household—to share their space and their food, to pester them with questions, to clamor about at night preparing my tape recorder, and to take up an inordinate amount of space with my inventory of tapes, camera equipment, notebooks, and materialist assortment of baggage. Neither did they know (although they certainly must have hoped) that I would bring them coveted luxury items such as salt, coffee, and sugar, nor that I would, on many occasions, make them weep with laughter at my inexperienced way of maneuvering in their world.

Although at times I was a tiresome, tape recorder–toting nuisance, from that first night I sensed that I was always welcome in this dignified family of leaders. With his brief but upbeat greeting, Agostim broke the ice to put me at ease (as he has done many times since). He helped me sling my hammock, and soon, cozy in my sleeping-bag cocoon, I enjoyed my first night in the bosom of this gracious and accepting family. I was exhilarated to be with them inside their thatched home, listening to their soft voices as they discussed the events of Warodi's trip to Barra do Garças. Even though I understood little Xavante at the time, and what I could hear was punctuated with slurps from juicy oranges and distorted by mouths sucking on hard candy, I knew Warodi's elder daughters were inquiring about me from their sleeping mats on the opposite side of the partition. All I could make out of this dialogue was *tsawi di* (she is nice) and *wẽ di, wa-ma wẽ di* (it's fine with us [that she will stay here]). To the comforting sounds of the family's discussion and the cockroaches and crickets chirping outside, I drifted off to sleep.

Had I continued to live apart from the village at the FUNAI post or in my own separate residence, I would have come to know the soundscape of this Xavante community only by day. But living in Warodi's house, I became privy to the soundspace of a Xavante home, as well as to the sounds of the village by night. Slung in my hammock, I listened to the sounds within our house and those of the village outside. Day and night the patterns of human voices weaved themselves through my ears, were captured on the tapes of my ever-present cassette recorder or transcribed in my notebook, or were guarded in memory as final thoughts to be added to my notes the next morning. Over the sounds of the family's breathing and Agostim's occasional snores, I grew familiar with the sounds of night—a baby's cry, an individual's tuneful weeping, dogs barking, the novitiates' calls, and their nighttime singing and dancing.

At first, as a new resident in Warodi's household, I found it difficult to adapt to sleeping in the afternoon. Since I tried to be alert for events during the day I was overwhelmed when I found that I needed to be up nights as well. In the dry season particularly, the time of many ceremonials when segments of the population are apt to be up at all hours, I felt like a hospital intern on rotation. Barring sickness, I tried to be at the locus of activity, tape recorder in hand. I learned to sleep lightly, to listen for the calls that summon performers to the *warã* village center after midnight or just before dawn. Often I fell asleep long after most in my home were swept up in their dreams, finding these moments when there was no singing to be the only precious times I had to myself. When I did drift off to sleep, I slept with one ear cocked to hear what kinds of talk or song my tape recorder might, as Xavante say, "listen to" that night.

SELECTIVE SILENCE

One night in July 1984, long after I thought my housemates had all gone to sleep, I heard the door creak open and the mysterious steps of someone slipping in. Palm fronds rustled—the intruder must have adjusted the sleeping mat as he lay down. For a while all I heard was the steady breathing of those who still slept a sleep untroubled by the appearance of this stranger in our midst. Then, peering over the rim of my hammock, I saw my eldest sister, Aracy, silently cross the room to Warodi and his wife, Irene's, side of the house, where Aracy's eldest daughter slept. Her flashlight located the sleeping girl in the tangle of heat-seeking little bodies. She whispered, loud enough for me to hear, "*Ĩ-tsaʔõmo ma we mo* (My son-in-law is here)!" "Uhhh," was her daughter's sleepy, protesting reply.

Cecita didn't go to her future husband that night; he slept alone in the partitioned enclosure, the "bridal suite" that Aracy had carefully made for them (Fig. 6). At 2:00 A.M. I began to hear the calls summoning the *ʔritaiʔwa* novitiates to sing. Beckoned, the novitiate groom slipped out as quietly as he had come.

The next day, when I asked my sisters who our nocturnal visitor had been, they could hardly contain their laughter over what was to them my incredible naiveté. "Really, you don't know?" I conceded my ignorance with a nod. Pointing with her lower lip in the direction of Etẽpa's house, she then replied, "From over there." Not speaking his name, Aracy observed the taboo against uttering personal names. But with her gesture she gave me a substantial clue as to the identity of her daughter's suitor. I guessed, and later confirmed by observation, that Cecita's beau was Suptɔ. When Suptɔ came the next night, Cecita slipped into the partitioned enclosure without prompting from her mother. Yet when I awoke the next morning I spotted her nestled against her cousins and younger sisters. Since at first these visits were brief, once Suptɔ joined his cohort in the central plaza Cecita would be left to sleep in the partitioned area by herself. After Suptɔ left, she snuggled back into her familiar position. It was too cold (without a sleeping bag!) to sleep alone.

Comings and goings such as Suptɔ's are hardly mysterious within Xavante households. Nearly everyone is alert to what is going on during these nocturnal rendezvous and has an interest in the success of such fledgling relationships. In fact, what we might think of as courting behavior between young lovers is actually the manifestation of a relationship that implicates many people in addition to the trysting couple. Suptɔ's family, for instance, had long since arranged with Cecita's that when she became of marriageable age, Suptɔ would be her husband. Likewise, the two families—members of the opposed exogamous moieties *poridzaʔõno* and *öwawẽ*—had agreed that Suptɔ's younger brothers were promised to Cecita's younger sisters. The parents, both biological and classificatory, in these two families—myself included—call and refer to each other as *watsini* our in-laws. As is typically the case, Suptɔ and Cecita's marriage is linked to the marriages of sisters and brothers and involves arrangements between entire extended families.

6. Warodi's granddaughter Jacoro in front of the partitioned area where her older sister and the sister's fiancé sleep. (Photo by Laura Graham, 1987.)

Given the Xavante pattern of uxorilocal residence, Agostim and Suptɔ's father, Etẽpa, had worked out an excellent deal. The arrangement was well suited to accommodate both the emotional and the political needs of those involved. As Agostim's daughters grew to maturity, they would marry Etẽpa's sons and nephews, his brothers' sons. One by one the four boys involved in this arrangement would eventually move into Agostim's household. There, since kinship is often the basis for political alignments, they would be able to reconstitute their basis of political support. For Agostim's daughters the arrangement also has its advantages: marrying a group of brothers, or—as in the case of Moriwadze and Joasi—sharing the same husband, maximizes their potential to stay together in the same household, or in adjacent households, into old age. Now that Cecita's breasts had begun to develop, it was time for Suptɔ to visit her at night. Their nuptial encounters were the first in a series, and their behavior served as an example for the other girls to follow in the future.

Xavante marriages are partnerships between individuals as well as between entire families. Marriage is a process, a state that evolves slowly over a period of years, involving individuals within family networks. Food exchanges between in-laws—tokens that model the contribution each partner makes to a household in marriage—begin to bind the two families even while the future couple are toddlers. A girl's mother sends her future in-laws cooked foods and produce she has harvested from her garden, while a boy's family sends a portion of the game the father, and later the boy himself, brings in from the hunt.[3] Unlike marriage in Western society, in which a single individual vested with particular authority alters social relations through a performative speech act, no Xavante individual can transform a couple's civil status by saying, for example, "I now pronounce you husband and wife."[4] The ceremony known as *adaba* that publicly represents a marriage is celebrated only after a couple has cohabited for at least several months, usually closer to a year. The *adaba* involves a ritual exchange: meat from a ceremonial bridal hunt (*da-batsa*) is given to the bride's family on behalf of the groom. In exchange, the bride's family offers ceremonial bread to the members of the groom's family who labored during the bridal hunt. As a civil state, however, marriage is considered stable only after the birth of the first child.

Once the bride is deemed old enough, the groom begins his nocturnal visits. Slowly the young couple begins to get acquainted, and a sexual relationship eventually develops. While the couple get to know each other, the bride's household gradually adjusts to the new man's presence. As Agostim put it, Suptɔ visits "just a little so we can all get used to him." This transitional period is a delicate phase, as Agostim pointedly acknowledges in this statement. Although both families have invested considerable energy in laying the groundwork for a successful marriage, the transitional period is a time fraught with potential instability. Will the young couple be compatible? Will the newcomer, possibly a member of a different political faction than his father-in-law, be perceived as posing a threat to his senior's authority?[5] Will the mother-in-law prevail upon her daughter to assume her new responsibilities as a wife? Will the young girl protest? Will she refuse to wash her new husband's clothes?

One night, almost a year after Supto's first visit, I heard the door open
as I lay in my hammock. I listened to the sound of footsteps, which I now
recognized as his, move across the room. I heard him rustle against the
palm fronds and enter the partitioned area where Cecita now awaited his
arrival. As usual, no one in the house said a thing. No one greeted him or
acknowledged his arrival. Although I heard him clear his throat and spit,
I didn't hear him speak. Cecita, on the other hand, giggled from time to
time. I could hear her voice pipe up in what was, at least for Supto, a very
muted conversation. By now the two had become friends and lovers and
each looked forward to Supto's visits.

Some time passed. Then Agostim spoke up from his sleeping mat. He
addressed his eldest daughter, using not her "child name," Cecita, but the
term for married girls who are not yet mothers: "*Tsoimba*, is my son-in-
law hungry? Does he like rice?" I heard whispers and the murmur of a soft
conversation from within the bridal partition. "*Īhe*, yes, he's hungry," Cecita replied. She emerged from the partitioned area to fetch the plate of
rice Agostim and Aracy had put aside for their son-in-law.

"What a peculiar conversation," I thought to myself. Surely, even though
he was out of sight in the partitioned area, Supto could hear the question
which, although formally directed to Cecita, was obviously meant for
him. Why didn't Agostim ask Supto himself if he wanted some rice? Why
didn't Supto answer directly his father-in-law's generous offer?

Almost as soon as I remarked on the curiousness of this circuitous conversation I recognized it as a beautiful example of avoidance behavior between in-laws—just where I might have expected it! Relationships between in-laws, particularly during transitional phases, are potentially
volatile in almost any society. In numerous cultures, various forms of
avoidance behavior surround this relationship. These behaviors, which often take the form of taboos, formally acknowledge the structural tensions
inherent in the affected social relationships.[6] Avoidance behaviors also
provide ways to guard against conflict by minimizing direct contact between individuals in certain structural relations at moments of potential
volatility. Moreover, in observing these behaviors, individuals show their
respect for or deference to socially significant others.

In witnessing the members of my household implement this speech taboo, it occurred to me that I was witnessing an elaborated version of a
similar behavior that might be called "no-naming," with which I am familiar as a member of middle-class Anglo-American society. No-naming
occurs between individuals who are in much the same position as Supto
and Agostim: a suitor, too familiar with future in-laws to use titles—
"Mrs.," "Mr.," or "Dr."—but not yet comfortable with, say, "Doris" or
"Phil," gets the addressee's attention by some other means, such as clearing his throat, "Ahem!" Then, having avoided the issue of naming alto-

gether, he politely asks, "Please pass the salt." No-naming enables participants in an unequal status relationship to avoid drawing attention to the tensions inherent in their relationship while engaging in congenial conversation. It enables them to formally avoid acknowledging the status and power differentials of their relationship.

The linguist R. M. W. Dixon documented one of the most striking examples of altered speech patterns between in-laws among the Djirbal, an aboriginal group of North Queensland, Australia.[7] In Djirbal, individuals were obliged to use a separate linguistic code, the "mother-in-law tongue," when speaking to the mother-in-law (or classificatory cousins of the opposite sex), *and* whenever the mother-in-law was within earshot. Xavante in-laws, instead of using an entirely different set of lexical items, simply avoid addressing each other altogether during the transitional phase when marriages are formalized. In the comings and goings within our household, Suptɔ and Agostim, as well as Agostim's wives, each upheld their end of the in-law speech taboo. They communicated through intermediaries and thus avoided speaking directly to each other. Until Suptɔ became a well-established presence in the household, after he had fathered several children, he employed his wife, his mother, a child messenger, or, innovatively, the visiting anthropologist as intermediaries.

The speech taboo elaborates a model of communication which, in the event of an actual conflict, can be effectively marshaled so that the parties involved may avoid face-to-face confrontation and the potential for public loss of face. Negotiation via intermediaries is one way of formally removing speech production from individual agents. When a message is communicated through another speaker, it is actually delivered to the receiver by someone other than its original producer. At the level of appearances, the message is not connected with its sender. This dissociation enables participants to broaden the space for their negotiation; it leaves open, for example, possibilities for each to rationalize or account for their differences. Perhaps the sender misunderstood a previous message. Perhaps the messenger confused the sender's words. At the very least, this form of communication buys time for those involved. It forces people to slow down when their "heads are hot," as Xavante say. It opens up a space for parties to consider further the matters under discussion. Moreover, the involvement of a third party formally allows for the expression of outside opinions and the possibility that such opinions might help mediate between opposing points of view.

The speech taboo thus offers a microlevel model of how individuals, should significant differences arise between them, might effectively buy time in the communicative process to consider other perspectives. Simultaneously, it enables participants to avoid direct confrontation and the possibility for public humiliation. The fact that the speech taboo is the operative mode of communication precisely during this transitional phase highlights the Xavante's sensitivity to the potential for conflict as a son-in-law disrupts the status quo in his wife's father's household. As we shall see in Chapter 5, Xavante formally manipulate discursive practice to dissociate speakers from the content of their speech—through different formal means but toward a similar end—in another potentially "hot" arena, the *warã* men's council.

In the case of Agostim and Suptɔ there was no conflict at this time, as evidenced by Agostim's generous offer of food. However, their relationship was one in which hostility or conflict could easily develop, particularly since, as a young novitiate, Suptɔ's political allegiances aligned with those of his father, not with Agostim's. Of course, as Agostim's offer of rice displays, a father-in-law is interested in currying his new son-in-law's favor in the hope that he will eventually earn his support in the political arena. Moreover, Agostim had his other daughters' marriages in mind, since they depended to some degree on the success of the first. Suptɔ's credibility in the political sphere of adult males depended, in turn, on the success of his marriage and the children he hoped to father. Clearly, both parties had an interest in the success of their relationship.

In the same way that a groom's allegiances lie with his father during the early phase of marriage, a young girl's bonds to her father are stronger than her ties to her new husband at the outset of marriage. Through her, the father-in-law is in a position to exert some control over his new son-in-law.[8] Thus, while both father-in-law and son-in-law have an interest in establishing a convivial relationship, theirs, especially in this initial phase, is not a relationship between equals. The interests of both are served by maintaining the appearance of mutual respect, even though theirs is clearly an asymmetrical relationship. They publicly signal this respect in their mutual observance of the speech taboo.

Despite what both young men and seniors label as mutual "respect," their behaviors in both speech and demeanor render the asymmetries of their relationship unmistakable. There can be no overlooking the fact that the novitiate newcomer is subordinate to his father-in-law's authority while in his wife's home. By literally muting his behavior, he displays a humble attitude toward his in-laws and respect for the status quo of their household. This "muting" is made most salient by his silence. A young suitor avoids calling attention to himself while in his in-law's home primarily by not speaking. He also visits his in-law's home sheathed under the cloak of darkness. Although other sounds belie his physical presence in the house—a yawn, a fart, a movement on the platform bed—he does not *speak* loudly enough for anyone but his new wife to hear. In the darkness, no one *sees* him. Thus, of all the sensual modes through which an individual's physical presence may be manifested, Xavante pick out speech and visibility as the most salient. A young groom makes himself physically and acoustically invisible to signal his respect for the status quo.

In contrast, other members of the family, including his father-in-law, carry on as usual. Agostim, for example, always in form when it comes to bedtime jokes, put on some of his best displays once Suptɔ had settled in for the night. At times it seemed to me that Agostim was pushing Suptɔ's unobtrusiveness to its limits, trying to get his son-in-law to laugh—but he never did. Agostim loved to entertain us by teasing imitations of complex speech from his smallest children, as well as from me. He also liked to tease me or one of his wives about one embarrassing thing or another that had happened during the day. Once he discovered my taste for *buriti* palm fruit, for example, I became an easy target. During the rainy season when *buriti* fruit, *udzu*, are ripe and abundant, he teased me incessantly. One night Agostim called out from his mat, "Reme?õ ate an entire basket of *udzu* today! I saw her chomp [snort], chomp, chomp [snort] like a wild pig!"[9] As my Xavante improved, so did my contributions to this repartee. No doubt my comebacks made the encounters that much more engaging to our audience. Over time our jokes escalated to outrageous proportions: "I saw him, my sisters' husband, drink a whole gourd of water—no, suck the river dry. Then, SHHHH, he pissed like a horse!" With entertainment like this, the entire household shook with laughter. But, when he was a newcomer and still a novitiate *?ritai?wa*, I never heard Suptɔ join us in our guffaws.

For girls, the in-law speech taboo hardly exists. A girl of marriageable age has few opportunities to encounter her father-in-law directly. She does not speak to him when she does. She may, in contrast, frequently meet her mother-in-law. For example, during her courting Cecita often sat and quietly listened to women's conversations when Suptɔ's mother came to visit our home. Within months, Cecita began to work at her in-law's home to assist with large food-processing tasks such as making manioc flour. In contrast to Suptɔ's behavior, Cecita soon spoke freely in the presence of Suptɔ's family.

This gender differential in speech taboo behaviors underscores the political nature of the relationship between a man and his wife's father. Since a girl does not move into her father-in-law's household at marriage, she poses no threat to the household's status quo. Most significantly, young men, as opposed to young women, are directly implicated in the male-dominated political arena. A son-in-law comes into his in-law's home as a political "unknown," and potentially as a member of a different faction whose political interests at the community level may differ from those of his wife's father. Relationships between men thus involve stakes that extend beyond the domestic sphere into the community-level political arena. The speech taboo formally underscores this very political nature of the men's relationship. Indeed, a boy observes this taboo and generally avoids direct contact with his future father-in-law even before he begins to visit his father-in-law's home.

Once a young man has established himself within his in-law's household, he will be able to begin to change his speech behavior, to speak freely and loudly, and eventually to address his father-in-law without going through an intermediary. When Suptɔ graduated from novitiate status to become a young adult, an ĩ-prɛdup-tɛ able to participate in the men's council, his "silent" phase came to an end. Also, as a young adult he began to come openly and in broad daylight to our house. He began to speak up: his voice could be heard at any time of day or night, even when Agostim was around. This "opening up" was publicly displayed after the next age-set was initiated. At that time the new novitiates' age-set sponsors stormed into our home, as well as the homes of the entire cohort of past novitiates, to dramatically rip out the partition that separated Suptɔ and Cecita's living area from that of her parents. The effect of this ritual act was to publicly expose Suptɔ's presence within our home. Without barriers, he could now be seen and heard. As a young adult, however, Suptɔ still avoided talking directly to Agostim. Although he had become a visible and audible presence, he maintained a humble demeanor around his father-in-law in particular.

Some four years later, after the next initiation in 1990, Suptɔ moved another rung up the age-grade ladder to become a fully mature male, an ĩ-prɛdu. Had their first child not died of a fever in the rainy season of 1987, Suptɔ and Cecita would have had two children. With a stable marriage, children of his own, and an active voice in the warã men's council, Suptɔ began to speak openly with Agostim and his wives. However, he continues to exhibit respect for his in-laws by not entering their living area within the home, an area separated from his and Cecita's by a resurrected palm-frond screen. When he addresses his in-laws, he speaks from his area of the home, loudly enough for them to hear.

In time, Suptɔ will be able to enter Agostim's area of the domicile just as Agostim was apt to visit Warodi. Eventually, when Suptɔ has many children, instead of spending most of his time at his own father's house he will be at ease in his father-in-law's home, as Agostim was with Warodi. Although Agostim generally avoided trespassing into his in-laws' space for anything other than political meetings, he often lay down beside his father-in-law, alongside those who frequently came to visit, to join the quiet discussion of political matters and issues that concerned the broader community. In the mornings and evenings, Suptɔ, too, will join the family to sit and talk around the cooking fire on the patio of our home. Listening to Suptɔ, I could hear that the process of social maturation is marked through sound and the control of expressive forms.

MICROLEVEL BEHAVIOR: HONORIFIC PERSON MARKING

As a mature man, an *ĩ-prɛdu*, with three of Warodi and Irene's daughters as his wives, Agostim has many children of his own. He "works hard!" as both men and women jestingly put it in Xavante: in 1987 he had eleven surviving children; by 1991 there were fourteen. So many grandchildren delighted Warodi, who consistently indulged the little ones, hardly minding their distractions as they crawled upon him while he conferred during long hours with his associates. Although Warodi was considered head of the household, as a mature male Agostim maintained a visible and acoustic prominence within the home. He came and went freely and spoke openly to his in-laws. As adults no longer bound by the speech taboo, they addressed each other face-to-face and engaged in conversation that spanned an unlimited range of topics, from domestic matters to issues of political and community concern.

Although they conversed openly with each other, there was something striking about this conversation between in-laws. They differentiated their discourse from speech to most other individuals by using a special set of grammatical features in pre- and postpositional person markings. As mature adults, these in-laws encoded their relationship at the microlevel of grammar rather than at the macrolevel of overt behavior. In doing so, they formally indicated, as well as called attention to, the social salience of their relationship.

To the unwitting observer, this grammatical differentiation is a much subtler way of highlighting the in-law relationship than the obvious avoidance behavior manifested in the speech taboo. For example, during the initial stages of my fieldwork when I struggled to achieve a basic command of the language, I was able to observe the operation of the speech taboo by being attentive to the visual and acoustic environment in our home: I could hear Suptɔ's silence by the absence of his voice; I listened as Cecita answered when Agostim formulated a question aimed at his son-in-law; I heard the door creak open and Suptɔ's footsteps as he traversed the room. Yet in the darkness I never *saw* him. My family's implementation of the speech taboo was a thing I noticed with my senses. Yet the ways in which Xavante speakers intertwine social relations with the actual forms of speaking remained invisible or, more aptly, inaudible to me during my first months of fieldwork. I was deaf to the rich and complex system of marking social relationships that operates at the very microlevel of grammatical organization.

When I began to focus on the transcription of Warodi's dream narrative, speech that I had recorded as a discussion unfolded between senior men—not speech that I had elicited—I began to notice the appearance of what are, in comparison with elicited forms, extremely unusual person markers. Eventually I was able to determine that certain person-marking forms (sets of pronouns, clitic person markers, and postposition verb endings) are used by adults to speak to and about particular kin and affines. I refer to these forms as a system of honorifics, using a conventional term for pragmatic phenomena of this sort.[10] In speech to and about individuals who do not belong to these salient groups, individuals use the socially unmarked set of person markers, the ones assistants give in elicitation.

Initiated men and adult women—women who have given birth—employ one set of person-marking forms in speech to and about first and second ascending generation kin and affines. A son-in-law, for instance, addresses his father- and mother-in-law in the same way that he addresses his biological and classificatory parents; the grammatical forms he uses are different from those he uses when speaking to and about his siblings and ceremonial friends, for example. With these formal markings he indicates his adult status. He also displays his kin and affinal relationships. Moreover, the forms he uses indicate equal respect for his parents and in-laws, thereby blurring the kin/affine distinction.

The same set of formal markings is also used in reference and address to second descending generation kin. Warodi employs forms from this set, for example, to indicate respect when speaking of his "descendants" in the dream narrative. A similar set is used in speech about the ancestors, thereby suggesting, from a formal point of view, a similarity between ascending generations (and second descending generation kin) and the ancestors.[11]

Adults use a second set of honorific person markings to address and refer to first descending generation affines—sons' wives and daughters' husbands. The most significant feature of this set is that its forms do not distinguish between second and third person. Therefore, a mother- or father-in-law uses third-person reference forms to address, as well as to speak about, a daughter's husband or son's wife. Using these forms, a parent-in-law creates the appearance of avoidance. For instance, when Warodi asked Agostim if he planned to go hunting, he said, "Is *he* going hunting?" instead of, "Are *you* going hunting?"

This particular grammatical arrangement is fascinating in light of the in-law speech taboo. The people who use it are the very same ones who spoke through intermediaries and avoided direct address in an earlier phase of their relationship. Ingeniously, the honorific forms permit address while simultaneously perpetuating the previous pattern of avoiding direct address. In using these forms, speakers project avoidance onto the level of grammar. They extend the overt "observable" behavior of the speech taboo into grammar as the in-law relationship matures. When Warodi spoke directly to Agostim, addressing his son-in-law to his face, he spoke to him as "he." Thus, while young men mark the passage of time and the maturation of their relationships with their in-laws by moving from silence to speech in the presence of their in-laws, a father-in-law moves from physically mediated speech to direct speech. However, this direct speech is mediated—by grammar.

NOCTURNAL RESONANCES

In December 1985, a year and a half after Suptɔ and Cecita's first nuptial encounters, Suptɔ was still a *Pritaiʔwa* novitiate. He was also a teaching assistant in FUNAI's primary school, a position for which he continued to receive a salary even though the school had not functioned during the past two years. Among the purchases he made with his earnings, and which he subsequently brought into our home, were a foam mattress for the double platform bed and a stereo boom-box.

Suptɔ's blaster was one of the first tape recorders to make its way into the village. Waldo, the tractor driver, had had a transistor radio as early as 1981. Occasionally I'd heard him play it as the morning men's council got under way. But, probably owing to the high cost of batteries, Waldo rarely played it for any length of time. In his own home it "sang" only for short periods. When I arrived, my tape recorder was a big hit. I was summoned daily to visit houses so that occupants could listen to singing I had recorded.

Although I enjoyed being able to bring such pleasure into their homes, these incessant requests proved to be a significant obstacle to my research. With twenty houses to visit and occupants in each demanding to hear a full forty-five-minute tape, I spent hours visiting people who were intent on listening rather than talking. Moreover, this activity occupied my tape recorder with playback rather than recording, as I wished, not to mention that it drained my precious supply of batteries. I schemed to visit only a few houses with the tape recorder on any given day, promising to let it "sing" for others on subsequent days. Nevertheless, members of some households perceived my activity as favoritism and complained to Warodi. One afternoon when I returned home, he scolded me. "You should visit *every* house with the tape recorder, they like to hear the music. Start there, at the *apmrã* [first house] and [pointing to each house in succession] go around." Plagued by these demands, I began to perceive my tape recorder as a hindrance to my work, rather than the asset I had expected it to be.

Consequently, when Suptɔ and soon other young men began to purchase tape recorders of their own, the constant pressure on me began to let up. Happily, I was relieved of the exclusive responsibility to let my tape recorder "sing." But Suptɔ, like other young proprietors, adapted his tape recorder to alleviate the pressure of the in-law speech taboo: at any hour of the night he turned it on full blast to provide a sound screen for his conversations with Cecita or to cover the sounds of their lovemaking. Once again, as I was jolted out of my exhausted sleep, I came to loathe the invention of the tape recorder.

Whereas I had tried to be discreet with my machine, never playing it loudly or at night, Suptɔ and those members of his cohort who owned boom-boxes worked the batteries past their limits or picked up mostly static from bad radio reception, literally filling their in-law's homes with noise. I silently gave thanks for the times when Suptɔ didn't play it, and for the occasional evening when one of his cohort borrowed the machine to keep another household of in-laws awake. To my chagrin, Agostim told me he liked the nighttime entertainment. My sisters did not, or so they said. Warodi just laughed. So far as I know, no one ever said a thing to Suptɔ or the other young men who visited our house to court our daughters.

Finally, in the summer of 1991, when Suptɔ's younger brother played his music too loudly for me to bear, I pulled rank as his mother-in-law. "Wĩrĩ (Kill it)!" I called out to my newly wed daughter. Respecting my wish, her husband turned off the machine. I negotiated with Suptɔ for a low-volume ordinance in our house after midnight. Once again I could hear the night sounds of the village without static or interference: the calls of the novitiate ʔritaiʔwa as they summoned their cohort to the central plaza, their singing around the village, and tuneful laments on the part of nostalgic or grieving adults.

Around midnight I began to hear "kai, kai, kai," the falsetto calls of the ʔritaiʔwa novitiates as they gathered in the warã central plaza. While most others sleep, the adolescents, who are housebound by day, take over the warã plaza by night. It is theirs to occupy until about 4:00 A.M., when it reverts to their seniors' domain. Meanwhile, the adolescents physically and audibly stake their claim to the plaza, periodically shouting summonses to their cohort while they talk quietly, lying on their mats or huddled around a blazing palm-frond fire to take the edge off the dry season's chill.

Hearing their calls, Suptɔ left, clicking his lighter to illuminate his path to the door. Beckoned like a novitiate myself, I groped for my flashlight, rolled out of my hammock, and bundled up to sit for an hour or two in the cold night air. Tape recorder and microphones in hand, I followed my flashlight's beam to where I could see the dark figures silhouetted against the flickering blaze. I heard giggles as I approached. Then someone, whose face I couldn't see in the dark but whose voice I recognized, inquired, "E aptöʔö õ di (Aren't you sleepy)?" "Ĩhe, aptʔö di! e aptöʔö ã bö (Of course I'm sleepy)," I replied, "aren't you?" "No, we're not tired," they boasted.

As novitiates, the adolescents took pride in their stamina and their marvelous ability to stay up throughout the night. What they failed to mention was that each had remained indoors all day, either napping or lounging by his father's side.

"Who dreamed?" I asked, "whose song are you going to sing?" "A-tsaʔõmo (your daughter's husband), rotsawẽrẽ petse di, õ hã (he dreams well, that one)," a voice in the darkness replied. I knew my interlocutor was teasing both me and Suptɔ because, at first, the adolescents found placing me in their kin networks to be most amusing. After a while, someone stood and the others followed suit. The interval between their falsetto calls diminished, and they gave the last call for those who had remained in the warmth of their beds. "Kai! kai! kai!" Then, tapping their hands against their mouths, they joined together in a boisterous final whoop. They were about to sing. If ever I'd remained in my hammock too long, I knew I'd need to rush, for, after completing this call, they launched into their low and hushed rehearsal, my favorite part of their performance. Another whoop and they set off for the first house on their singing/dancing tour around the village.

Da-ñoʔre: Collective Singing

Their song, composed by Suptɔ's cousin Jé Paulo, was a marawaʔwa, an early morning song, the kind that can be performed between midnight and about 3:00 A.M. Maraʔwaʔwa are a type of da-ñoʔre, a collectively performed combination of song and dance. When performing da-ñoʔre, participants sing and move together, forming a circle with clasped hands. Indeed, when Xavante speak of da-ñoʔre, they refer to a unified performance complex, not simply to the acoustic features produced by voices. Since movement is an integral part of this expressive form, readers should think of da-ñoʔre as referring to both song and dance. I write of da-ñoʔre as "song" following Xavante's Portuguese translation, but the term "song" actually denotes a song/dance complex.

Xavante classify three distinct performance types under the generic term da-ñoʔre. Da-praba, da-dzarõno, and da-hipɔpɔ are differentiated on the basis of the accompanying physical movements of the dance steps and the time of day suitable for their performance. Da-praba are performed in the late morning and throughout the day when the sun is full and strong. Male dancers mark time by stepping one foot to the side on one beat and bringing the other to join it on the next stressed beat. In this fashion the entire circle rotates in one direction. At transitional breaks in the song, the movements are reversed and the circle doubles back in the opposite direction. The physical movements that accompany da-praba

are the most vigorous of all the *da-ño?re* dances; *da-praba* are also performed at the quickest tempo. By engaging in this fast-paced and energetic
dance form under the hottest sun, men display their physical stamina and
endurance.

Xavante call songs sung in the late afternoon and early evening *da-
dzarõno*. Male dancers performing *da-dzarõno* remain in a fixed spot
while forcefully stepping one foot slightly forward and to the side. *Da-
hipɔpɔ*, literally "leg shaking" or "leg bouncing" (*da-hi*, "leg"; *pɔpɔ*,
"to shake or bounce") are performed at night and early morning. Standing
performers bend their knees outward in time with the metric pulse of the
music. The knee bends cause the dancers' feet to shuffle back and forth.
Pre-initiates, with their senior age-set sponsors, sing *da-hipɔpɔ* between
10:00 and 11:00 P.M., before the novitiates take over the plaza. When
the novitiates sing after midnight, they perform a subgenre of *da-hipɔpɔ*
known as *marawa?wa*. Then, on the occasions when the senior men
sing after reclaiming the plaza from the novitiates—between 4:00 and
5:00 A.M.—they perform a type of *da-hipɔpɔ* known as *awẽ?u*. The
novitiates' *marawa?wa* and the seniors' *awẽ?u* are sung at the slowest
tempo of all *da-ño?re*. According to Lino, the slow tempo and mature
men's rich, deep voices compliment the early morning hours.[12]

After the novitiates performed Jé Paulo's *marawa?wa* in front of Sãsão's
home, the father of one of the performers and the elder household head
expressed his appreciation by uttering the phrase *he pãrĩ, he te pãrĩ*. This
is an utterance spoken exclusively by senior men; it is the closest thing
there is in Xavante to "thank you." At the other houses on the novitiates'
tour around the village, senior men expressed their appreciation in the
same way. The seventh house we stopped in front of was Serebu?rã's, Jé
Paulo's father. As we approached the patio, the novitiates formed a circle
around me, and standing in the middle, I positioned my microphones. The
performers clasped their hands, cleared their throats, and shuffled their
feet in preparation to begin. A few seconds into the performance, after the
barking dogs had silenced, I began to notice another sound, a woman's
tuneful lament. Known to Xavante as *da-wawa*, ceremonial keening is
a form of vocal expression that elder people harness in exceptionally
charged emotional situations. The mournful sound was coming from the
house next door. It was Pedze, Serebu?rã's mother, grandmother to both
Jé Paulo and Suptɔ.

Da-wawa: Tuneful Laments

Prompted to wail by their singing, Pedze continued her lament even after
the novitiates had finished their song and moved on to the next house on
their itinerary. As they left Serebu?rã's patio, none of the boys commented

on the tuneful weeping their singing had provoked.[13] I remained alone, standing in the dark, mesmerized by the beauty of the woman's lament as she continued to wail. Even without words, the melodic phrases of Pedze's lament suggested nostalgic sentiments. The formal features of the expressive style enabled her to proclaim her deep-felt emotion. Her creaking voice, wavering vocalic utterances, high-pitched falsettos, and audible gasps for breath recalled "natural" or spontaneous expressions of grief.[14] Pedze embedded these microfeatures of crying—features which appear to be universal expressions of grief—into her tuneful expression of emotion. The feelingness of her vocalization, as formally encoded in features of the style, was unmistakable.

When I returned to the central plaza with the novitiates I inquired about Pedze's lament. "Why did she cry?" I asked. "*Mɛ, wẽ-te, ãte pedze-te, te ti-wawa* (Because she thought it [our singing] was beautiful, I guess. Perhaps she weeps from nostalgia)." Another chimed in, "*Ĩ-tsi-hudu tsawi-te dza* ([She weeps] because she loves her grandson)!" Even without asking Pedze herself, my young companions had theories about her wailing. As novitiates, each one had heard *da-wawa* laments many a time. From these experiences each had constructed an interpretive frame which enabled him to infer the meanings embedded in each instance of *da-wawa* performance. From experience, the novitiates could suppose that she wept for the beauty of the song as well as from nostalgia. They understood Pedze's keening as an expression of her appreciation for her grandson's composition, as well as a public demonstration of her affection for him. Later, when I inquired for further explanations from elders, their responses supplemented those of the youths. From their comments I could perceive that age and experience deepen one's interpretation of the meanings embedded in expressive performance. For elders, hearing the youths singing recalls memories of loved ones who had sung before and the songs of a bygone era. No doubt Jé Paulo's song and the *ʔritaiʔwa*'s singing reminded Pedze of her youth and of her loved ones' performances in years past.

Although Pedze's lament sounded like singing to me, Xavante do not consider *da-wawa* to be singing in any way. They classify *da-wawa* as a distinct expressive type, even though, in comparison with other forms of Xavante vocal expression, lament compositions are highly melodic. In contrast to their melodic complexity, however, *da-wawa* minimally exploit linguistic resources. Their texts consist of a limited number of vowel sounds: [a], [e], and [i], which combine with a consonantal onset, either [ʔ] or [h]. As such, *da-wawa* texts transmit no propositional meaning. Stripped of any referential content, the texts foreground the lament's message of affect. Without words, their unique combination of formal features fits together to connote the intimacy of an individual's sentiments.

In the darkness, Pedze's thin voice spoke to my senses, not to my mind.

My skin tingled and the hairs rose on my arms as I listened. I felt her memories in a tangible form, through the creaking of her voice, its wavering tones, the drawn-out, high-pitched *ʔi ʔi ʔi* with which she ended her phrases. Had she simply said, "Your beautiful singing makes me sad, it reminds me of the singing of my youth and the songs my husband used to sing," I would have understood her feelings with my intellect. Through her wordless lament, I felt her nostalgia with the whole of my being.

Features of performance, as well as formal characteristics of *da-wawa* vocalizations, emphasize intimacy and the experience of individual sensibilities. The arena appropriate for expressions of this sort publicly signals the intimacy of profound sentiments and the solitude of the weeping individual. Individuals perform *da-wawa* from the most intimate of social spaces, the sleeping mat or the bed, far from the village center, the center of social space.[15] Keening from her sleeping mat, Pedze sent her sentimental message from the most private space within the village.

The time of day appropriate for ceremonial keening highlights the liminality of intense emotion as well. Except when moved to keening by a specific event, such as hearing a song or seeing a photograph, individuals wail at transitional periods of the day, at dawn or dusk. Immediately after an experience of profound loss, such as a death, an individual may wail at any hour. In situations where wailing takes place in the presence of others, it is not a coordinated group expression. Individuals retain their separate forms and seemingly lose themselves, as if entranced, in their individual expressions of grief. The linguistic texts and highly melodic musical organization compliment these features of performance to formally emphasize the individuality of nostalgic experience.

At the same time Pedze expressed profound feelings through wailing, she expressed, as Urban and Briggs have pointed out for ceremonial lament, a desire for sociability.[16] People engage in ceremonial wailing precisely at periods of potential disorganization, when a death, absence, or overwhelming emotion threatens to disrupt the normal order of things. During these moments, an individual is able to represent her sociability by expressing herself through the culturally appropriate form for the expression of grief and sentimentality. Hearing Jé Paulo's singing may have provoked such a sentiment for Pedze. When she heard her grandson's song, she publicly represented herself as a sentimental grandmother. Simultaneously, because her lament was intended to be overheard by others, she expressed her desire for sociability.

In contrast to *da-ñoʔre* singing, which is an expressive genre primarily associated with men, both women and men perform *da-wawa* laments. Age, rather than gender, determines who can use this expressive form. During the senior phase of the life cycle, both men and women can express themselves this way. Occasionally children imitate the laments of adults by picking out the salient formal features of the style; in these imitations they only "wail" loudly enough for those in close range to hear. Elders, however, project their voices loudly enough for their voices to be heard across the village in the stillness of night or at dawn. According to all Xavante whom I asked, an individual may receive *da-wawa* through dreams only after she or he has at least several children. Lament's association with senior status, not gender, emphasizes that the experience of intense emotion cuts across gendered divisions.[17] Laments also display how feelings of loss and nostalgia become more profound as one moves toward the end of the life cycle. In all the Xavante villages I have visited, the eldest people are the ones who wail the most.

MORNING SOUNDS

I awoke the next morning to the soft murmur of the morning men's council. In comparison with the evening meetings, this one is poorly attended; its youngest members, the young mature males (*ĩ-predup-tɛ*)—most of whom now spend the entire night with their wives—are conspicuously absent. From my hammock inside Warodi's house I occasionally made out the voice of an individual, but for the most part the seniors' sonorous voices blur, merging into a subdued rumble. The murmur of the morning men's council is a comforting sound to awake to.

In our house, Warodi, who rarely attended these morning meetings, made his way across the packed dirt floor to the centerpost where the water gourds were stored. He lifted one to his lips and I heard its glug, glug, glug as he poured the cool liquid into his mouth. Then, cupping his hands to catch the stream of water he released from his lips, he splashed his face. I rolled out of my hammock when he finished, splashed my face in the same manner, and put on my contact lenses before emerging from the house. Squinting against the bright morning light, I made my way to the cook shed where my sisters competed with the dogs for a warm space next to the fire as the coffee pot came to a boil.

While the morning men's council fizzled out, activity in the semicircular ring of households swung into gear. Knowing that there would always be coffee at Warodi's while I was there, a number of men made their way toward us for a taste of the coveted (but overly sugared!) savory brew. My mother's younger brother Luis, for whom I had great affection, smiled as he approached. "*Ĩ-ra waptɛ! E mahata wedepro?* (My sister's daughter! Where's the coffee?)" Joking, I replied, "*Mɛ, wato dzörene dzaʔra ni. Baba di!* (I don't know, I guess we all drank it. It's gone!)" Then, amidst the protests of my deserving uncle, I pulled out my thermos and poured him a steaming cup. Luis never tired of this joke, since as a "request-for-food" greeting (such as, "What are you eating?"), it conformed to a typical Xavante greeting between close kin and affines.

Everyday Speech: Indexing Seniority, Gender, and Affect

As we sat around the cooking fire sipping coffee, both men and women discussed their plans for the day. Listening, I learned who planned to go to the garden, who would look after the children, and who would set out to collect forest fruits, and raw materials for baskets, ceremonial cords, and so on. These exchanges took place in a formally unmarked conversational style which I shall call everyday speech. Common everyday speech, particularly the speech of senior men and women, is often characterized by overlapping utterances. In this respect Xavante conversational patterning differs markedly from the organized pattern of turn taking found in middle-class Anglo-American society.[18] Participants often punctuate the principal speaker's utterances with affirmations—*ĩhe* (yes), *tanε* (like that), *ãnε* (like this)—or glottal releases. In comparison to their North American counterparts, Xavante conversations are acoustically thick interactions. Senior men's speech especially, particularly the plaza speech of the evening men's council, elaborates this feature of overlapping voices. Xavante also employ a good deal of quoted speech in their conversational narratives. Speakers generally set off quoted from descriptive material by speaking in a noticeably higher pitch, with optional tags such as *ãnε te tinha* (s/he spoke like this), or the quotative particle, *ʔu*.

Intonations of declarative statements generally follow a regular pattern. Utterances begin high and may ascend slightly at the outset. Pitch then descends and falls off toward the end of the utterance. Questions follow the typical pattern of intonational rising. For example, when Warodi asked Irene what she would do during the day, she often responded, "I'm going to the garden." The intonational contours of these interrogative and declarative sentences are diagramed in Figure 7.

In everyday conversational speech, speakers relax their glottal chords phrase finally, and utterances typically end with a phrase final voiceless vowel: *buru ʔu wa dza moo*. This pattern contrasts with acoustic features of the formal speech style used in plaza and elders' speech, in which speakers tense their glottal chords phrase finally. Seniors' speech has a distinctive acoustic shape characterized by a slight intonational rise phrase finally and a staccato effect produced by the emphatic word final postvocalic glottal stop and aspirated release.

As the morning's conversation continued, one of Agostim's young daughters, Supara, snatched at a piece of corn bread her older sister held

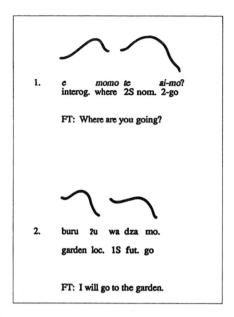

1. e   momo te   ai-mo?
    interog. where 2S nom. 2-go

    FT: Where are you going?

2. buru ?u wa dza mo.

    garden loc. 1S fut. go

    FT: I will go to the garden.

7. Intonational contours of Xavante interrogative and declarative sentences.

tightly in her hand. "It's mine," the older sister growled. Interceding before the two girls came to blows, their mother, Aracy, enforced the obligatory rule of sharing between siblings. "Give her some!" she commanded.
Speaking with tense, rasping voice, Aracy gave her command an aggressive tone. Individuals frequently employ this voice quality to make emphatic statements as well as to convey the impression of hostility or anger.
Sometimes people marshal this voice quality without making propositional statements. Children, particularly siblings, often growl at each
other to make demands for food or to claim space on a sleeping mat. In
the same way, Xavante vehemently reprimand their dogs.

Apart from a few lexical differences, there are no linguistically
marked gender distinctions in everyday speech. For "what," men say
marĩ, whereas women say *tiha*; men say *mare di* for "no," while women
say *madze di*.[19] Both women and men add diminutives to nouns and some
verbs to express affection in everyday speech. For example, the morning
of Warodi's dream enactment, Daru, an elder, spoke affectionately in response to the question, "Where did your wife go?"

atsaro dzo te   ti-mori-re
rice   for 3S nom. 3(dim)-go-dim.
FT. She is going for rice [said affectionately].

Unmarked for affection, the same statement would be:

atsaro dzo te   mo
rice   for 3S nom. 3-go
FT. She is going for rice.

Hedza: Hymns

Whereas everyday speech minimally distinguishes gender through a few lexical distinctions, unequal access to other expressive resources underscores a gender-based power differential in Xavante society. Unlike men, women do not engage in distinctive expressive behaviors such as *da-ño?re* singing or plaza speech, through which men define and represent their participation in extradomestic corporate domains. Moreover, apart from wailing, most of the distinctive expressive practices available to women are, in fact, controlled by men. For example, women occasionally participate in *da-ño?re* performances. However, when women sing and dance they participate with men in performances that are called for by the senior males.[20] Men lead these collective performances and sing songs that have been composed by men. The songs which are performed in community-wide performances are associated with men's age-sets and the male solidarity of youth.

In calling for these community-wide performances, the senior men, who do not participate themselves, demonstrate their privilege over both women and younger men. Senior men, however, can't force women or their juniors to participate. The seniors' subordinates may opt for a strategy of nonparticipation as a way to publicly register their protest. In fact, women sometimes elect to show their resistance to male dominance by refusing to sing with the men.

When senior men consider that the women have stepped out of line, they often deem it appropriate to call upon the women to sing what are known as *hedza* (from Portuguese *resa*, "prayer," "prayer song," or "hymn"). *Hedza*, however, are always composed by elder men, and are always led by a senior male. Although men may join the women in singing *hedza*, the principal performers are women. As musical compositions, *hedza* are slightly more melodic and less rhythmically pronounced than *da-ño?re*. Senior men call the women to sing *hedza* in the early morning, after the men's council, or in the evening.

Hedza appear to be adaptations of religious songs that were initially introduced by missionaries. Their lyrics speak of *Jetsutsi* (Jesus), *wamama* (our Father), and *wa-ñoreptu-?wa* (our Savior). This religious association may account for the fact that the men, now familiar with the Western work week, call the women to sing *hedza* on Sundays as well as on occasions when there is strife within the village. The sermons which inevitably follow *hedza* performances further underscore Xavante's patriarchy. The leader, typically Warodi's younger brother Sibupa, who is considered to be a spiritual leader, launches into a sermonlike lecture in a rhythmically even monotone. His speech bears remarkable similarity to the style priests use to deliver a Catholic mass, and I suspect that Sibupa had picked up formal features from the Salesians who visited the village to say mass from time to time. In his lectures Sibupa exhorts the women to behave, to keep their homes clean, and to bathe their children frequently.

DAYTIME SOUNDS

After a cup of sweet, hot coffee and a piece of roasted manioc, corn, or potato, or sweet bread if we had it, the members of our household dispersed to conduct their business for the day. If they didn't stay home to process manioc into flour or, as in July, to boil up a batch of *urucum* for body paint, most of the women set off with the elder children for the garden or, accompanied by female members of a neighboring household, left for a day's collecting excursion. Usually one or two women stayed at home to watch the house, take care of the small children, wash clothes, and boil up a huge pot of rice for a midday meal. Despite the women's covert complaints that they never received anything from those to whom they were so generous, my sisters—the chief's daughters—always offered heaping plates to any men who happened to be visiting Warodi when the rice was ready.

Throughout the day our home experienced a constant stream of male visitors who came to confer with Warodi and the members of his faction. Our most frequent visitors, Warodi's younger brothers and his wife's brothers, entered the house as familiars, joking with my sisters, me, or the children by asking for something we had—like food. Alternatively, they came in without a word. I most frequently heard, "My sister's child, where's the coffee?" Each visitor made his way to Warodi's sleeping area, where, on his four-poster bed, Warodi lay on his back. Sibupa, Warodi's closest confidant and usually the first to arrive, took his place beside him; without greetings the two launched into intense but muted discussions (Fig. 8). As they spoke quietly, often with one hand covering the mouth, sometimes gesticulating by extending an uplifted arm in a downward motion, others nonchalantly took places on the sleeping mats beside the bed.

For hours our visitors kept up their sotto voce conversations. From time to time, one or another would rise, perhaps leaving briefly to urinate in the area planted with manioc behind the house, or perhaps returning

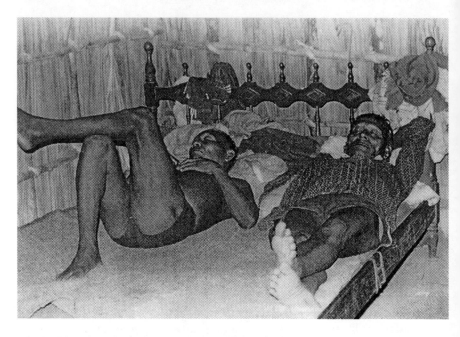

8. Warodi and Sibupa conversing on Warodi's bed; they do not look at each
other as they speak. (Photo by Laura Graham, 1986.)

only the next day. Undisturbed by these and other disruptions, the men
kept up their hushed conversations, their voices intermingling and overlapping in a manner precedent to the discursive practices of the evening
men's-council meetings (see Chapter 5). In these meetings, men spend a
great deal of time discussing politics—their business with FUNAI, for
example—as well as practical matters in the village having to do with
planting, hunting and fishing trips, and the calendar of ceremonial events.
Enthralled by the soft sound of the men's quiet, overlapping voices, I
wished to tape-record these secluded meetings. My requests met with firm
denial. "In the *warã* central plaza, you can 'listen' with the tape recorder,
only in the *warã*."

For their participants, these private meetings were confidential. Here
they worked out positions and strategies which they would present in the
men's-council meetings. In these discreet meetings, the business of factional
politics was done. Our home was by no means the only one in which such
meetings took place. The homes of other prominent senior men buzzed
with similar gatherings throughout the day. As I visited other houses I was
welcome to lie by the men's sides to listen, but with my ears only. In the
warã, when positions were publicly articulated, I was welcome to record.

In addition to discussing politics in these meetings, senior men shared their intimate, personal thoughts and experiences, such as dreams, with their companions. Sons and nephews also lay by their seniors' sides to learn the stories of their pasts. For example, when Warodi's nephews Cipassé and Jurandir came to visit from Goiânia during their scholastic holidays, Warodi shared his stories of their family's past; he imparted pride in his family's history, their connection to the past as the descendants of the first creators, and the dignity of leadership. On such afternoons, Warodi often called me to lie by his side, to teach me tales of his family's past and demonstrate the connection between the world of the creators and the world the Xavante live in today.

Late in the afternoon the men dispersed and Warodi went to bathe in the river. When he returned, as the sun sank lower in the sky, he joined the family as they began to gather on the patio to share news of the day and to eat. Slowly the senior men began to make their way to the central plaza for the evening men's-council reunion. Tired and elderly, Warodi rarely attended the men's council. Nevertheless, members of his faction with whom he had met for lengthy discussions during the day carried his thoughts and words to the meeting for him. As the mature men gathered in the *warã* for the men's council, the novitiates—primly coiffed, bodies oiled, heads bowed, with woven mats before them—made their way to an area just to the side of the men's council. Now that evening had begun to cast its shadow over the village, the novitiates prepared to sing *da-dzarõno* around the village. While they provided entertainment for the women and children who remained at home, the men's council got under way.

Da-hörö: Shouting

As the evening men's council broke up, the men stood and slapped their sleeping mats loudly. This signaled that the meeting had ended. Then, as each man turned outward to face the households, he shouted loudly, broadcasting decisions that concerned the women and adolescent males. "Tomorrow the women will work their rice plantations!" Or, "Log race tomorrow!"

Xavante call any shouting *da-hörö*, but mature men's *da-hörö*, calls shouted across the plaza or across long distances, have a distinctive acoustic shape.[21] Pitched higher than a caller's everyday voice, the intonation contour of these calls is nearly flat. Phrases end with an emphatic release as the caller relaxes his constricted vocal chords. Good callers, such as Sibupa, Barbosa, and Serebu?rã, project their voices extremely well. Their calls are generally clearly audible from every point in the village.

Occasionally women respond to the men's shouts, and often humorous, sexually antagonistic public shouting dialogues ensue. In December 1985, when the village's male population returned from a trip to Barra do Garças, a senior woman, Carmelita, gave voice to the women's suspicions about the increasing frequency of the men's trips to Brazilian cities. In my recording, Carmelita's calls are difficult to make out. However, the microphone picked up Barbosa's voice loud and clear as he bellowed from the opposite side of the plaza. Carmelita, of the *öwawẽ* moiety, accused the men of sleeping with Brazilian women on their trips to Barra do Garças: "And when you all go, where do you wake up?" Booming into the night, Barbosa, a member of the opposite moiety (*poridzaʔõno*), negated the charge: "Don't say that! *Öwawẽ*, your speech is filthy!" Warodi, Irene, Agostim, and my sisters, as well as all the children gathered on our patio, listened delightedly to this exchange. As families did on every other patio around the plaza, our entire household stood under the stars listening and chortling to the entertainment Carmelita and Barbosa provided.

Although most *da-hörö* calling takes place at night, it does occur during the day as an alert or call to action. With *da-hörö* shouts the men call each other to arms: the village resounds with urgent calls from every corner when a herd of wild peccary is sighted near the village. Men also call the women to paint for ceremonial activities, to sing, and to take part in log races. Shouting can also be used to jest; for instance, a caller may publicly ridicule someone who makes an outrageously unreasonable demand for food or humiliate someone for his stinginess. Hilarious banter across the plaza then takes place as individuals call out obscenities and accuse each other of various sorts of social transgressions so that everyone can hear. If for some reason the men's council does not meet—if it is raining too hard or the men have returned from some arduous hunting trip or excursion to the city—elders shout out from the patios of their homes. On these occasions, decisions that would normally be made in the men's council are made in a public forum which all can hear.

As the *da-hörö* die out, quiet descends across the plaza; *da-hörö* are the last sounds to travel across the plaza before the singing performances of the youths once again take over the nocturnal soundscape. Between 10:00 and 11:00 P.M. the village becomes the domain of the *waptɛ* pre-initiates; during this time they may make a tour around the village with their senior sponsors, singing *da-hipɔpɔ* night songs. By midnight the novitiate *ʔritaiʔwa* begin to gather in the *warã* and their high-pitched calls begin to pierce the night. Between 1:00 and 2:00 A.M. they make their way around the village singing the *marawaʔwa* early morning songs. Once again the cycle of sounds that creates a palpable continuity to daily life begins anew.

THE SONIC CYCLES OF SEASONAL AND CEREMONIAL LIFE

Seasonal changes and the cycles of ceremonial life lend variation to this basic soundscape in Pimentel Barbosa. In the rainy season, for example, Xavante run their *uiwede* (*buriti*) log relay races to pit the members of one agamous moiety against those of the other. Following each race, members of the moieties sing *da-praba*, "midday songs." Year after year during the rainy season, *uiwede-ño?re*, "*buriti* log-racing songs," resound throughout the village. When the rainy season ends, the dry season, *wahu*, ushers in the best hunting. The men embark on collective hunting trips known as *du*, or "grass," in which, to flush out game, a fire brandisher from each exogamous moiety sets the savannah grasslands ablaze. As part of their ceremonial preparations for each *du*, the mature men gather in the central plaza to sing *du?u-ño?re* (*du* songs). The seasonal recurrence of such vocal arrangements extends the continuity of sound from one season to the next. Sounds persist across seasons to foster a sense of continuity from year to year.

Similarly, the recurring sounds of ceremonial cycles that span larger blocks of time bring a tangible sense of continuous re-creation to longer stretches of time. The cycles of both male initiation and the *wai?a* complex span approximately four to five years. Each phase of these two ceremonial complexes has its characteristic songs and other acoustic arrangements. In the initiation cycle, for instance, there is the silence that accompanies the induction of each group of bachelors into the bachelors' hut, *hö*, and the faltering, high pitch of the youthful voices as they sing for the first time with their senior sponsors. Before the *wa?i* wrestling matches there is the eerie moan of the *tsidupu* bamboo trumpets that the sponsors play before launching into the spectacular *wa?i* song, a song punctuated by collective shouts. After their residence in the bachelors' hut, the initiates undergo ear piercing, a ceremony that is accompanied by women's profuse laments and the distinct dances and rattle sounds of the *pahöri-?wa* and *tɛbɛ* performances.[22] Then there are the laments of the *a?ãma*, ceremonial parents, who weep for the initiates as they run the exhausting *tsa?uri?wa* race to complete their initiation into manhood.[23]

The final phase of the male initiation cycle takes place when the men of the mature men's council embrace a new set of mature males into their rank. In December 1985, when the *tsada?ro* age-set was to move up the age-grade ladder to become new mature men, the council's eldest members reached back into their memories to recollect the singing format the elders of their youth had used to ceremonially welcome the previous *tsada?ro* age-set over a generation ago. The elders who ran the ceremony in 1985 patterned their re-creation of their predecessors' ceremony according to the memories of Serebuʔrã, the man who articulated the clearest recollection of events that had taken place when he was just a boy. In modeling the contemporary ceremony after remembered events that had taken place during their childhood, the elders attempted to recreate the soundscape that had accompanied the *tsadaʔro*'s welcome over a generation earlier. The individual songs they sang were new, which imbued the ceremony with contemporary creative vitality. Nevertheless, by patterning the singing after their image of the past, the elders endeavored to bridge an entire generation and collapse the time in between. In planning the ceremony they attempted to give the impression of a soundscape that persists across time and generations.

Despite the elders' overt preoccupation with reconstructing soundscapes to represent continuity across generations, not all genres of verbal behavior persist to lend continuity to the soundscape. The women's naming ceremony, for example, was last performed in Pimentel Barbosa in 1986. Since contact, up through the 1970s and into the 1980s, this was the only Xavante community that continued to perform this ceremonial. To fit into its place within the cycle of male initiation, it should have been staged in June 1991. However, for various reasons, including changing attitudes with respect to the extramarital sexual relations involved, the elders elected to abandon it. As a result, no longer will the falsetto voice of the *aiʔute mañariʔwa*, the elder who "watches over the women" of the ceremony, be heard in any Xavante village. No more will male name givers enter a woman's house to sing as they offer her the names they have dreamed.[24] Thus, although the continuity of the daily, seasonal, and ceremonial soundscape creates a sense of endurance and persistence through time, the soundscape itself is creative, dynamic, and ever-changing. Aside from distinctly noticeable changes, such as the abandonment of the women's naming ceremony, the soundscape changes daily at a very micro level, since each new act of expression is itself a creative act. Yet even as the soundscape is ever-changing, the recurrence of patterned sounds promotes a sense of continuity and persistence through time, from day to day, from season to season, and across generations.

The Time of Sounds: Illusions of Perpetuity through Age-Sets and Age Grades

In November 1986, Warodi, accompanied by his younger brother Sibupa, came to fetch me in Goiânia where I was working on translations of his dream narrative. "*Tɔ tsoimba, ʔri tɛmɛ! Waptɛ* (*Tsoimba*, let's go to the village! There is going to be a *waptɛ* [a ceremonial induction of boys into the bachelor's hut])."[25] Like most everyone else in Pimentel Barbosa, Warodi took pride in the beauty of ceremonials and expressed his desire for me to see them. But Warodi was especially eager for me to see *this waptɛ*. An elderly man who was not feeling particularly well at the time, he had made the strenuous journey to Goiânia to get me. In Pimentel Barbosa, construction of the new bachelors' hut for the *hötörä* age-set was complete, and the first group of *hötörä* was to be inducted as soon as Warodi and Sibupa returned. Warodi was himself a *hötörä*, now a *hötörä-ʔrada*, a member of the preceeding generation of the *hötörä* age-set. This inauguration was an important and joyful event in his life. I was touched that he wished to share it with me.

A new age-set comes into being when a group of boys between the ages of about eight and ten, from both exogamous moieties, are inducted into the bachelors' hut during the *waptɛ* ceremony.[26] Age-set members are added to the initial group of inductees, the *ĩ-rõ-ʔrada* (first group), in two successive inductions: the *da-wawa ĩ-rõ* (middle group) and the *ĩ-rõ-tɛ* (new group) join the first group at approximately one-year intervals. The members of an age-set live together in a state of semi-isolation for about five years; of course, the most recent inductees spend the least amount of time with the other members of their cohort. During this time of collective residence, under the guidance of their senior sponsors, they engage in various solidarity-building activities. One of the most important of these is *da-ñoʔre* singing. The pre-initiates also practice various skills that require group coordination, such as hunting, fishing, and gardening, which will be important in their adult male lives. These activities, particularly singing, foster sentimental attachments between age-set members. Men nostalgically recall this period throughout the remainder of their lives.

Facing the river, the *hötörä*'s new home was set slightly apart from the horseshoe-shaped ring of houses on the left side of the village opening. This contrasted with the placement of the previous bachelors' hut, that of the *anarowa* age-set, which had been situated on the right side of the village opening. Since consecutive age-sets belong to opposite agamous moieties (Table 3), the alternating location of the successive bachelors' huts spatially represents the moiety affiliation of each. Those who reside in bachelors' huts located on the same side of the village opening refer to each other as *wa-ñi-wĩm-hö*, "bachelors' huts of our side" (*wa*, "our," possessive, first person plural; *ñi*, reflexive; *wĩ*, "side"; *hö*, "bachelors' hut"). They distinguish themselves from those whose bachelors' huts are located on the other side of the village opening by referring to the others as *õ-ñi-wĩm-hö* (*õ*, "that, there," demonstrative pronoun).[27] Various other activities, such as log races and patterns of singing around the village, represent the complementary opposition of age-sets of the agamous moieties.

Since Warodi and the members of the previous *hötörä* age-set had had their ears pierced and been initiated into adult male society, seven named age-sets had been inducted into bachelors' huts and subsequently com-

TABLE 3. AGAMOUS MOIETIES AND AGE-
SETS OF PIMENTEL BARBOSA IN 1986

Moiety A	Moiety B
	hötörä [-ʔrada]
aiʔrere	
	ɛtẽpa
tirowa	
	nodzöʔu
abareʔu	
	tsadaʔro
anarowa	
	hötörä

Note: In November the first group of *hötörä* was inducted
into the bachelors' hut. According to the pattern of recycling
age-set names, the age-set took *hötörä* as its name, thus recom-
mencing the cycle of repeating age-set names. Warodi and Apöwẽna, the eldest men in the village, were also *hötörä, hotora-
ʔrada* (past or previous *hötörä*).

pleted the cycle of initiation ceremonies. Warodi's initiation had taken
place before his father, Apöwẽ, had called out to Chico Meireles, saving
him and the members of the SPI "attraction front" from other groups of
hostile Xavante. When Warodi's father saved the white men, his *hötörä*
cohort had been *ʔritaiʔwa* novitiates. In 1986, when the next group of
hötörä were first initiated, the only living members of the earlier cohort
were Warodi and his age-mate Apöwẽna.

Because Xavante recycle age-set names over time, Warodi's age-set
name had finally come around again. In the years intervening between the
creation of the previous *hötörä* age-set and the present one, the Xavante
had experienced phenomenal changes: Apöwẽ had created the whites; the
village had fissioned and relocated numerous times; the SPI had come and
gone, as had the *fazendeiro* ranchers. Now, via FUNAI, rice—the creators' bland innovation for white people—had become a Xavante staple;
its production brought diesel tractors and enormous harvesters onto their
lands.

Although the Xavante had experienced dramatic changes, changes uni-
maginable to the earlier *hötörä* at the time of their initiation, the recurrence of the age-set names promotes the illusion of persistence and continuity through time. Xavante create a chimera of cyclic continuity by
invoking the same age-set names according to a pattern that spans generations. Although the constituent members of a named age-set change, and

thus each new age-set is a unique configuration of personalities, the repetition of age-set names gives the impression that social groupings continuously renew and regenerate themselves over time. The patterning of age-set renewal fosters a sense of internal stability and continuity within a society that is ever in a process of dynamic evolution.[28]

In Xavante society, the illusion of persistence and renewal is created not through the age-sets in and of themselves but through the repetition of age-set *names*. It is the name that gives the members of an age-set their distinct, collective identity and aligns them with an age-set of a bygone era. Behaviors such as singing in a particular pattern around the village signal an age-set's affiliation with one or the other agamous moiety. However, other behaviors, such as body painting and ceremonial participation during the life-cycle phases when age-set activity is prominent, make one age-set look very much like the next. An age-set's banner is its name.

At the same time a boy becomes a member of a named age-set, his induction into the bachelors' hut defines him as a member of the *waptɛ* pre-initiate age grade. Maybury-Lewis, in his pioneering study of Xavante social organization, was the first to observe that Xavante classify individuals at different life-cycle phases according to age grades, and that these intersect the age-set system. An individual belongs to an age-set for life, but passes through age grades according to processes of social and biological maturation (Table 4).

As named social categories, age grades appear to be stable and constant; individuals and age-set groups seemingly "pass through" as they move through the life cycle. Up to the point of induction into the bachelors' hut, age-grade classification for both boys and girls is reckoned on the basis of physical maturation. Thereafter, transitions in an individual's biological life cycle, such as the birth of children, tend to correspond to the continuous cycling of age-sets as they move up the age-grade ladder. However, unlike the Northern Gê Suyá, among whom an individual moves from one age grade to the next only when changes associated with biological processes occur (a Suyá man becomes a member of the mature men's age grade—"already with child"—only after he has fathered several children),[29] among the Xavante, the initiation of a junior age-set pushes all members of senior age-sets into the next age grade, irrespective of the biological processes of individual members. For example, Adzima moved into the mature men's age grade along with the members of his cohort, most of whom had fathered at least one child, even though he still waited for his child bride to mature.

Females are considered to be members of the same age-sets as males their age. However, no ceremony publicly signals that a new girls' age-set has formed, nor do ceremonies mark the movement of girls' age-sets through age-grade phases. For women, individual physical processes tran-

TABLE 4. AGE GRADES OF THE MALE LIFE CYCLE:
THE LIVING AND THE IMMORTALS

Non-initiates:	*ai?ute*	(baby)
	waptɛbrɛmi	(little boy)
	airepudu	(boy)

INITIATION	*waptɛ*	(bachelors' hut resident)
Initiates:		
	?ritai?wa	(novitiate)

Mature men:	*ĩ-prɛdup-tɛ*	(new mature adult, *waptɛ* sponsor)
	ĩ-prɛdu	(fully mature)
	ĩ-hi	(elder)
DEATH --		
Immortals:	*abadzehire/wadzapari?wa*	
	höimana?u?ö	

scend the movements of corporate age-sets: girls progress into the mature women's age grade as a result of biological changes rather than social ones. The birth of her first child, not her age-set position, establishes a woman's social status as a mature adult. Thus, Agostim and Aracy's daughter Cecita became a mature woman after the birth of her first child, even though the father, Suptɔ—several years her senior and a member of the preceding age-set—remained a novitiate. Despite the emphasis on biological processes, which enables women to move up the age-grade ladder independently rather than in groups, women are nevertheless associated with the age grades of men approximately their same age.

As they move through the life cycle, men and women have different sorts of social experiences. Women's attachments, principally to the members of their domestic group, remain consistent throughout the life cycle. Men, on the other hand, experience an ebb and flow of extradomestic attachments.[30] As in all Gê groups, ceremonial activities involve men in corporate groups that extend their loyalties and affections beyond the domestic level in a way that is unique to their gender.

Among men, the distinction between initiates and non-initiates is fundamental. The major life-cycle transition for boys is not induction into the bachelors' hut, but initiation. After the period of collective residence in the bachelors' hut, a series of ceremonials which culminate in the ear-piercing ceremony initiate the pre-initiate *waptɛ* into adult male society. Having passed this critical life-cycle transition, they become *ʔritaiʔwa* novitiates. As *ʔritaiʔwa*, the novitiates are formally recognized as adult members of society. Like all initiated men, they wear earplugs, the emblems of adult male status. However, despite their adult status, novitiates are not yet considered fully mature. Correspondingly, a novitiate is obliged to observe certain restrictions which limit his movement within the village and minimize his contact with women outside of his domestic group. Except for the now-popular afternoon soccer matches, novitiates remain indoors during the day.[31] It is during this time that a novitiate spends long hours lying by his father's side learning the stories of his family and its past.

The solidarity characteristic of the bachelors' hut *waptɛ* phase remains intact throughout the *ʔritaiʔwa* phase. However, ties among members of age-set cohorts become increasingly attenuated as males mature. When the next age-set is initiated to *ʔritaiʔwa* status, the previous *ʔritaiʔwa* become young mature men, *ī -prɛdup-tɛ*. The young mature men are embraced into the men's council in the *da-tsi-tɔ*, literally "the joining ceremony." As an *ī-prɛdup-tɛ*, a young man is finally able to sit with the other mature men in the men's council. Young mature males move to fully mature adult status after the next age-set is incorporated into the men's council. This usually corresponds with the time when a man has several children. At this point, a man is truly a member of adult society. As men grow into fully mature adults, *ī-prɛdu*, factional matters assume greater significance, and affective ties to age mates diminish as men become increasingly concerned with political affairs and family. During this time a man may become an audible presence in the men's council proceedings. By the time he has many grandchildren and several age-sets have joined the ranks of fully mature men, he becomes an elder *ī-hi*. At this point, as Maybury-Lewis observes, he may achieve some personal eminence, although, owing to the fissive tendencies in Xavante society, he must always have the support of his lineage or others who support it.[32]

As a male moves through the age grades, he moves between two poles of solidarity. Solidarity is at its peak during the *waptɛ* (pre-initiate) and *ʔritaiʔwa* (novitiate) age grades, when age-set ties are established and strongest. Opposition between alternate age-sets is also maximal during these phases. Maybury-Lewis argues that the period of semi-isolation in the bachelors' hut, age-set solidarity, and uxorilocal residence operate to weaken the bonds of patrilineal dominance and factional ties at the point in the male's life when he begins to formalize affinal ties. Once a man matures, the solidarity of his age-set weakens in proportion to the strength of his exogamous moiety and factional affiliations.

The relationship between individuality and corporate solidarity for Xavante men is a continuum between the poles of collective age-set solidarity during youth, on the one hand, and an increasing tendency toward individuality within the factional group, on the other. As he moves through the life cycle, a man experiences varying degrees of attachment to others within ceremonial and political arenas. The interplay and variable strength of these attachments continuously sustain a dynamic equilibrium in the individual's social life through time.

Expressive performance plays a key role in the differential strength of affective bonds between males at distinct life-cycle phases. Men establish and represent qualitatively different sorts of relationships with each other through their participation in expressive forms that are appropriate for different phases. The particular configuration of formal and performance features of Xavante vocal modalities creates and signals the differential strength of affective bonds between males as they move through the life cycle. Similarly, through their participation in different expressive forms, men experience different relationships with the immortals, the "always living" creators of whom Warodi speaks in his dream narrative.

Warodi: because they [the immortals] care for us
            because they care for us
                they are turning [thinking of] to us
                they are turning [thinking of] to us
                    always Xavante
                    for us to forever remain always Xavante
                    for us to forever remain

            they
            they gathered as always
            they gathered as always
            there, like this, they
                like this
            ʔã'
                suggested
                suggested
            they, for us,
            they, for us, suggested something according to their knowledge

```
        I
        I, in [the meeting]
        I, in [the meeting]
          tried
          tried to fight
Sibupa:   yes

Warodi:   tried to fight tried
            to remain always Xavante
            to remain always Xavante
            to forever live as Xavante always
            to forever live as Xavante always

          because they care for us?
          because they care for us?
            the thought
            the thought
            their thoughts
              they joined as al[ways]
              they joined as always

          I [share] these, like this
            like this, according to their speech, for you to think about
              for you to think about . . .
```

The Living and the Dead

Brazilianists have often spoken of Gê societies as societies which are "this-world oriented."[33] This is so because Gê peoples are renowned for their representations of social reality through the use of social space, for example, as well as for their use of other representational media such as body ornamentation. In all Gê societies, forms of body decoration, which are especially elaborate among some Northern Gê groups, signal membership in different social groups and categories.[34] Because of their developed use of observable representational media, the Gê have been contrasted with peoples such as those of the northwest Amazon. Many of these, particularly Tucanoan and Tupian groups, emphasize the social reality of other worlds—worlds which may be entered through the use of hallucinogenic drugs, for example.

Contrary to this characterization, Xavante are indeed "other worldly." I once commented to Warodi's nephew Jurandir my observation that in his discourse Warodi appeared to be absorbed with the world of the creators. He was involved in the creation of the always living *höimanaʔuʔö*. Jurandir responded, "The elders are like that," and, using a colloquial Portuguese expression, he characterized his uncle by saying, "My uncle is always in the clouds." The problem for ethnographers has been that this other world is not a world that is *seen;* the world of the immortal creators is a world that is *heard.* One cannot see the immortals, yet their presence can be heard and felt among the living.

Xavante bring the immortals into being as a category within the final age grade of the life cycle (Table 4). They do this through discursive practice. After death, individuals move from the realm of the living into the realm of the dead. Evil people are said to be transformed into what are called *abadzehire.* Most people, however, become what are known as *wadzapariʔwa.*[35] Although many fear contact with the *wadzapariʔwa,* who may take on animal as well as human form, in general they are spoken of as beings who watch over the living. They live in a subterranean settlement beneath the sierra that stretches to the east of the village, from which Pimentel Barbosa takes its name, Eteñitɛpa (*ɛtẽ,* rock or sierra; *ñi,* reflexive; *pa,* long).

Warodi:	over there stands the rock
	over there
	over there they gathered together
	over there they gathered together
	over there stands the rock
	it's not far away
Daru:	they are surrounding us
	they are many
Warodi:	it's not far
Sibupa:	for this they always tire of us [continually watch over us]
Warodi:	there stands the rock
	there stands the rock

Xavante only utter the name *wadzapariʔwa* in hushed tones. In conversation they call them *tsareʔwa,* or even *aʔuwẽ* (Xavante). They are the dead others who, although spoken of with some trepidation, are thought of as benevolent, unlike the feared dead among other Gê groups.[36] "When the *piʔã* bird calls in the forest," Roberto told me, "it is a *wadzapariʔwa* warning a Xavante of some danger."

Before I learned that when Xavante speak of the *wadzapariʔwa* they refer to the dead, I understood that the "always living" *höimanaʔuʔö* were the ancestors, the ones who created the world the Xavante live in. When I learned of the nature of the *wadzapariʔwa,* I began to inquire if all

Xavante become *höimanaʔuʔö* when they die. Suptɔ told me, "When *aʔuwẽ* die, they continue living as *wadzapariʔwa*. I don't know if they all become *höimanaʔuʔö*, but I know that my father, a *cacique* chief, is now *höimanaʔuʔö*." Unlike the *wadzapariʔwa* who are said to live in the sierra, the *höimanaʔuʔö* are said to live in the sky. "When Xavante die," explained Sidanɛrɛ, one of Warodi's younger brothers, "their spirit [*da-höibawarõ*] goes to the sky and meets the *höimanaʔuʔö*. *Höimanaʔuʔö* sends most spirits back to the earth, to the *wadzapariʔwa*." Warodi's sister-in-law Fernanda confirmed that only exceptional people— counselors and chiefs—become *höimanaʔuʔö*. The rest become *wadzapariʔwa* or *abazehire*, depending on their lives. She told me that the world of the *wadzapariʔwa* is like that of the living: there are *öwawẽ* and *pordzaʔõno* exogamous moieties, and age-sets as well. These explanations correspond with accounts of dreams I heard from Sasão and Wautɔ. Both recounted dreams they had had during bouts of severe illness, in which they traveled to the sky. There each met an elder male, whom they labeled *höimanaʔuʔö*, who sent the dreamer back to earth.

The relationship between the *wadzapariʔwa* and the *höimanaʔuʔö* thus appears to be one of status and gender. Both groups continue an immortal existence, one in the sky, the other on earth. Both groups reveal themselves to living Xavante in dreams. Ceremonials are for both the *wadzapariʔwa* and *höimanaʔuʔö* to see. The difference is that the *höimanaʔuʔö* appear to be a special class of immortals, males who have played exceptional roles during their time among the living. They are made up of the original creators, and their ranks have been augmented by exceptional counselors and chiefs of the more contemporary world. The ones Xavante immortalize through tellings are males.[37] They are the ones whose individual memory is perpetuated in the tales Xavante tell of the creation.

Together, the *wadzapariʔwa*, *höimanaʔuʔö*, and *abadzehire* make up what can be thought of as the final age grade of the Xavante life cycle. After death, an individual moves from the realm of the living into the realm of the dead, to become an *abadzehire*, a *wadzapariʔwa*, or, in exceptional cases, one of the "always living" *höimanaʔuʔö* creators.

Xavante society is thus a totality that includes both the living and the dead. The major life-cycle transition is initiation, when a boy becomes a member of adult male society, or—for a girl—the birth of a first child, when she is considered to be a woman. Death merely marks one's transition into the final age grade of the Xavante life cycle. Then an individual becomes one of the immortals.

Xavante bring the immortals into the realm of the living through their expressive practices. In the same way that the distinct forms of expressive behavior appropriate to the different life-cycle phases shape and represent different sorts of affective bonds between living performers, these expressive practices shape and represent the different sorts of relationships that performers experience with the dead. Each expressive mode engenders qualitatively different relationships, appropriate to their associated life-cycle phase, between performers and the immortals. Thus, through these expressive modalities, Xavante continuously engage in attempts to establish continuity between the living and the dead, to align the present with the past, and to promote cultural continuity over time.

The elders spoke of the immortals' singing like this:

Sibupa: okay
             okay, let's listen for ourselves, like this
                 listen for ourselves
Aiʔrere: before the whites they had this custom
                 the custom
             for this you are telling their story to the end
             really, they remember this in each generation
             really
Sibupa: yes
             yes
Warodi: yes, that's it

4

Singing Dreams, Dreams of Singing

> ah Xavante
> to be always Xavante
> in order to live as Xavante always
> > according to their [the creators'] customs
> > according to their customs
> i[t], it [*da-ño?re* singing] is for that
> it is for that

In August 1984 I returned to Pimentel Barbosa for the second time. Given the turmoil of my previous visit, I thought it wise to make a reconnaissance trip before submitting grant proposals and committing myself to two years of doctoral research. I wished to know whether members of the community were willing to accept my project and to have me live and work with them. I also wanted to know how the community's relationship with FUNAI had evolved in the year and a half since I left. I couldn't imagine that I would be able to work productively in Pimentel Barbosa if Boanergis continued on as post chief, and I wondered how I would get along with whatever new staff FUNAI had sent to the area. I also wanted to identify which, if any, of the young men who spoke Portuguese might agree to work with me translating recordings I made of contextually situated speech. Most importantly, I needed to know that members of the community would continue to endorse my project and support my work.

In the dry season, the bus trip from Barra do Garças to Matinha passed quickly. The dirt road's treacherous rainy season ruts had hardened to a washboard surface; the trip was dusty but uneventful. When I stepped off the bus I was surprised to encounter a group of Xavante from Pimentel Barbosa—both men and women—who were hanging about Chico's bar and restaurant. Chico's also housed the local office of the Empresa Xavante bus company and thus cornered most passengers' business when drivers stopped for breaks or to conduct official business. The group from Pimentel Barbosa welcomed me.

A rush of voices simultaneously attempted to explain the unusual presence of so many Xavante in town. I was astonished to learn that more than fifty people from Pimentel Barbosa were in Matinha for, curiously enough, a soccer match. I could see that this was no ordinary game: a number of men were armed with *uibrɔ* clubs and bows and arrows. Many had painted their foreheads red with *urucum*, making the men appear ready for a battle. The atmosphere was tense.

I tried to make sense of the information coming at me. Pimentel Barbosa had agreed to the soccer match, to pit their players against those of a rival community, the name of which I didn't recognize. This was where I first heard the allegations that Sõrupredu, Warodi's former secretary, had secretly been selling off the community's cattle for cash. I gathered that factional rivalries had flared and strife between members of Sõrupredu's faction and others within Pimentel Barbosa had become intolerable. I learned that just a few months before, the trouble had come to a head and Sõrupredu had left with his supporters to found a new village, Tangure, not far from Matinha and the road.

As I attempted to understand the reason for such a tremendous gathering of Xavante for the Matinha soccer game, I discovered that hostilities had raged between members of the two communities since the separation. Gossip and rumors of sorcery fanned resentments, breathing life into longstanding antagonisms. Speaking of events that led to the breakup, Roberto told me, "Sõrupredu tried to kill Warodi with sorcery. Now no one will defend him [Sõrupredu] and he will have sorcery put on him." He explained that rumors of sorcery prompted many from Pimentel Barbosa to travel to Matinha to witness the match. "Sõrupredu planned to poison [Pimentel Barbosa's] soccer players with *abdze* [sorcery] that [players from Tangure's team] would rub on their bodies. Two of us were marked, myself and Bomfim; you know, Kariri's husband." I understood then that the Xavante who met me had traveled to Matinha to defend their young men and, if necessary, to challenge Sõrupredu should any harm befall the players.

In the sleepy settlement of Matinha, where the most exciting events of the day are the arrival of the two buses that stop on their routes between São Félix do Araguaia and Nova Xavantina, the match itself was a tremendously thrilling event. Nearly all the locals attended, as well as Xavante. To everyone's relief, none of the soccer players suffered injury. But the day's excitement did not cease after the game's final play. In fact, the match was but one small part of the activities that absorbed the attention of the Xavante who had traveled to Matinha. After the game, senior men from both sides took over the field and plunged into heated debates and aggressive dialogues—the intense arguing which has often struck me as the preferred sport of mature Xavante men. Long after the sun had set, men from each side continued to hurl accusations of sorcery or to counter with fierce defense. The Brazilian spectators who witnessed the day's events still remember these debates as singularly peculiar proceedings.

Eventually, after dark, those of us bound for Pimentel Barbosa piled into the well-worn secondhand transport truck FUNAI had purchased for the community. Strong men hoisted my heavy gear up and over the railing onto the flatbed. I had a backpack, a suitcase full of cassette tapes and batteries, and a few boxes of food. The truck was clearly overloaded. But Elio, Matinha's gas-station attendant, confirmed that he would be able to drive us the sixty kilometers back to the village if everyone agreed to descend from the truck at treacherous points on the sierra.

About half way, the first tire blew. The truck lurched and tilted under its heavy load. Elio kept going. The tires were double, so unless we lost the mate to the one that had blown, Elio assured me, the truck would be able to make it. About fifteen minutes later, I thought I heard a gunshot. The truck pitched violently. Elio slammed on the brakes and we came unsteadily to a stop. Men, women, and children clamored to descend from the flatbed. Still a long way from the village, we prepared to make the remainder of the journey on foot in the dark.

I was relieved to see that several stout men had willingly lifted my baggage onto their shoulders. I would collect it in the morning, after a good night's sleep. In the time it took to unload my things, many passengers had set off along the road that stretched before us. Those in front lit dried palm fronds and touched them to the dried grass in the road's median strip to light the way. Myriad fires—spots of burning grass and flickering torches—illuminated the path up and over the next hill as far as I could see. Led by this spectacular vision, in which spots of light on the ground mirrored the stars above, those of us toward the end of the line followed the lights ahead as we advanced steadily toward the village. As we approached, the dark silhouettes of houses loomed in the blackness. For me, the exhilarating walk and striking nocturnal arrival accentuated the thrill of being back in Pimentel Barbosa.

Accompanied by my mother's brother Luis, I arrived at Warodi's house around 2:00 in the morning. The door creaked familiarly on its hinges and I stepped across the threshold onto the packed dirt floor. Alerted by the dogs' barking that had heralded the approach of those before us, someone had lit the little kerosene lantern and placed it in the center of the house. Its warm light flickered, casting shadows about the large thatched room. Warodi, Irene, my older sisters, and Agostim were all there waiting to greet me with warm hugs. They had been expecting me. The letter I'd written several months before had reached them, and the now-helpful FUNAI staff in Barra do Garças had radioed news of my arrival the day before. Too tired to sling my hammock, I nestled alongside the children on a sleeping mat near Warodi and Irene's bed. In my exhaustion, I soon drifted off to sleep, hardly bothered by the fleas that pester those who sleep on the floor.

On the second day of my visit, a festive mood vibrated throughout the community. The senior men had decided to hold a celebration to welcome me back to Pimentel Barbosa. The festivities were, Warodi said, "for me to look at" and to photograph. I was moved by this gesture of goodwill since, during my previous stay, I had heard many people express skepticism toward visitors: "They lie, they never come back. They just take photos and we never see them." My return evidently signaled a commitment they had sensed from only a very few outsiders; many marveled that I had traveled so far, ö poʔre dzaʔra ʔu (over the ocean), waradzu dzaribi-na, adzatu-na (in an airplane, in a jet), to visit them again.

Perhaps it was also significant that the day before, I had begun to share my ideas with Warodi and other senior members of the community about returning to spend at least a year tape-recording, translating, and writing about their speech. They became animated with the discussion of my proposal: I was coming, "ĩhe! ĩhe! (yes! yes!)," to write their speech and tales as they told them. Even Etẽpa's novitiate son, who had previously been skeptical of my work, informed me that he wanted to help me write when I returned. To certify their position, the elders charged Roberto with the task of writing up an official document inviting me to return. This I could show to FUNAI (and granting agencies) to prove that the community approved my project and welcomed me to their community. At the FUNAI post, on FUNAI's typewriter, Roberto laboriously pecked out an invitation. Then, ceremoniously, Warodi slowly and deliberately signed his name next to his *urucum* thumbprint. That afternoon both men and women decorated themselves with body paint. Gathered in the plaza as the sun sank low in the sky, they sang and danced.

The day after the welcoming celebration, discussion in the evening men's council meeting inevitably turned to the troubled situation with Sõrupredu. In the short time I'd been in the village, this issue had been the predominant topic of conversation. Nearly everyone I'd spoken with had been preoccupied with rumors of sorcery and witchcraft: four people had already been killed in another village, or so the talk went. The meeting went on for some time before Warodi stood to give an oration. Calmly he addressed the rumors. Sõrupredu's plans to kill people in Pimentel Barbosa were just lies, he said. The ill will and bad feelings had been disruptive enough; people in Pimentel Barbosa, he counseled, should not make war. The time had come to restore a healthy atmosphere. As the discussion came to a close, the senior men began to call to the women. They invited them to join the men in singing *da-ñoʔre*. The singing was for fun; it was to lighten spirits that were heavy from gossip and unrest.

The next day I began to hear discussion of plans for yet another celebration, and I wondered what this ceremony might be. I knew that the dry season is the time for many important festivities: it is the time of the initiation and ear-piercing ceremonies and also the time when men perform ceremonies of the *waiʔa*.[1] None of these ceremonials, however, was scheduled to take place this year. In fact, free of any ceremonial obligations, about half the village was off on trek. Could Warodi be planning another event "for me to look at"? Perplexed, I asked Agostim if he could tell me what this ceremony was to be about. "*Höimanaʔuʔö* (the always living)," he replied. Scarcely enlightened by his answer, I wondered if, as he'd done during my last visit, Warodi might be planning a dramatization of one of the creation stories.[2] I was eager to learn what this *höimanaʔuʔö* ceremony would involve.

Early on the morning of August 8, the novitiates began removing brush from the forest clearing (*mará*) where ceremonial preparations and parts of male rituals that cannot be witnessed by women are often carried out. Occasionally their sharp cries—"*kai! kai!*"—shot through the air. At about 8:00 Warodi stood up from the bench where he was sitting under the cook shelter and indicated he was ready to leave. "*Tɔ tsoimba* (Let's go, *tsoimba*)," he said, and he gestured for me to follow. "Take your tape recorder!" Agostim called out to me. I fetched it and then followed Warodi down the path to the *mará*. Except for Abdzuká, who had gone with his wife to gather palm hearts, and Simão, all the elder men who had stayed in the village were already there waiting for Warodi to arrive. Abdzuká and Simão showed up later. I noticed that *buriti* palm fibers had been strung between trees about four feet apart and that several men were weaving the strands into three loose mats. Other men had built a small fire in the center of the clearing and were talking softly among themselves as the novitiates raked the periphery to widen the clearing. Warodi seated himself next to Etẽpa, and the elders who had been weaving left off their work to join the circle.

From the ceremonial preparations I'd seen before in the *mará* clearing, I knew that these men were preparing to learn and rehearse a song. After arranging my recording equipment to tape their singing, I sat down next to Warodi. Very softly, he began to sing. After he sang a few phrases the others began to join him and their voices blended together. I was surprised that the elders clapped when they finished the song. No one I asked subsequently gave me a satisfactory explanation for this unusual behavior. I suspect some of the elders had seen Brazilians clap after vocal performances, and, perhaps for my benefit, they incorporated it into their rehearsal to acknowledge their familiarity with Western customs.

Even more surprising to me was that after the first song, Warodi led the elders in singing two more. In most ceremonials, participants learn, rehearse, and then perform only one song at a time. Performers repeatedly sing the same song as they move to various places within social space. After completing one performance they may go on to perform more songs, but typically only one song is rehearsed and then performed at a time. In Kuluene in 1980, I learned this bit of information in a rather embarrassing way during the first ceremonial I witnessed. Distracted by the novelty of events, and to the amusement of my hosts, I tape-recorded the same song several times before I realized what the performers were doing.[3] No wonder the Xavante thought I had tape to burn.

Then, quietly, at first almost imperceptibly, Warodi began to speak. Once again, I was confounded. By this time I had witnessed numerous song rehearsals but never had I witnessed anyone elaborate the rehearsal with a narrative. I moved my microphone in closer to pick up the sound of Warodi's soft voice as he spun his tale.

> like this, like this, so
> so you all may think about it
> ?ã'

As he went on, his speech was frequently supplemented by comments and questions from the others present. Both I and my tape recorder "listened to" the sounds of the elder men's voices; they mingled and overlapped and were punctuated by bird calls, the buzz of cicadas, and the voices of the novitiates who continued to work nearby.[4] Warodi spoke softly in a style I recognized as ĩ-hi mrɛmɛ (elders' speech). He was using short phrases, a great deal of repetition, and words and expressions that differ from those used in everyday speech. He was also employing a distinctive intonation pattern; at times he even whispered. Although I found his eloquent speech extremely difficult to follow, this extraordinary arrangement of voices and forest sounds was acoustically stunning. Curious to know what Warodi was saying, I leaned over toward Sibupa, who was seated on my right, and ventured to mix the sound of my voice with those of the others. I whispered, "E tiha te tiña (What's he saying)?" "Huh?" Sibupa replied, then added in Portuguese, "Tsodzu (a dream)."[5]

A dream, I marveled. What was Warodi doing telling a dream as part of the process of teaching songs? I was baffled by this. From Agostim I had understood that this celebration was to have something to do with the creators, with the always living höimana?u?ö. Now Warodi was "telling a dream"! As I contemplated the convergence of expressive vocal forms embedded within the preparations for this performance, I began to realize that my comprehension of the celebration's meanings would depend on a great deal more than merely translating the text that the elders intricately wove with their comingling referential statements. I recognized that discerning the meanings associated with the various vocal forms that comprised the ceremony would be equally important. Besides telling a story, the elders were doing things with words and sounds.

To make sense of this innovative undertaking, each participant must have drawn upon his or her individual experiences of the celebration's constituent expressive forms. Therefore, to unravel the meanings associated with the performance, I, too, needed to look at the discursive practices embedded in this particular celebration. Learning more about meanings associated with the discursive practices that circulate within the community would, I hoped, afford insights into the meanings they imparted to this particular event.

Since *da-ño?re* singing formed the expressive anchor of the celebration, I needed to elaborate my understanding of its performance practice and the meanings associated with it as an expressive form. By learning more about the ways in which individuals and groups use *da-ño?re*, and toward what social ends, I hoped to deepen my understanding of what Warodi and the elders were attempting to accomplish by using it as a scaffold for this event. What was the significance of Warodi's sharing a dream narrative, an expression of a uniquely personal, subjective experience, with the members of a group? Could Warodi's choice of *da-ño?re* be relevant to the current political circumstances in the community? How did *da-ño?re* fit into Warodi's personal strategies as a community leader and as an elder? To seek answers to these questions I turned to *da-ño?re*, a type of discursive practice that literally circulates—both physically and acoustically—within Xavante communities.

SINGING SOLIDARITY

By 1986, when I saw the *wapte* ceremonial induction of *hötörä* preinitiates into the bachelors' hut with Warodi, I knew more or less what to expect. I had read David Maybury-Lewis's description of the ceremony,[6] and in November 1981 in Kuluene I had witnessed one. However, when I witnessed the 1986 *wapte* in Pimentel Barbosa, the ceremony was more meaningful for me. I knew the participants and I was aware of Warodi's sentiments about this life-cycle milepost. Also, unlike my experience in Kuluene, where those involved hardly knew me, nor I them, in Pimentel Barbosa my hosts encouraged me to approach the central plaza to take close-up photographs of the inductees as their senior sponsors, the *tsimñohu* (members of the first ascending age-set of the same age-set moiety, in this case, the *tsada?ro*), led them one by one to the plaza. By this time those in Pimentel Barbosa knew I would bring them copies of photographs I took, and they were eager for me to capture the moment on film. I also knew that these photos would be cherished mementos that their owners would keep along with other valuables (such as cloth, identification documents, and, even though most couldn't read, addresses and telephone numbers of people Xavante men had met on excursions to Brazilian towns and cities) in dusty suitcases stashed inconspicuously in the darkest recesses of their homes.

In the central plaza I photographed the sponsors of the previous *waptɛ* group as they accepted ceremonial offerings from the new pre-initiates. They took the arrows that each inductee brought with him and removed the boys' neck ornaments of macaw feathers and spun cotton wrapped in *buriti* fiber. These offerings would supply the receivers with raw materials to be used in the preparation of future ceremonial regalia. As soon as an inductee had been relieved of his ornaments, his accompanying senior sponsor led him into the bachelors' hut (*hö*). Each pre-initiate was thus introduced to his new home, the residence he was to share with the members of his age-set cohort for the next several years. When this new group of boys took up residence in the bachelors' hut, eight age-sets after Warodi's group, a new group of *hötörã* was born.

Inside the bachelors' hut, the residents anxiously awaited their numbers to be complete.[7] Once all the inductees were gathered, they were joined by their *tsimñohu* senior sponsors, the *tsadaʔro*. Amid the animated chatter of the new pre-initiates, Benedito, one of the senior sponsors, began very softly to sing. Gradually the members of his cohort joined him, and in hushed voices the *tsadaʔro* completed the song. Immediately they went on to sing the song at full volume. Thrilled to be able to sing with their seniors, the young *waptɛ* began to chime in on the loudest repeated phrases, which were easiest for them to pick out and imitate. In this rehearsal, as in all other instances of *waptɛ/tsimñohu* performance, the *waptɛ* joined the sponsors more and more as they began to perceive the pattern. Indeed, this is the manner in which all *da-ñoʔre* are taught and rehearsed by the members of a group; it is the same pattern that the elders followed when learning and rehearsing Warodi's songs in the *marã* clearing. As they rehearsed, the *waptɛ*'s voices blended with those of the *tsimñohu*, and the two groups acoustically merged into one.

After practicing the song in this manner, the pre-initiates filed out of the bachelors' hut and made their way to the patio of the first house of the village arc opposite the location of the bachelors' hut. They formed a semicircle and waited nervously, staring at their feet.[8] The *waptɛ* were obviously self-conscious and anxious about their first public appearance. As they fidgeted, senior men and women, young girls and small boys all good-naturedly admired the new group: the boys were handsome in their red body paint and *buriti* palm-frond headbands, the corporal decorations that signaled their *waptε* status. After a few minutes, the *tsimñohu* sponsors nonchalantly emerged from the bachelors' hut. Comporting themselves with cool confidence and poise, they joined the *waptε* to sing and dance at the first house on their performance itinerary.

Depending on their agamous moiety affiliation, groups perform around the village in either a clockwise or a counterclockwise direction: facing the river, the *hötörã*, like all age-sets of agamous moiety B, move around the village in a clockwise direction; age-sets belonging to agamous moiety A proceed in a counterclockwise direction (Fig. 9). Correspondingly, bachelors' huts of each moiety are located on opposite sides of the village opening: facing the river, bachelors' huts for age-sets of moiety A are located to the right; for the age-sets of moiety B, bachelors' huts are located to the

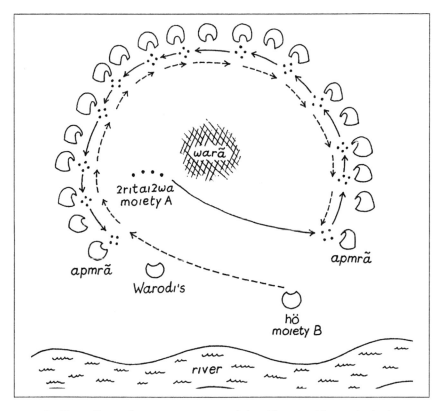

9. *Da-ño?re* performers move around the village in either a clockwise (moiety B) or counterclockwise direction (moiety A), singing on the patios of designated houses. The location of the bachelors' hut alternates between sides of the village opening.

left. The path performers follow when singing and dancing around the village, as well as the location of the bachelors' hut, physically represents the complimentary opposition between age-sets of the opposed agamous moieties. As the *waptε* followed the patterned itinerary, singing and dancing with their sponsors through social space for the first time, they publicly represented their status as an official age-set and their agamous moiety membership.

Benedito, who led and taught the song, established the rhythm by beginning the dance movements. As the song's composer, he had the right to wear an elaborate leg rattle, the *popara*, which he shook to start the dance (Fig. 10). He then added his voice to initiate the singing. The *popara*, and the fact that Benedito initiated the dancing and singing, highlight his individuality. However, all other features of the performance minimize attention to any one performer. As we shall see, *da-ñoʔre* performance effectively highlights the cohesiveness of the singing group rather than the identity of individual performers.

Singing with the *tsimñohu* sponsors is the first activity the pre-initiate *waptε* engage in collectively as an official age-set. Being novice performers, *waptε* make plenty of mistakes, to the amusement of adult spectators. Not only do their high-pitched voices distinguish them as novice singers, but *waptε* also frequently miss breaks and make errors in the accompanying dance steps. Pre-inititates often bump into each other, particularly in *da-praba* performances, when, at breaks, dancers switch their movements to rotate in the opposite direction. *Waptε* singers also tend not to sing at full volume on all loudly sung notes. The sponsors tend to carry the melody and responsibility for continuing the rhythm, while *waptε* chime in on the highest and loudest notes where they are most confident. These features make the *waptε*'s voices stand out against the blended voices of their sponsors. Notably, these outstanding voices correspond with the initial phases of the collective experience and effectively mark the fact that the young pre-initiates have neither fully internalized the *da-ñoʔre* form nor solidified into a firm collectivity. With time and practice, boys miss breaks less frequently, and this serves as an index of their coordination and hallmark of their cohesiveness.

As they made their way around the village, the performers sang the same song once in front of each house designated for *da-ñoʔre* performance.[9] They therefore sang the same song many times on their performance tour; this repetition is a form of parallelism that repeatedly calls attention to the *da-ñoʔre* form itself as well as to the collective identity of the performing group.[10]

After a complete round of singing, the *waptε* and their *tsimñohu* sponsors made their way back to the bachelors' hut, where the boys learned

10. Pre-initiate *waptɛ* (right, wearing headbands) performing *da-ñoʔre* with their *tsimñohu* sponsors; the song's dreamer wears the *popara* (feather leg-rattle). (Photo by Laura Graham, 1987.)

another song. This process was repeated all day as each one of the sponsors taught, rehearsed, and then led a public performance around the village. The songs they sang are known as *waptɛ-ñoʔre* (songs of the ceremonial induction of pre-initiates into the bachelors' hut). By singing the
seniors' *da-ñoʔre*, the pre-initiate *waptɛ* expressively linked themselves to
their sponsors. In this fashion the sponsors' *da-ñoʔre* would continue to
be heard and performed within the village at a time when they had retired
as independent performers. The performances therefore physically and
acoustically brought the sponsors back into the public arena. Moreover,
since the sponsors were themselves expressively linked to other sponsors,
by singing and dancing with their seniors the *waptɛ* demonstrated their
connection to an even larger group—the agamous moiety to which they
now belonged. Through their expressive performances, participants promote continuity between age-sets of the same agamous moiety and create
a cohesive soundscape within the village over time.

REPRESENTATIONS OF DREAMS

Benedito, like Warodi and, indeed, all initiated men who teach *da-ñoʔre*
to a group, "received" the song he taught in a dream. According to most
Xavante adults, both men and women, individual *da-ñoʔre* originate with
the immortals and *höimanaʔuʔö* creators whom people see and hear in
their dreams. Some young men claim not to know the identity of figures
who appear in their dreams. For example, Lino described his dreams of
obtaining *da-ñoʔre* as visions of singing and dancing men, although he
said that he did not usually recognize the members of the dancing group.
Most seniors, however, elaborate that these are the immortal *höimanaʔuʔö*. In fact, it is older people like Warodi who tend to make the connection between dream visions and the immortals. For seniors who speak
of them, the figures that appear in dreams are the dreamed personifica-
tions of the ancestors. Despite the difference in their acknowledgment of
sources, all Xavante—young and old, men and women—concur that
sleeping Xavante men, especially adolescent novitiates, are the most prolific dreamers of *da-ñoʔre*.

"Everyone experiences dreams," I have been told by all I have spoken
to about the phenomenon known as *rotsawẽrẽ* in Xavante. The ways in
which an individual publicly represents his or her dream experiences,
however, vary according to gender, position within the life cycle, and the
accessibility and appropriateness of distinct discursive practices. Seniors,
both women and men, publicly represent their dreams as *da-wawa* (sung
laments).[11] Young men, in contrast, represent their dreams as *da-ñoʔre*.
Some small children, boys in particular (and their parents), often say they
hear songs in their dreams. These individuals are quick to qualify their

remarks, stating that since the dreamer is young he doesn't remember his dreamed songs; when a boy has his ears pierced and becomes a ?ritai?wa novitiate, they say he will dream and remember.[12]

As I pondered my interlocutors' discussions of their dreams, I thought it particularly interesting that the public representation of dreams should vary according to gender and life-cycle phase. I realized, of course, that I could never know what an individual's actual sensory experience had been during a dream, since only the dreamer is privy to its visual, tactile, and acoustic imagery. A dream is, after all, a uniquely individual and subjective experience: conceived of as a series of internal psycho-physiological processes, a dream can only be experienced by the person who "has" it. As Supto once told me, "One's dreams are very personal." The dream itself necessarily pertains to the domain of individual subjectivity.[13]

Yet as soon as an individual attempts to share this personal experience, she or he must put it into a culturally interpretable form using the culturally appropriate means of signification—narrative, song, or visual imagery. These expressive forms, moreover, must fit within the appropriate context or contexts for dream sharing.[14] Thus, external expressive practices shape the way in which a dream experience is expressed (possibly even its presentation to consciousness), as well as how it is manipulated and interpreted by members of a society.[15] There is a dialogic process at work between the individual's conscious experience of a dream and the social context that influences the way a dream is outwardly expressed, indeed, the way it is publicly re-presented.

Dreams, then, are analogous to the "word" or "utterance" in the Soviet linguist Vološinov's theory of expression.[16] Like speech, dreams consist of an "inner experience," a semiotic process located within individual consciousness, and an "outward expression," the formal means through which dreams are communicated in social interaction. Vološinov's theory of expression presupposes the reciprocal interaction of the two: consciousness exists through its dialogue with exterior, social expressions; it conveys the material of its inner processes through acts of objectification. "Consequently, the whole route between inner experience (the "expressible") and its outward objectification (the "utterance") lies entirely across social territory."[17] Regardless of where they are culturally positioned along a continuum between sleeping and waking realities,[18] dreams, like Vološinov's utterances, take place in the individual consciousness, draw from cultural and social circumstances, and are publicly expressed in socially interpretable forms.

The variability among ways in which Xavante re-present dreams illustrates the inseparability between dream expression and publicly circulating discursive practice. Moreover, it illustrates that the way people talk about dreams accords with the discursive practices that circulate within a community. Thus, regardless of whether or not Xavante men actually "experience" *da-ñoʔre* in dreams, it is nevertheless the case that, in talk about *da-ñoʔre*, they situate the compositional process in this arena: through their discourse, Xavante link *da-ñoʔre* compositions with dreams and with individual subjective experience.

Since dreams belong to the domain of individual subjectivity while their expression depends upon socialized forms of signification, dream re-presentation offers a particularly potent means of signaling both the uniqueness of individual subjectivity and the sociability among individuals. Xavante celebrate the complex dialogic processes between subjectivity, or "inner experience," and "outward expression" in the course of sharing songs, represented first as individually dreamed compositions and then performed collectively, when the dream-song, representing subjective experience, becomes socially shared experience. In speaking of a "song's dreamer" and of "receiving" songs, I employ expressions as Xavante use them.

THE INTERSECTION OF "INNER" SUBJECTIVITY AND EXTERNAL DISCURSIVE FORM

A young man's ability to re-present his dreams as songs is an important criterion of his social status as an adult male. Male initiation culminates with the ear-piercing ceremony, *da-pɔʔre puʔu*. At this time an adolescent novitiate, *ʔritaiʔwa*, receives his earplugs, and with them the means to, as men say, "receive" songs from the ancestors through dreams. Today young men make the analogy between earplugs and antennae: they say their earplugs give them the ability to "tune in" to the ancestors in their dreams. Typically men receive only one song per dream. For this reason, when he first heard my tape recording of Warodi's dream narrative, Lino marveled that Warodi must have been an exceptionally potent dreamer as a young man to have received three songs at once.

It is particularly significant that the ability to re-present dreams as *da-ñoʔre* co-occurs with a man's formal recognition as an adult member of Xavante society. *Da-ñoʔre* publicly display his direct contact with the immortals. They represent his new role as an active bearer of Xavante tradition and signify his participation in perpetuating this tradition through time.

The novitiates, whom the Xavante consider to be the most prolific dreamers of *da-ñoʔre,* are generally unmarried or only recently married. Xavante men cite this as an important fact to explain novitiates' particularly prolific abilities to receive songs in dreams; sexual relations, men say, interfere with one's ability to receive and remember *da-ñoʔre*.[19] Decreasing *da-ñoʔre* composition thus signals an increase in the sharing of subjective experiences between partners in marriage and diminishing solidarity among members of an age-set cohort. Notably, the decrease in dreaming and sharing *da-ñoʔre* with members of his age-set correlates inversely with increasing intimacy between a young man and his wife. The *ʔritaiʔwa*, who have relatively little sexual contact or none at all, have not yet "clouded" their reception by relations with women. Mature men do continue to re-present dreams in *da-ñoʔre* form, although with less frequency than novitiate *ʔritaiʔwa*: the songs associated with particular ceremonies such as the *waiʔa* are said to be dreamed exclusively by adult men.[20] Generally speaking, however, Xavante consider that novitiate *ʔritaiʔwa* and young men, *ĩ-prɛdup-tɛ* (who are the *waptɛ* sponsors), have the greatest facility to dream *da-ñoʔre*.

Before novitiates can publicly present dream-songs of their own, they must complete an apprenticeship with their sponsors during their pre-initiate *waptɛ* phase. Pre-initiates, not being adult members of society and not possessing the earplugs which Xavante cite as providing the means for acquiring *da-ñoʔre* through dreams, are unable to receive *da-ñoʔre* on their own. Instead, they learn and perform the *da-ñoʔre* of their age-set sponsors, the *tsimñohu*. The *waptɛ* boys learn the sponsors' repertoire and with it the form for their own future compositions. The teaching process primes them for the eventual process of receiving personal *da-ñoʔre* from the ancestors. Furthermore, this teaching process models the technique they will later use to incorporate individually dreamed *da-ñoʔre* into their age-set's repertoire. Finally, the teaching method illustrates the correct way of performing *da-ñoʔre* publicly.

Seen according to Vološinov's scheme, it is during the pre-initiate period that a boy begins systematically to internalize expressive forms that will become the sign material for his inner expression in dreams.[21] Only later, after his initiation, will he outwardly re-present his dreams in *da-ñoʔre* form. Indeed, once a *waptɛ* has been initiated and possesses the earplugs that enable him to receive songs from the ancestors, he will be expected to share his song with the members of his group for them to perform without the *tsimñohu* sponsors.[22]

Throughout the pre-initiate *waptɛ* phase the bachelors repeatedly sing *da-ñoʔre* together with their sponsors. In these joint performances, the *waptɛ* learn, in addition to the *da-ñoʔre* form and proper performance practice, the entire *da-ñoʔre* repertoire of their sponsor group. Through these repeated performances, the pre-initiate *waptɛ* construct an image of *da-ñoʔre* as a *type* which each individual will later draw upon in the composition of his own songs.

In a very literal sense then, young men receive songs, as a general type, from the ancestors. They learn the *da-ñoʔre* form by singing with their senior sponsors, who learned the form by singing with their seniors, and so on back through time. Actual songs themselves, however, are only transmitted from one generation to the next: one generation of performers learns the songs of its senior sponsors, and then, after initiation, its members compose and perform their own new songs. Only these new songs are eventually passed on to a group's juniors when the group eventually becomes the *tsimñohu* sponsor. The life of any given song therefore spans only two generations of *da-ño?re* performers.[23]

DA-ÑO?RE AS TYPE: BLENDING VOICES TO MINIMIZE INDIVIDUATION

Da-ño?re are performed primarily by men, particularly during those phases of the male life cycle in which solidarity is at a peak (Fig. 11). *Da-ño?re* performance is, indeed, instrumental to the creation and maintenance of affective bonds between males, and male solidarity varies in proportion to the frequency of *da-ño?re* performance. During passage through the pre-initiate, novitiate, and young men's age grades, when age-set members frequently engage in *da-ño?re* performance, the strength of bonds between performers is maximal. Later, during the mature phases of the life cycle, domestic concerns and political factionalism displace the solidarity of youth, and men engage less frequently in *da-ño?re* performance. In those instances when mature men do engage in collective singing performance—for instance, prior to collective hunting trips, in curing ceremonies, or when embracing a new age-set into the mature men's age grade—participation effectively engenders a spirit of cohesiveness which prevails over the factionalism that typically characterizes their life-cycle phase.

In *da-ño?re* performance, a complex intersection of formal characteristics and features of performance practice combine to promote participants' experience of merging their individuality into a cohesive whole. Singing and dancing formally emphasize group cohesiveness and foreground collective identity while minimizing differentiations among individual performers. Thus, each instance of *da-ño?re* singing acoustically and visually represents the merging of individual identities. As in Suyá unison songs, *ngere*, in which men try to blend their voices, the individuality of the singers is not important; what counts is with whom one sings.[24]

Repetition, a key feature of *da-ño?re*, instantiated at multiple formal levels and in performance practice, effectively absorbs individuals into the group.[25] Repetition is a prominent feature of the process of *da-ño?re* transmission across generations and of the process by which novel compositions are incorporated into a group repertoire. Through repetition of a composition itself, an individual's song becomes the property of the age-set, which then performs it publicly around the village. The pattern directly parallels the process by which distinct groups become part of larger

11. Some *ɁritaiɁwa* novitiates performing *da-ñoɁre* in 1987.
(Photo by Laura Graham, 1987.)

collectivities: the pre-initiate *waptɛ* become part of an agamous moiety by repeating their sponsors' songs, and novitiate *ɁritaiɁwa* become part of society as a whole by first hearing and then joining their voices to sing the songs of the ancestors.

Within a composition itself, repetition of multiple formal elements blends the individual dreamer's voice with the voices of others.[26] In addition to repetition, voice quality, pitch range, melodic contour, and rhythmic and linguistic structures are each used in *da-ñoɁre* composition so as to minimize individuation and promote the experience of cohesiveness. Features of *da-ñoɁre* performance practice, such as the physical dance movements, choreography with respect to village space, and body paint design, also advance the spirit of group solidarity and distract attention from any one individual.[27] Performance illustrates the socialization of bodily movement and sound production. Moreover, *da-ñoɁre*'s simple melodic and rhythmic structures render composition relatively easy once a man has internalized the form through repeated performances with the *tsimñohu* sponsors. In fact, I have never heard of anyone who was not able to compose at least one song. Consequently, as Ellen Basso notes regarding expressive performance among the neighboring Kalapalo, formal

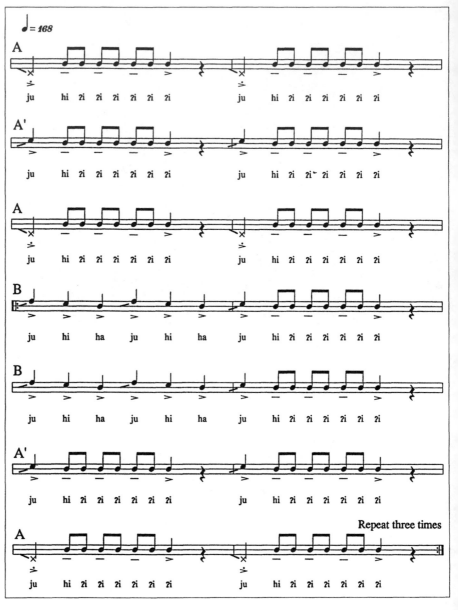

12. *Da-ño?re* transcription, Benedito's song (*da-hipɔpɔ*). Musical transcription by T. M. Scruggs.

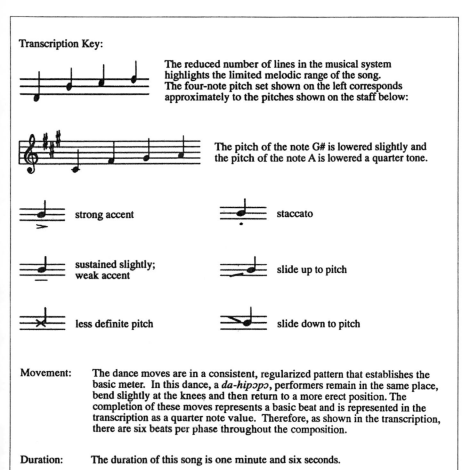

Transcription Key:

The reduced number of lines in the musical system highlights the limited melodic range of the song. The four-note pitch set shown on the left corresponds approximately to the pitches shown on the staff below:

The pitch of the note G# is lowered slightly and the pitch of the note A is lowered a quarter tone.

strong accent

staccato

sustained slightly; weak accent

slide up to pitch

less definite pitch

slide down to pitch

Movement: The dance moves are in a consistent, regularized pattern that establishes the basic meter. In this dance, a *da-hipɔpɔ*, performers remain in the same place, bend slightly at the knees and then return to a more erect position. The completion of these moves represents a basic beat and is represented in the transcription as a quarter note value. Therefore, as shown in the transcription, there are six beats per phase throughout the composition.

Duration: The duration of this song is one minute and six seconds.

complexity does not lead to a class of virtuoso composers from which certain individuals are excluded by virtue of their lack of musical talent.[28] However, some men do attempt to promote their individual interests by composing many songs—an issue to which I shall return.

The blending process that is achieved through repetition at multiple formal levels is mirrored in each singing performance. Each *da-ñoʔre* consists of repeated combinations of only a few short phrases. For example, the *da-ñoʔre* (*da-hipɔpɔ*) transcription in Figure 12, which I have selected to illustrate features common to the *da-ñoʔre* type, divides the musical material into three sections of two phrases each. In the transcription, each section occupies a system, a line of modified staff notation, and is labeled

A, A', and B. The first two sections are labeled A and A' because they show similarity in their melodic and rhythmic structures; the third section is labeled B because of the distinct melodic and rhythmic structures of its first phrase. The performance consists of repetitions of these sections; the overall form of the performance, as indicated by repeat signs in the transcription, is

A A' A B B A' A B B A' A B B A A'

Several features of the performance are not indicated in the transcription. For example, the song's initiator, who is generally the dreamer, sings the first phrase alone; the rest of the group joins in throughout the second phrase.[29] In most performances, the initiator gives a solo cue to initiate new phrases during the singing. Again, through the repetition within each singing performance, the initiator's voice is absorbed into the others. Outside of these phrasal introductions, if ever an individual's voice stands out above the rest, or if someone misses a break between phrases, Xavante consider the aesthetic to be disturbed. Ideally, no individual voice should stand out during a break.

The voice quality characteristic of the *da-ñoʔre* delivery style further obscures the distinctive identity of individual voices. Marked pharyngeal constriction, together with loud, forced voice, characterizes delivery, and the frequencies of *da-ñoʔre* are low. The acoustic timbre thus produced lies somewhere between singing voice, as Westerners conceive it, and shouting. This voice quality is similar to that found elsewhere among lowland South American groups in forms of ceremonial dialogue, and it may be used as an index of masculinity.[30] Indeed, a continuum seems to exist between song and speech voice in *da-ñoʔre* singing; at some points musical pitch becomes obscured. The only occurrence of speech voice in this *da-ñoʔre* example occurs at the first utterance in each phrase of the sections labeled A in the transcription, as shown by the special ⤬-shaped note. In other performances, pitch identification can be more problematic.[31] The voice quality renders distinct pitches and individual voices difficult to identify.

To the degree that pitches are distinguishable in each short phrase, they are found within a very narrow frequency range. With the exception of the less definite pitch that begins each phrase within section A, the pitch range is less than a minor third in the standard Western well-tempered scale. The melodic contour thus remains within a relatively narrow range, as can be seen in the transcription.[32]

Da-ñoʔre have a distinctive melodic contour characterized by movement between proximate pitches. The proximity of pitches facilitates the shouting delivery style. Although the Xavante gloss *da-ñoʔre* as *canto*

(song, in Portuguese), songs are considerably less melodic than ceremonial wailing, which the Xavante do not consider to be song in any way. Both the melodic contour and the narrow pitch range operate, in this case, to minimize features of individual voice quality and obscure individual differences, since the physical requirements for the production of the full pitch set do not vary considerably.

Rhythmic structure—the horizontal organization of sound in time—rather than linguistic text and vertical parameters of pitch, is the principal organizing feature of *da-ñoʔre*.[33] Rhythm is what coordinates singers' movements in space and time. The importance Xavante attach to rhythm is evidenced by their descriptions of receiving *da-ñoʔre* in dreams. Young men say that one first perceives the rhythm and dance steps, and then the text and tune.

Rhythmic parameters include tempo, or speed, systematic organization of pulses into discernible phrases, and the rhythmic structure within each phrase in a composition. The three basic *da-ñoʔre* types exhibit some variation in tempo: *da-praba* (late morning to afternoon songs) are fast and danced with energetic sideways stepping; *da-hipɔpɔ* (night and early morning songs) are performed much more slowly and are accompanied by pulsing or slightly bouncing knee movements; and *da-dzarõno* (late afternoon to early evening songs) are characterized by an intermediate tempo and are danced with a shuffle step in which one foot moves slightly forward on stressed beats, then back with the next unstressed beat. In all three *da-ñoʔre* types, the dance moves set the tempo. Physical movements therefore coincide with pulse. Indeed, each performance begins with the initiator's setting a steady, immutable pulse before adding his voice. After establishing the pulse, others join the initiator, and the same tempo is maintained throughout the performance of each composition. There can be some variation in tempo between villages. Lino, for example, marveled at the fast tempo at which *da-praba* were performed in Pimentel Barbosa relative to the performance tempo in his own community, São Marcos. However, within a given village the tempo for each *da-ñoʔre* is re-created with as much consistency as possible across performances.

The systematic grouping of pulses into discernible phrases, like the rhythmic parameter of tempo, varies across the three basic *da-ñoʔre* types. For example, *da-hipɔpɔ* consistently have six beats per phrase, as shown in the transcription, whereas *da-praba* are less regular. The patterning of phrasal organization is, however, consistent in a composition; Xavante do not improvise in *da-ñoʔre* performance.

Within a given *da-ñoʔre* composition, each phrase has a unique rhythmic structure built up from the pattern of stress, or accented beats, and utterance duration. Stressed beats, especially pronounced in *da-praba* and *da-dzarõno*, are marked by strong attack and loud volume; unstressed beats are sung softer with a weaker attack in the voice onset. The sound envelope, the shape of the utterance's wave form for each stressed utterance, has a large initial amplitude that tapers off toward the end of the utterance. Unstressed utterances, having a smaller initial amplitude, display less differentiation in sound envelope owing to the relatively uniform amplitude throughout the utterance. The repetition of this envelope form produces a rhythmic pattern that is distinctive to *da-ño?re* within the Xavante expressive repertoire.

The texts of *da-ño?re* are vocables, either syllables or words from the Xavante language; they do not communicate any propositional or referential meaning and thus neither permit nor encourage the metapragmatic differentiation of individual identities through dialogue. The entire linguistic inventory of the *da-ño?re* transcribed in Figure 12 is typical; the text consists entirely of the syllables *ju, hi, ?i,* and *ha*.[34] Moreover, in contrast to canonical dialogic forms, which highlight individual differentiation, the linguistic structures of *da-ño?re* do not involve dialogicality, and therefore pragmatically deny overt recognition of the "other."[35] Instead of formally representing acknowledgment of individual difference, *da-ño?re* utterances, in the form of vocables, ideally take place simultaneously.

The elders, whom young Xavante identify as the target audience, do not participate as interlocutors in any way. They rather "overhear" and comment on the performance from their position outside the circular boundary described by the dancers; at the end of a song, elders often express their approval by uttering, with a good deal of diaphragmatic explosion, the phrase *he te pãri te pãri*, which young men gloss in Portuguese as *obrigado*, "thank you," although the expression is used exclusively by men to indicate appreciation for *da-ño?re* performances. Apart from these comments there is generally little, if any, verbal evaluation.

While I think it is unreasonable to assume a relationship of inherent causality between the absence of referentiality and the experience of sociability, such as Leanne Hinton proposes for Havasupai vocables,[36] the Xavante *da-ño?re* provide an especially interesting case in support of Hinton's thesis. *Da-ño?re* vocables are only one among many modalities that function pragmatically to promote and signify a spirit of collective solidarity. All participants move identically and simultaneously utter the same vocables and short phrases over and over. This complex repetition of multiple identical units and multiple performance modalities effectively effaces individual differences and promotes group solidarity. The intersection of these expressive modalities signals the merging of individual experience into collective experience by formally displaying the absorption of individual expression into collective expression.

The pattern by which an individual composes a song and then shares it with the members of his cohort so that it becomes part of a group repertoire for public collective performance further underscores the movement from individual subjective experience into shared experience. The locus of individual creativity lies within the process of dream-song composition, while the sharing and subsequent performance promote sociability between performers as well as the continuity of *da-ñoʔre* performance practice over time.

INDIVIDUAL CREATIVITY AND GROUP REPERTOIRE

Once a boy's ears have been pierced and he has been reintegrated into society as a *ʔritaiʔwa* novitiate, he is eligible (in fact, obliged) to receive his own *da-ñoʔre* through dreams. By composing his own song, he signals his initiate status and represents his personal dream-contact with the ancestors. Simultaneously, his composition demonstrates his individual creativity, since each *da-ñoʔre* composition is unique and no two tokens of any *da-ñoʔre* type are exactly alike.

Each new *da-ñoʔre* composition constitutes a varied manipulation of melodic pattern and rhythmic structure, as well as an entirely novel vocable text. For example, within the basic restrictions of a song type, the composer can vary the number of beats per phrase and the ordering of these phrases within a composition. In *da-praba* afternoon songs in particular, the dreamer-composer enjoys a certain latitude in choosing the number of pulses to group into phrases, not all of which must be equal in number. For all *da-ñoʔre* types, an individual may vary both the number of accents within a phrase and the pattern of accentuation. The song dreamer also determines the tempo, setting it by beginning the dance movements when initiating a *da-ñoʔre* performance.

The second principal arena of individual creativity in *da-ñoʔre* composition is the text. The text of each composition is unique—a novel combination of referentially meaningless vocables. To Western ears, innovation at the level of texts is perhaps the most obvious and easily detected area of formal manipulation in *da-ñoʔre* composition. The three sample *marawaʔwa* texts below, representing a type of *da-hipↄpↄ* that is performed between midnight and 2:00 A.M., illustrate the unique texts of each individual composition.

 1. *marawaʔwa* by *aihöbuni* (*anarowa* age-set)[37]
     warã hu ma are wa jɛɛ
     warã hu ma are wa jɛɛ
     wa jɛ warã hu ma are wa jɛɛ

2. *marawaʔwa* by Suptɔ (*tsadaʔro* age-set)
waĩ hörö ha hi hã ri ha ha ha
i i hi hi ha i i hi hi
ha i i hi hi ha ha ha
waĩ hörö ha hi hã ri ha ha ha

3. *marawaʔwa* by Bill (*anarowa* age-set)
wa ʔraʔãi hörö
hã ʔã hã hã
wa ʔraʔãi hörö wa ʔrã
hã ʔã hã hã

According to Xavante men, a composition results when, in his sleeping dreams,[38] an individual sees and hears the figures in his dream—the immortals and "always living" *höimanaʔuʔö* —sing and dance *da-ñoʔre*. All the men I spoke with reported hearing many more *da-ñoʔre* than are actually mentally "recorded" for later recall. According to young men, to remember a song after seeing and hearing it in a dream, the dreamer wakes and sings the song through softly one time. They say a man "sings quietly so as not to forget" (*te ti-ñoʔre tsiru di tete waihuʔu da*). He then repeats the song loudly to etch it indelibly in his memory.

At this point, Xavante consider the dreamer to be the "owner" of the song; the composition represents an intimate and highly personal experience, a unique expression of his individual subjectivity. At the next appropriate opportunity, however, the dreamer will call the members of his age-set together and teach the song to them.[39] The process of imparting the individual's song to the group mirrors the process by which men say an individual receives a song in his dreams. This, in turn, mirrors the process by which *waptɛ* pre-initiates learn the songs of their *tsimñohu* sponsors. The process unfolds in the following manner. After the members of the *ʔritaiʔwa* age grade have assembled, for example in the *warã* central plaza after midnight, the song dreamer begins to teach his song. He sings it, first softly, then loudly a second time. The others join as they pick up the pattern. Through repetition the individual's voice blends with the other voices, producing a sound that is more or less monophonic.

In teaching and then performing the song with the members of his age-set, an individual moves his inner experience outward, making his individual experience accessible to others so that, in collective performance, it can become a shared experience. Through song, an expressive form which is discursively represented as a dream experience, an individual opens a window into his personal domain; his expression exposes part of his most intimate self to others. By sharing his intimate experience through song, a young man publicly signals his sociability in ways similar to those in which elders signal their sociability through ceremonial wailing.[40] However, in contrast to ceremonial laments, which among lowland South American Indians are compositions sung exclusively by their composers, a dream-song is offered by its composer as an expressive experience to others. In collective performance, others partake of his personal experience.

In singing and dancing the da-ño?re composition of one of its members, a group collectively experiences what was originally presented as the song dreamer's personal, highly subjective experience, his dream. Together, in performance, they *feel* the composer's dream experience. At this point, the song becomes the property of the age-set. It no longer belongs exclusively to the individual who dreamed it. Via performance, ownership of the song is transferred from its original dreamer-composer to the performing group.

Through this sharing, a composition becomes part of an age-set's repertoire, an aggregate constituted of the expressive contributions of individual selves. Each age-set member contributes compositions which are expressive representations of subjective experiences of his individual self. Indeed, the repertoire is an expressive whole analogous to the age-set's social formation itself: a group of boys establish themselves as a cohort through the process of sharing experiences over time, and, notably, da-ño?re performance publicly displays this sharing of experience.

The process of taking a dreamed composition into an age-set repertoire transforms what was originally the material expression of an individual's subjective experience into a collective experience and expression of group solidarity. Through this sharing the expressive self becomes coextensive with a community in which the expressions of similar selves make up the whole.[41] The expressive pattern of da-ño?re sharing and performance thus crystallizes the monologic model of the relationship between self and community which Urban identifies for central Brazilian societies and the Gê in particular. In da-ño?re, "the boundaries of the self are extended to encompass others—and they do not encompass just one or a few others but the entire community."[42] In sharing da-ño?re a dreamer extends the boundaries of himself to embrace those who may enter into his experience through performance. The shared experience thereby transforms the experience of individual subjectivity into group experience.

Although Xavante identify da-ño?re songs first and foremost with an age-set, people who have close kinship or emotional ties to a song's dreamer continue to associate the song with that individual even after the composition has been incorporated into a group repertoire. In most cases, when asked to identify a song's dreamer, Xavante first respond by giving the name of the age-set—tsada?ro-ño?re (the tsada?ro age-set's song), for example. However, for the members of a group and those closely associated with the group (tsimñohu sponsors, close kin and affines), the identity of the song's dreamer remains salient long after ownership has been transferred from the individual dreamer to the group, and from one age-set to its juniors. For most men, recalling the repertoire of the *tsimñohu* sponsors invokes fond memories of days in the bachelors' hut, details of who dreamed which songs, and discussions of events recounted by individuals who dreamed particular songs. Similarly, in afternoon and other conversations, fathers and uncles sing their own songs and the songs of members of their group, as well as recount memories of their performances to sons and nephews. And, in some instances, hearing an individual's song may provoke an elder to *da-wawa* lament. This occurred, for example, when the *tsadaʔro* age-set, in performing its repertoire around the village, included the song of one of its deceased members. When the singing began on the patio of the house belonging to the father of the deceased composer, the elderly man began his tuneful weeping. Stimulated by the sound of his son's song, he wailed to express his personal experience of grief and his sorrow that his son was not physically present among the performing group.[43] For intimates, as this example shows, a composition continues to bear the mark of individuality.

While all novitiates and young men are expected to dream *da-ñoʔre* to signal their maturity, contact with the ancestors, and ability to bring the voice of the ancestors into the present, some young men represent themselves as especially prolific dreamers and share more songs with the members of their cohort than others. Such an individual creatively draws upon *da-ñoʔre* as an expressive means to advance his personal prestige and notability within the community. Composing and sharing *da-ñoʔre* is, for an ambitious novitiate or young man, the principal expressive means by which he can publicly demonstrate his ambitions to positions of prominence and leadership. At one level, in choosing *da-ñoʔre* he signals his conformity to established norms and thereby his sociability.[44] Further, getting the members of his group to repeatedly sing *his* compositions effectively demonstrates an individual's prominence among his peers. Yet the features of performance practice, combined with the formal features which mitigate against the prominence of any particular individual, effectively minimize the chances of any one person's gaining *too* much notability.

DA-ÑOʔRE IN WARODI'S DREAM PERFORMANCE

The insights afforded by the preceding discussion help to shed light on the uses and meanings associated with *da-ñoʔre* performance that Warodi and the elders engaged in when they organized the innovative *höimanaʔuʔö* ceremony, their celebration of the "always living" creators. With the understanding that Xavante regard *da-ñoʔre* compositions as originating with the immortals, compositions that the ancestors transmit to the living in dreams, Sibupa's response—"A dream"—to my inquiry, "What's he telling?" makes sense. Agostim's explanation of the ceremony as "*höimanaʔuʔö*" also becomes less opaque.

For Warodi and the other Xavante who participated in the celebration, Warodi's *da-ñoʔre* compositions are the material expressions of his dream; they outwardly portray Warodi's intimate dream-communion with the immortal creators, the *höimanaʔuʔö*. Appreciated and even talked about as dreams, the songs are considered to be expressions of Warodi's "inner," subjective self. The songs also demonstrate Warodi's sociability. They signal his ability to publicly portray his "inner" experience in a socially appropriate form, and they mark his membership in society as a whole, a whole that includes both the living and the dead.

By sharing his personal dreamed songs with the elders and later with the entire community, including the women, Warodi offered something of his "inner" self; he imparted an expression of his self to members of the community. In the process, Warodi actually gave more of himself to others than is typical of other men. He shared his songs not only with the members of his age-set but with all members of the community who were present in Pimentel Barbosa at the time. He therefore expanded the quotient of himself within the community in a very literal sense: when the community performed his songs, men and women, seniors as well as youths from both agamous moieties, experienced and represented expressions of Warodi's subjective self. Distributing his experience throughout the community, Warodi in effect contributed something of his personal self to further advance his prominence.

No doubt Warodi's dream sharing also called attention to his exceptional ability to enter into contact with the immortals, as Lino's comment about Warodi's extraordinary faculties as a dreamer suggests. Moreover, since dream-songs are normally performed by pre-initiate *wapte, ʔritaiʔwa* novitiates, and *ï-prɛdup-tɛ* young men, the fact that Warodi, an *ï-hi* elder, was able to secure the participation of the entire community for this unique event testifies to an impressive status. Certainly, Warodi's history of long-standing prestige influenced others to agree to participate in performing his dream. Their involvement points to the high regard and fondness they felt toward him. Also, by participating in this performance soon after the village had fissioned, performers demonstrated their commitment to Warodi as opposed to Sõrupredu.

In some measure then, the performance proclaimed and promoted Warodi's stature as a distinguished individual. At the same time, because *da-ñoʔre* sharing is understood to be an act that transforms an individual's subjective experience into a collective experience, Warodi's sharing of not the usual one song but of *three* signaled a remarkable altruism. Further-more, as discussed above, the formal features of *da-ñoʔre* performance operate even at very microlevels to expressively counteract the public pro-motion of personal interests. In singing, as the others learned Warodi's songs and then joined their voices to blend with his, Warodi's promi-nence as the song's dreamer and as a distinguished individual diminished. Through their singing and dancing, participants combined the formal fea-tures of *da-ñoʔre* performance to promote solidarity. In performance, the overall effect of blended movement and vocalization compellingly down-played the public display of whatever distinction Warodi may have had.

Despite the representational effect of *da-ñoʔre*'s combined formal fea-tures, the key to Warodi's success in harnessing the others' enthusiastic participation lay in his ability to represent the performance as an activity designed to benefit the entire community at that particular time.[45] Warodi explicitly represented his dreamed songs as gifts to the Xavante from the immortal *höimanaʔuʔö*. In the magnanimous spirit of the immortal crea-tors, Warodi portrayed himself as one who, by sharing "their thoughts," was benevolently passing on the creators' gifts to the community. The ob-jective of sharing these songs, according to Warodi, was to provide a means for the Xavante to remain Xavante forever.

Immediately after finishing the song rehearsal with the elders, Warodi initiated his dream narrative in this vein:

> like this
> like this
> > so
> > so you all may think about it [the dream] . . .
> ʔã'

> everything is fine
> everything is very fine
> everything is fine
> this is the way it is
> this is the way it is
> ʔã'

> the Xavante
> > after they [the creators] taught the Xavante
> > after they taught
> they[46] [the youth] don't remember us anymore
> they don't remember us anymore
> they don't remember us anymore

those there
those there our blood
our blood
our younger brothers
our younger brothers
they don't believe in us anymore

because they [the creators] care for us
because they care for us
    they are turning to [thinking of] us
        always Xavante
        for us to forever remain always Xavante
        for us to forever remain

they
they gathered as always
they gathered as always

there like this
    they like this
ʔãʼ
        suggested
        suggested
    they, for us,
    they, for us, suggested something according to their knowledge

I
I, in [the gathering]
I, in
    tried
    tried to fight
    tried to fight tried
        to remain always Xavante
        to remain always Xavante
        to forever live as Xavante always
        to forever live as Xavante always

because they care for us
because they care for us
    the thought
    the thought
    their thoughts
    they joined as al[ways]
    they joined as always

> I [share] these like this
>   like this according to their speech
>   for you to think about
>   for you to think about

Warodi presented his dream to the elders as counsel from the immortal "always living" *höimanaʔuʔö*. He framed his dream-songs as messages from the creators—in order for the Xavante to continue as Xavante forever—which they offered to the Xavante at a time when, according to Warodi, the faith of the youths was waning. In relaying these thoughts, "the creators' thoughts," Warodi positioned himself as an intermediary. He represented himself as one who unselfishly communicated the immortals' advice to the living.

Later, when the women came to the *mará* clearing,[47] Warodi again represented his dream-songs as gifts from the immortals, gifts that had been offered for the benefit of the entire community. However, in contrast to his presentation to the men, this time Warodi represented the objective of the songs as a gender-specific complement to the general message he relayed to the men: because the inhabitants of the community had ceased to remember the lives of the ancestors ("living according to their teachings"), the creators had stopped "working" (sending babies).

> have you learned it?
> all right, think about the song
> their [the creators'] thoughts
>   in order for you to learn
>   I called you
>   to think about their thoughts
> you all think about it
>
> it is only there [in other villages]
>   according to their [the creators'] ideas
>   that they
>   it is only there
>   that they [the creators] continue to work
>   that they work according to their teachings
>   they continue to work
>
> that is why
> that is why to protect you
>   to protect you
>   they gathered to give these songs to you

these
these you must learn
it is only over there [in other villages]
it is only over there
it is only over there that they work

all of us, we are the forgotten ones
  we are the forgotten ones
  we are really the forgotten ones
  we are the forgotten ones

they only work over there [in other villages]
they only work over there
for that, babies one after another
  they send babies

As these excerpts illustrate, Warodi represented himself to both the men and the women as someone who had the interests of the community, not his personal self, in mind. By sharing his songs and his dream narrative, Warodi extended the creators' benevolent message to all those living in Pimentel Barbosa. He addressed his message, the ancestors' message, to the entire community. It was a message designed to restore the community's spiritual well-being. He suggested that restoring spiritual health would enable the Xavante "to remain Xavante forever." It would also, his words imply, ensure the community's physical survival: Xavante can only continue as Xavante forever if more babies are born.

It is not fortuitous that Warodi chose this particular time to convey his message, the "creators' message," to members of the community (and to me). The community was in a state of social turmoil. Sõrupredu and the members of his faction had only recently departed to settle in Tangure, and in the wake of this disruption, the village teemed with rumors of sorcery and witchcraft. Only a few days before the performance, the encounter in Matinha had fueled the ongoing gossip and fanned volatile tempers. The separation had clearly disrupted the social order, and the continuing gossip and rumors were hindering the healing process.

Warodi spoke directly to this gossip in his dream narrative. He yearned for the time when peace prevailed, the time when the Xavante resided in a big village and lived according to the influence of the *wamarĩ* (wood of peace).[48] The festering rumors and gossip had disturbed the elders' ability to receive counsel from the always living creators. Specifically, the scandals and bad feelings had disrupted the capacity of Sibupa, a renowned peacemaker, to dream and have communion with "the father in the sky."

Warodi: our [bad] thoughts
            with our thoughts
                they always ruin our ideas
                they always ruin our ideas
                with our thoughts

            where is the time of the big village
                with the *wamarī* [wood of peace]
                with the *wamarī*?

            where is it?
            with us
            with us
                when we had good ideas [with us]

            since then
            since then you
                our ideas
                [you have] killed our ideas [with bad thoughts]

            so
            so they
            they
            they gathered their ideas for us

            also
            also this is the thought
            this is the thought of the father in the sky
                and my younger brother [Sibupa] he
                my younger brother he
                my younger brother he
                he
                he is having trouble thinking

            his ideas
                his ideas you have killed them
                you have killed them
                all of you
                all of you have killed them

Warodi portrayed the creators' songs and counsel to the living as a salve, a remedy to heal the social wounds that plagued Pimentel Barbosa.

By remembering the lives of the ancestors, Warodi says, healing will take place. In his narrative, as we shall see in Chapter 6, Warodi does, in fact, embed tellings that recount the creators' lives. Thus he metapragmatically frames these tellings as acts of spiritual healing. Framed in this way, his tellings of the creators' lives become performative acts that promote healing effects themselves. Warodi *does* the very thing he prescribes. In telling of the ancestors' lives he remembers. Moreover, he causes others to remember as well.

The songs themselves are also ways of remembering, particularly since—through his narrative—Warodi makes their links to the creators explicit. As ways of remembering the lives of the ancestors, the songs will help restore spiritual well-being to the community. Each song was given by the creators for a lofty purpose, which Warodi recalls: the *uiwede* song (*buriti* log-racing song, a *da-praba*) is for peace; the *da-dzarōno* is for celebrating when children are born; the *da-hipɔpɔ*, given by the öwawē-ʔwa (the one who made the sea), is for health—it cures sickness.

Warodi: continuing with this
             continuing
                 you won't have sickness
                 you won't have sickness

             while you are well
             while you are well
                 continue the custom
                 continue the custom

             this is the word
             this is the word

Sibupa: that's it

Warodi: so
             so they shake [dance] removing the sickness
             so they shake removing the sickness

             like this again when you are sick
             when you are sick
                 again
                 you will walk again
                 you will walk again

again
again you will all be fat [healthy]
you will all be fat [healthy]
ʔãʔ'
like this their speech
like this their speech

Sibupa: that's it really
we go on like this [we continue in this way]
really like this we go on

Even without having made the connection to the creators explicit, through their own experiences as *da-ño?re* performers Warodi and the other elders who collaborated to stage the performance knew that the very actions of singing and dancing would promote well-being among participants. In the same way that the formal characteristics of *da-ño?re* performance foster feelings of togetherness among boys and young men, the principal performers of *da-ño?re*, they could be expected to have similar effects in this performance. Furthermore, just as the songs of an age-set's repertoire represent connections to their sponsors, the sponsors' sponsors, and so on back through time, Warodi's songs also recalled these connections. In a very potent way, his songs conjured up feelings of continuity.

These are the associations that Warodi and the other elders drew upon by anchoring this ceremony with *da-ño?re* performance. In singing and dancing, the participants heard their voices blend and felt their bodies move together. In performance they renewed and reexperienced their collective solidarity to heal the community's social wounds. Singing the creators' songs, moving together as an integrated whole, they actively reaffirmed their continuity with the past and their connection with the first creators. They remembered the creators' lives by singing their songs. Remembering in this particular way—the way each generation has remembered in its time, as Ai?rere says in the dream narrative—the Xavante will continue as Xavante forever.

before the whites they had this custom, the custom
for this you [Warodi] are telling their story to the end
truly, they remember this in each generation
truly

5

Depersonalizing the Dream:
The Politics of Narrative Performance

After Warodi had taught and led the elders in their rehearsal of his songs that August morning in 1984, I listened carefully to the acoustically fascinating arrangement of voices as he spun the tale of his dream. Frequently the other elders interrupted his narrative with questions, contradictory statements, and asides. Their voices often obscured Warodi's calm, quiet utterances; from time to time overlapping comments and simultaneous discussion overwhelmed the sound of his voice. Warodi responded to many of the elders' ongoing remarks and regularly wove their comments into his telling. From the outset, Warodi's voice was not the only one that told the tale of his dream.

Warodi:	like this, like this, so
	so you all may think about it
	ah
	[various unintelligible aside comments]
Aiʔrere:	ah, I'm not certain
	I'm not certain
	I'm not certain how
	I'm not certain how you are telling
	that the men in all the villages always sang loudly
	I'm not certain
	I'm not certain
	I think it was in the dry season
Sibupa:	it makes us sad
Aiʔrere:	[they] always sang loudly
Warodi:	everything is fine
	everything is really fine
	everything is fine
	this is the way it is
	this is the way it is

Each of the elders who sat around the embers of the dying fire after Warodi first taught his song contributed something to Warodi's dream telling. Later, when the women arrived and learned the songs, while the youths remained in the background, Warodi again elaborated his telling, weaving in the comments of others.

Warodi: this [song] here, this *da-dzarōno*
           this *da-dzarōno*
           this here
             that I
             that I began for you
               it is his [the one who made the sea]
               it is his
Sibupa: what is it for?
Warodi: this
           well ah
           what is it for?
           he taught this for [us to sing] when white [beautiful, healthy] babies [are born] [1]
           [he taught it for] his descendants
           it is an arm moving
           it is an arm moving song
           it is an arm moving song
           he taught it for [us to sing] when white babies are born

Again, the elders who stood by his side as he told the tale to the women joined their voices to elaborate his narrative. His dream account was a veritable collage of voices.

I reflected on this multivocal narrative with the knowledge that Warodi was telling his dream, as Sibupa had said. Warodi's manner of sharing his dream-songs did not conform to the typical pattern. Normally, when individuals share their dreams as songs to a group, they do not offer narratives of the dream visions. It seemed curious that others would jointly produce a telling of an individual's dream, a phenomenon that is conceptualized and talked about as a personal, indeed "inner," experience. I wondered if this manner of constructing a narrative might be interpreted as an instance of an individual's spreading more of himself throughout the community, as discussed in the preceding chapter. Was Warodi allowing others to apprehend his experience more profoundly by permitting them to share in the narrative construction of his dream? Might there be a political component to this form of discursive practice? By bestowing partial responsibility for the construction of the narrative on others, might Warodi be dispersing accountability for its message among those gathered? Might this form of discursive practice promote the public appearance of an understated personal prominence and simultaneously minimize Warodi's individual distinctiveness?

I also wondered why the other elders would be so invested in collaborating with Warodi to stage this performance, going so far as to collaboratively produce the narrative of his dream. That the elders would be interested in promoting collective singing as a way to mend the social crisis Sõrupredu's departure had precipitated didn't surprise me: the elders often prescribed collective singing to remedy social disruption. In 1976, following the death of the renowned leader Apöwẽ, Warodi's father and the one who "saved" the whites, the community had staged an impressive *da-ñoʔre* performance to commemorate his greatness as well as to assuage the pain of their sorrow.

I could also understand that the elders would embrace an opportunity to dramatize the lives of the creators for didactic purposes. By embodying the creator figures who appeared in Warodi's dream, the performers gave material form to the personages the elders remember when they tell the stories of the Xavante creation. The embodied performance made the creators more real for those who had heard, as well as for those who told, of their phenomenal deeds. But why would the elders be so interested in performing Warodi's *dream* of the creators as opposed to dramatizing the *events* the elders tell of when they relate the stories of the creation?[2] Could the elders as a group have some political investment in staging this performance? Did they conceive of the performance as a means toward advancing the interests of the entire community in some novel way? Particularly, how did my presence influence their perception of the dream performance's objectives?

After learning Warodi's dream songs, the elders conducted themselves in a manner that bore similarities to senior men's comportment in political meetings. Speech in political meetings, as in most (if not all) gatherings of adult individuals generally, is truly polyvocal in the Bakhtinian sense. Discourse is literally constituted by a diversity of voices. Understanding the meanings associated with the multivocal discursive practices of the Xavante political sphere can shed light on the expressive power of the collaboratively constructed dream narrative, just as the insights about *da-ñoʔre* illuminated meanings associated with the *da-ñoʔre* of the dream performance. The social ramifications of this type of discursive behavior, and the ways in which these practices inform participants' interpretations of the narrative, can best be appreciated by examining the discursive practices of *warã* meetings, the quintessential arena of polyvocality in Xavante social life.

PERSONALIZED DISCOURSE

In analyzing the discursive practices of *warã* political meetings, it is help-
ful to consider the presuppositions of discourse ideology in Habermas's
notion of the public sphere and in Western philosophy of language, specifically speech-act theory. Rather than being grounded in actual discursive practice, Habermas's model reflects a particular ideology of discourse
that views positions discussed in the public forum as originating in individually ratiocinating speakers.[3] From a Bakhtinian perspective, the notion that discourse can be anything other than the product of discursive
interaction, or that public discourse can be constituted by anything but
multiple voices, is problematic.

Xavante practices fit poorly with Habermas's perspective on the relationship between discourse, the individual, and the collectivity. Whereas
Habermas argues that communicative action—action oriented toward
reaching an understanding—is achieved by means of a consensus among
individual selves who must account for intersubjectively recognized claims
of validity,[4] the Xavante organize discourse to be the product of multiple
selves in the form of multiple voices. The thought-provoking contrast between this theory and Xavante practice stimulates questions about the locus of political action in the Xavante *warã* or, for that matter, any social
formation, regardless of the formal arrangement of speaking voices.

Reflecting on the eighteenth-century public sphere, an institutional
space which provided a framework for the formation of public opinion
and criticism, Habermas attempts "to establish a social theory in which
reason and discourse can constitute the core."[5] His view of discourse, embedded in the tradition of Western philosophy of language, implies a particular ideological position with respect to the relationship between a
speaker and his or her utterances. Conceptions of discourse from this traditional perspective—and in this respect Habermas's views present no exception—conform to an essentially individualistic model; discourse is
composed by individuals, not, as in a Bakhtinian perspective, by interactions among individuals. In Habermas's view, individually conceived and
produced utterances can be theorized in terms of validity claims (ratio-
nality, truth, legitimacy, sincerity, or authenticity); discourse is understood
to represent an *individual* speaker's intentions and experiences. Searle, for
example, in discussing speech acts (his proposed basic unit of communication), suggests that "there are a series of analytic connections between
the notion of speech acts, what the speaker means, what the sentence (or
other linguistic element) uttered means, [and] what the speaker intends."[6]
Because, according to this model, discourse is the product of individually
ratiocinating speakers, its production is essentially an individual undertaking. It is social insofar as the formal linguistic code itself and the rules

of use are socially governed phenomena.[7] However, the general framework of Western speech-act theory presupposes a relationship of personal accountability between the individual speaker and his or her utterances, even in situations such as the courtroom, where one individual (an attorney) may speak for another (the defendant).[8]

Such a conception of the relationship between discourse and individual speakers lies at the foundation of contemporary notions of Western democratic tradition. Democratic power as Habermas envisions it, for example, accrues to the people through the accumulation of individual voices critically articulating their views in a public sphere. Discourse that circulates in the liberal public sphere is constructed of individually produced statements; it is based on rational notions of universal truth and universal validity claims. The pertinent question, from an anthropological point of view, is whether or not this relationship between discourse and the individual is teleological. The possibility that other relationships may exist among discourse, the individual, and the collectivity does not figure into the model.

Recently, work describing discourse production and interpretation as socially situated interaction has begun to challenge prevailing notions of individual agency, intentionality, and truth in Western speech-act theory.[9] Work in conversational analysis—in Anglo-American middle-class society, for instance—has been steadily chipping away at the primacy of individual agency, underscoring the interactional nature of conversation as a socially coordinated achievement in which the utterances of one actor influence those of others.[10] Webb Keane's work on ritual speech in Anakalang, Sumba, in which he argues that performance formalizes discrete participant roles to separate voice from agency, also suggests the need for expanded notions of agency.[11] In work along these lines, John Du Bois and Alessandro Duranti offer critical perspectives on the issue of intentionality.[12] Duranti, for example, illustrates that the meanings of utterances in Samoa are neither a priori nor personal but are derived from and are dependent upon interaction.

These and other studies have begun to undermine one of the unquestioned views of Western speech-act theorists: that doing things with words is "an achievement of autonomous selves."[13] Perspectives that conceive of discourse and meaning as personalized are being replaced by ones that see them as the product of cooperative, dialogic interactions between individuals. These interrelational perspectives on discourse resemble those of Bakhtin and members of his circle: "Language, for the individual consciousness, lies on the border between oneself and the other. The word in language is half someone else's."[14]

In Xavante political discourse—a strikingly literal institutionalization of Bakhtin's polyvocality—much of what an orator says is explicitly that of another speaking self; *warā* discourse is formally represented so as *not* to be construed as the product of individual speakers. Rather than evincing a set of one-to-one correspondences between *individual* speakers and discourse, *warā* discursive practice represents discourse as a collage of multiple, articulating voices. It pragmatically illustrates the emergent intersubjectivity inherent in any discursive interaction. In the Xavante model, truth is not a universal standard against which individual statements can be measured; truth can be contested, for it is constructed from many voices.

DISCOURSE AND THE PRINCIPLE OF ANONYMITY

In a brilliant treatise on the public nature of print in late-eighteenth-century America, Michael Warner argues that print—only one of many linguistic technologies, including speaking, reading, and writing—itself obeys no natural teleology.[15] He claims that norms of domination such as race, gender, and status influence the ideological character of print; social ideologies determine print's value, meaning, and interpretation. The same can be said of spoken discourse, when discourse—actual instances of speech and other forms of verbal expression—is conceived of as a semiotic phenomenon.[16] Like print, speech in itself has no natural order. Furthermore, the relationships among discourse, a speaker, and a collectivity follow no natural teleology. The interpretation of discourse as a system of signs is mediated by the ways in which members of a society understand the relationship between a speaker and discourse production in actual instances of performance and against the backdrop of previous performances.

Ethnographic studies of speech practice and linguistic ideology document many instances in which members of a social group attribute considerable significance to an individual's speaking abilities. For example, in many societies an individual's ability to manipulate expressive vocal resources can be used to enhance his or her social status or to create a social persona.[17] Rhetorical abilities may also allow people to attain particular social roles or positions of power.[18] Moreover, success in influential positions may be dictated by expressive proficiency,[19] and expressive proficiency may be instrumental to the enforcement of relations of power and domination.[20] Insofar as institutionalized practice limits access to certain expressive forms—along age or gender lines, for instance—it may also restrict access to positions of social power and authority, thereby reproducing social relations of domination.[21]

The seventeenth-century Quakers, on the other hand, whose linguistic ideology and linguistic practice were marked by a fundamental ambivalence toward speech and language, present a salient contrast to social groups that place a premium on the individual's expressive capabilities.[22] Quakers, Richard Bauman states, coupled "a basic distrust of speaking with a recognition that it was essential and desirable for certain purposes which were central to the religious goals of the Society of Friends."[23] Such an attitude posed a peculiar paradox for the Quaker ministry. Quaker ministers balanced precariously between two poles: on the one hand, they felt a pull toward ministering (speaking) to guide newcomers to the experience of Inner Light; on the other hand, they were drawn to silence, the expression of Inner Light. The seventeenth-century Quakers saw the discourse of the ministry as a reflection not of an individual will but of the Truth and the divine Spirit.[24] The ideology of the ministry depersonalized the discourse of individual speakers.

Depersonalized discourse corresponds to what Michael Warner describes as the principle of negativity and what I prefer to call the principle of anonymity (or self-effacement): the negation of self in public discourse as a condition of legitimacy.[25] Warner articulates the principle of negativity as a corollary to Habermas's principle of supervision (the axiom which demands that all proceedings be made public) to explain the particular relationship between printed discourse, private individuals, and the reading public in late-eighteenth-century America. During the eighteenth-century republican era, when the prevailing ideological framework championed public virtue as opposed to individual or private interest, anonymity constituted a form of political validity. Certain assumptions about discursive norms and print as a form of representation gave printed discourse, particularly political discourse in the form of pamphlets, a special legitimacy. This legitimacy stemmed not from any inherent or "natural" feature of printed discourse but from the fact that print was "categorically differentiated from personal modes of sociability."[26] The general reading public, not the individual author, was responsible for gauging the truth of any particular statement. According to Warner, late-eighteenth-century colonists did not construe writing as a form of personal presence. Political pamphlets were characterized by the absence of personal authorship, a practice that expressed the general principle of negativity in representational politics. The colonial preference for fictitious personae exemplified the principle of negativity; it removed the individual's persona from discourse and bestowed responsibility for the supervision of discourse on the reading public.

Although print easily lends itself to anonymity, a similar anonymity or self-effacement can be achieved in spoken discourse, as many studies focusing on speaking and verbal art attest. For example, a large number of ethnographic studies document strategies such as the use of metaphor, allegory, and proverbs that allow a speaker to obfuscate the relationship between his or her individual persona and the content of the discourse.[27] Such strategies are frequently (but by no means exclusively) found in societies with an egalitarian ethos, where they are used as means of avoiding direct confrontation between equals; metaphor, for example, can be employed to disguise the source of and diffuse the potential for conflict. Other means of denying subjectivity and personal will or of disclaiming accountability in discourse are the invocation of social positions or roles and the attribution of positions taken in discourse to an external authoritative source.[28] In situations of potential or real conflict in societies where speech helps create and sustain an egalitarian polity, indirect speech can be critical to the maintenance of social relations.[29]

There is, however, nothing inherent in the various modes of "indirect speech" that necessarily *makes* them a means of avoiding conflict, as Michelle Rosaldo points out in the case of metaphor.[30] How indirect speech is understood has to do with how such speech is regarded in a particular society, indeed in particular speech situations. Take an example from contemporary American society: indirect speech between partners in a marriage can be construed as incitive and more likely than not to escalate, rather than diffuse, the potential for misunderstanding; counselors encourage partners in this type of contractual relationship to be frank and direct. Elsewhere, ambiguous speech may operate in complex fashion, protecting a speaker's anonymity while simultaneously promoting his or her individual status and self-interest. In Mount Hagen, New Guinea, according to Andrew Strathern, orators use ambiguous speech to express dissatisfaction while preserving social relations. Yet skill in the use of figurative speech can, according to Strathern, be used to enhance a speaker's personal status.[31]

When indirect discourse operates to dissociate the author's person from his or her speech, the principle of anonymity functions referentially. Metaphor, "winding words," "crooked speech," allegory, and the like are discourse strategies that work at the level of content. An effaced presence can, however, also be achieved by other means, for example, by manipulating features of performance itself. In co-performances such as the *pancayats* and gossip sessions of the Fiji Indian villages of Bhatgaon described by Don Brenneis, the boundaries between performer and audience may become permeable and the question of authorship remains open.[32] In the *pancayats* and gossip sessions, two or more individuals together produce a narrative. *Pancayat* participants, for example, construct a public account of an event using a question-answer format in which "the committee member's question and the witness's answer comprise a single proposition. No one is solely responsible for any claims. The public narrative is constructed through the propositions collaboratively stated by questioner and witness." [33] In these situations, the truth of the narrative is not at issue; "the committee is not presenting an account of its own but is contributing to its composition." [34] This officially constructed version will set the baseline against which all future discussions are measured.

The discourse of co-performance in which authorship is negotiated is, as Brenneis notes, truly multivocal in a Bakhtinian sense. [35] The question of authorship remains open, as does that of accountability—an openness suitable to the quasi-egalitarian society of Bhatgaon. [36] In contrast to the Western democratic view of discourse that Habermas describes, the discourse is not linked with the individual ratiocination of its producers, although individuals participate in discussion in an atmosphere of social parity. Indeed, decoupling individual authorship from speech is arguably a factor that helps create egalitarian relations. [37]

In Bhatgaon, according to Brenneis's descriptions and analyses, anonymity is achieved through referential as well as performative means. However, in the Xavante warã meetings, anonymity is achieved almost entirely through performance practice. Indeed, the Xavante example may offer a limiting case with regard to the achievement of anonymity through performance. To explore the limits of anonymity in the Xavante case, let us turn to the discourse practices of Xavante political meetings, warã. These are the same practices that the elders invoked in the construction of Warodi's dream narrative.

WARÃ: THE MEN'S COUNCIL

Even before the first rays of sun break over the horizon, one of the mature men manages to leave the warmth of his bed and make his way to the village center, the warã. [38] Huddled in a blanket against the morning chill of the Central Brazilian Plateau, he begins the high-pitched calls that beckon others to join him. The calls cease after one or two others arrive, and the village awakens against the sonorous backdrop of the men's quiet voices as the soft murmur of their discussion emanates from the plaza.

The mature men meet twice daily in the warã, once in the morning and again in the evening. Here men openly discuss events that affect the community. The topics span a wide range, from economic activities such as gardening, hunting, and fishing to planning for ceremonial events, resolving interpersonal disputes, and assessing the community's general health and well-being. Whenever a group returns from a hunting or fishing trip or an excursion outside the village, a designated member makes a report.

Typically, morning reunions proceed in a less structured manner than evening ones. Attendance is considerably lower and the younger men are noticeably absent. Men gather in the morning to discuss their plans before setting off for their various activities. They normally keep the topics light and the meetings relatively brief. Men tend not to embark on speech making or serious decision making in their morning assemblies. These they reserve for evening meetings.

Around dusk, men again begin to gather in the central plaza. The first to arrive make high-pitched cries to summon the others. Ambitious men, those who aspire to positions of leadership, set the example by their attendance and early arrival at the *warã*.

Men come to the *warã* prepared to camp out comfortably for the evening. Traditionally men lie on *wɛtɛñamrĩ* (sleeping mats) or deer hides.[39] Today they arrive with these and whatever else may be available to sit on. Recent innovations in portable *warã* furniture include bashed-in ten-gallon drums, which make nice stools, and handmade wooden benches. Some men bring wooden chairs in various states of repair and recognizability that have been looted from nearby abandoned ranches or the FUNAI post. One or two cloth-covered folding beach chairs or stools, which can be purchased at many Brazilian urban discount stores, have been imported into the village as luxury items. These began to turn up in the *warã* in the mid-1980s and are the latest novelty in *warã* lounge furniture.

Men's-council meetings take precedence over whatever activity has been going on in the central plaza. Frequently the mature men displace the novitiates and younger men from the plaza, which sometimes doubles as a soccer field in the afternoon.[40] Usually by the time the mature men begin to gather, the sweaty players are on their way to the river. However, I recall more than one evening when the youths, engaged in an especially exciting tournament, had not begun to make any signs of disbanding before the elders started to arrive. While balls whizzed past and runners dodged benches, mats, and empty oil-can "stools," some intrepid elder men proceeded to make themselves comfortable for the upcoming *warã* meeting. Seated in the midst of the playing field, they watched and rooted for their favorite teams while dodging the final plays. Despite their enthusiasm for the youths' soccer matches, the elders' ability to displace them from the *warã* playing field underscores the existence of unequal power relations based on seniority in Xavante society.

Men can appear at or leave the men's council whenever they please. Attendance is by no means obligatory. If a man is tired he may forgo his usual appearance or leave early. Sometimes men sleep right through the *warã*; it is not uncommon after a hard day's work for a man to doze off while lying on his back gazing up at the stars. Occasional snoring may provoke a wisecrack or laughter, but generally nappers are left in peace. A man who has to relieve himself is not obliged to excuse himself. Without being impolite, he walks just a few feet from the circle, where he can still hear what the others are saying and not miss a thing.

Pre-initiates, novitiates, and women do not attend the *warã*. Pre-initiates (*waptɛ*) remain in the bachelors' hut while novitiates (*ʔritaiʔwa*) gather on the side of the mature men's council and prepare to sing around the village. As the men's council gets under way the youths begin to sing. Women and small children remain at home. Occasionally, women visit the homes of their kinswomen while men attend the *warã*. Most often they display little interest in the men's council proceedings, although they may strain their ears to listen to speeches when something particularly interesting is under discussion. I have witnessed only two occasions on which the women congregated in the central plaza to follow the *warã* debates. They ventured near the meeting place only after the proceedings were well under way. Then they seated themselves several feet behind the men and conversed quietly among themselves without commenting openly on the men's discussions.

Usually, women await the return of their husbands and fathers to express their opinions openly. When families are settled on their sleeping mats or sitting on the patio to enjoy the fresh air, women and men openly discuss the evening's proceedings. Indeed, women are not entirely excluded from access to knowledge of community issues; they are often present when men gather in their homes to discuss political matters. And since most issues are discussed in households before they are brought up in the *warã* forum, women's opinions probably do have some impact on political decisions. However, women, explicitly excluded from the forum for public debate, are a disfranchised group; their participation in community decision making is largely mediated by men.

Contrary to Maybury-Lewis's initial observation,[41] men always sit in the same positions at the evening gatherings. This order is not strictly adhered to in the morning gatherings because many men are absent. Some men may sit slightly forward of or behind their neighbors, but each one's position relative to others is always the same. Mature men sit in a circular arrangement, although the circle itself is rather roughly defined.

Seating positions are established at the *da-tsi-tɔ* (joining) ceremony, when the new members, *ĩ-prɛdup-tɛ* (new mature men), are received into the men's council circle. A new participant is supposed to sit between members of the opposed exogamous moiety who are his immediate age-set seniors (Fig. 13). In this arrangement, individual age-sets are not differentiated: the members of adjacent age-sets are integrated and the members of a given age-set occupy a general area within the overall circle. The death of a mature man leaves a hole in the ideal integrated pattern. Among the eldest, age-set areas become indistinguishable. The seating arrangement thus represents not only the diminishing significance of age-set allegiances as men age but also the dynamic balance between members of exogamous and agamous moieties.

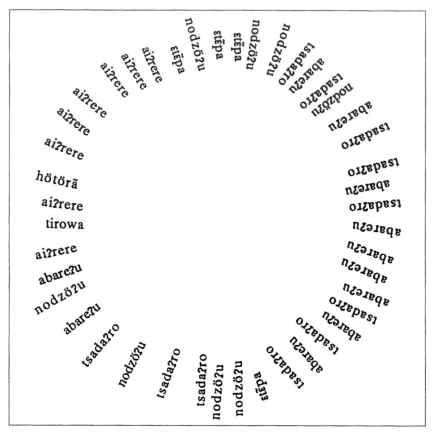

13. *Warã* seating arrangements after the 1985 *tsadaʔro* age-set *da-tsi-tɔ*
(joining ceremony).

Once darkness falls over the men's council, it is difficult to see individual speakers. In the night, when the voices of multiple speakers interfere with and obscure the definition of an individual's voice, location becomes an important key for speaker identification. The familiar seating arrangement assists members of the audience in their attempts to identify speakers. Men can identify a speaker not only by the familiar sound of his voice but also by the location from which it comes. Listeners thus have two sets of clues with which to identify a speaker who is shrouded in darkness.

As the number of participants grows, men talk quietly among themselves and occasionally shout out to others across the circle. Whoever has a tape recorder and batteries is urged to bring it. The men often exhorted me to play songs I'd recently recorded; in fact, it seemed that they preferred listening to recordings of previous performances than to the novitiates' live performances, which typically occur as the men's council is getting under way.

After a period of visiting, one individual stands, clears his throat, and spits. He may also shuffle his feet a bit. These are attention-getting devices that signal the beginning of a speech. If a tape recorder is blasting, the speaker orders its owner to turn it off with an emphatic imperative *wĩrĩ* (kill it!).

WARÃ DISCURSIVE PRACTICE: FACTIONALISM AND THE PRINCIPLE OF ANONYMITY

While the men's council offers a forum for the open discussion of conflicting viewpoints—a "public sphere"—the speech conventions themselves pull the members of different factions together. The organization of speech in the men's council counteracts the centrifugal forces of Xavante factionalism, forces that constantly threaten to rend a village. Men's-council discourse structures speech between individuals of different factions to display centripetal forces opposed to those of factionalism. In mature men's speech, Xavante harness their expressive resources to create a balance between factions and to counterbalance the omnipresent tendency toward fission. They do not succeed in all instances, and when they do not, a minority faction may leave to form a new village, as Sõrupredu's did in 1983.

While the discursive practices of men's-council gatherings counteract factionalism, they simultaneously promote cohesiveness among the members of each faction. Speakers normally address the men's council on behalf of their factions and only occasionally represent their individual interests. Thus, when a man addresses the men's council his factional identity takes priority over his individual self. Mature men's speech contrasts with *da-ñoʔre* (collective singing), in which no individual voice is supposed to stand out. In mature men's speech, individuals do have the opportunity to speak up and let their voices be heard. When a man speaks up, however, he addresses the group more as a representative of his faction than as an individual self.

Consequently, a tension between individualism and factional identity inheres in men's council discourse. The formal features of this discourse, together with certain characteristics of its performance practice, effectively minimize the focus on a speaker's individual identity. Yet the very act of public speaking itself contributes to individual prestige. A man who speaks in the men's council does so with the support of his faction. Those without such support hesitate to raise their voices. Young men, who have not yet had the opportunity to build up factional alliances, rarely address the men's council. Moreover, because the youngest members of the mature men's age grade engage in certain ceremonial activities, such as collective singing, in which their seniors do not, their age-set ties promote interfactional solidarity. Seniority as well as gender, then, affects the participatory franchise.

To become a village leader, a position characterized more by prestige than by any real power or authority, a man must take the initiative to speak up in the men's council. Through speaking he becomes increasingly adept at manipulating the unique formal features that elders and most eloquent speakers employ in their speech. Public speaking moves a man closer to mastery of the verbal art known as *ĩ-hi mrεmε* (elders' speech). Yet simultaneously, features of performance and *warã* discourse metacommentary overtly deny the presence of individuality. This tension is similar to that described by Warner in discussing individuals such as Benjamin Franklin, who, during the American republican era, wished to assert their individual leadership but at the same time had to consider the principle of negativity as a condition of legitimacy.[42] This tension is the result of the opposing pulls between the principle of negativity on the one hand and what might be called the principle of notability on the other.

Unless directly addressed by one of their seniors, young men generally refrain from speaking in the men's council. They listen and learn, absorbing the expressions and stylistic features of the elders' speech for future use. Young men claim to enjoy the privilege of attending the men's-council reunions not only because it offers them an opportunity to learn firsthand about decisions affecting the community but also because it enables them to listen to and learn the *ĩ-hi mrεmε* speech style used by the elders. Aspiring young men practice with the members of their cohort and in smaller groups. Once a young man has garnered sufficient support to begin to speak in the men's council, he actively begins to employ the features of the *ĩ-hi mrεmε* style. Adeptness with the code thus corresponds to socialization. Those who are more adept are more fully socialized and, being more adept, tend to speak more frequently, opening possibilities to acquire still greater eloquence and greater prestige. Consequently, by controlling the discursive resources of *warã* debate, those who are more fully socialized actively define and reproduce relations of domination based on gender and seniority.

The more a man engages in public speaking, the more he gains confidence in his oratorical abilities. Likewise, the more confidence he gains, the more readily he addresses the group. As Maybury-Lewis observed, those who speak up generally enjoy a certain esteem by the time they begin to orate.[43] Speaking itself demonstrates both a man's confidence and the support of his political faction. To be considered a village leader, a man must be perceived as one who represents the interests of the community at

large. Confidence, the support of one's faction, and skill in addressing the
council not as a self-interested individual but as a member of a group are
among the essential ingredients for success in Xavante society. The more
fully socialized the individual, the more he can represent his own interests
as those of a broader group; he can thereby increase both his prestige and
his opportunities to manifest his sociability.

The man who begins the evening's proceeding is a leader, a man of established prestige. During the early and mid-1980s, when Warodi was
cacique, either he or his younger brother Milton carried out this task. The
leader commences his address by introducing the issues to be discussed.
These have come to his attention in meetings at his household throughout
the day, when the village buzzes as men visit with members of their factions to discuss their interests and positions; they raise issues to be discussed in the evening's reunions and use this forum to lay out their views
before meeting with members of other factions. Consequently, most subjects discussed in the men's council have already been addressed by individuals in small groups. Discourse practices employed in these private
meetings are the same as those used in the *warã.*

When a leader opens the men's council, making general introductory
remarks, he speaks on behalf of the entire community. His statements
merely open the floor for discussion; they do not prevent others from rais-
ing additional topics. They define a flexible agenda that can be modified
as the meeting progresses. As the meeting proceeds, any issues he has neglected to raise can be brought up by anyone who wishes to do so. In
making his opening remarks, the leader acts as an initiator, a term appropriate for this role because he has no more power or authority than any
other member of the men's council. The initiator's job is to get the proceedings under way. At this point he refrains from stating his personal
opinion about specific issues. Just like anyone else, he may later comment
on subjects as they arise.

As the initiator's speech continues, men from the circle begin to speak.
Their increasingly frequent comments obscure the initiator's voice, and as
others become involved he sits down. His voice is absorbed into the voices
of multiple speakers. This blending of voices signifies the fact that as an
individual, he has no special power or authority to sway the decision-
making process. He is a facilitator who begins discussions in which all
men may participate.

Several features of men's-council discourse combine to play down a
speaker's individual identity as he orates. These help a speaker to disen-
gage his individual identity from the content of his speech, as do aspects
of the physical setting and performance practice. Effectively reducing an
individual's personal accountability for what he says, they simultaneously

enable him to serve as a representative of a group rather than of his individual self. The formal arrangement of the discourse pulls the members of a group together. At the same time, *warã* discursive practice binds speakers of different factional groups. Thus, while the *warã* provides a forum for the articulation of differing points of view, its discursive practices restrain the forces of factionalism. The discursive practices of *warã* meetings counteract forces that otherwise exert pressures to pull men apart.

WARÃ DISCOURSE: FORMAL FEATURES
AND PERFORMANCE PRACTICE

Xavante men's-council discourse contrasts sharply with customs in other societies that highlight an individual speaker and make a clear distinction between the speaker and the audience. In the *warã* many people talk at the same time; there are no podiums, no spotlights, and no public announcement systems. Moreover, men avoid looking at whoever is addressing the group; most lie on their backs staring up at the sky (Fig. 14). An individual speaker is thus not the explicit focus of audience attention.

By the time the initiator has finished his opening remarks, night has enveloped the central plaza and the speakers are cloaked in darkness. In the dark it is difficult to distinguish the forms of the men as they sit and lie on the ground. A full moon casts the participants' shadows and illuminates their profiles. Moonlight makes it easy to detect their movements, yet individual faces and expressions remain veiled, with the light of the full moon or without it.

The difference between the audience and the speakers is minimal. Indeed, one of the most striking characteristics of the men's council, as David Maybury-Lewis noted, is that most men keep up a running commentary throughout the entire evening.[44] Many men are simultaneously speaking at any point in time. The volume of their commentary, as well as the volume of many of the individual speeches, is usually quite soft. The men's council rumbles in a constant murmur that often obscures the individual voices. Some speakers cover their mouths with a hand while speaking, further obscuring their voices.

From time to time someone rises to put forth an issue to the group from a standing position. The act of standing adds emphasis to his speech and signals that he wishes to make an extended statement. Those who remain seated make shorter comments and often prompt a standing speaker. As the one who stands talks, the other men continue their comments and asides, thereby diminishing the acoustic prominence of the speaker's voice. Although by standing a speaker acquires a certain physical prominence (notability), this is mitigated by the fact that he faces the horizon, thus diminishing the acoustic prominence of his voice (anonymity).

14. Elder men lying on their backs, listening to the *warã* men's council. Sibupa is the figure nearest the camera. (Photo by Laura Graham, 1986.)

When a *warã* participant finds a subject uninteresting, he may turn to his neighbors and strike up an unrelated conversation, or he may simply doze off until a more interesting topic arises. His apparent lack of attention is not considered rude. In any case, most men keep one ear cocked throughout the meeting and merely feign sleep so as not to be bothered.

A man who wishes to follow another's speech with an address of his own may rise even while the other speaker is still standing. He detects the end of his predecessor's speech when the speaker begins to talk less and listen to comments more. Speakers may also end their addresses with closing statements such as *toibö* (that's all) or *tane ñ-mremε* (that's my speech). To indicate his readiness to take over the floor, the waiting speaker often makes muffled sounds and clears his throat repeatedly. A second speaker does not necessarily wait for the first to finish before he himself begins to speak. In this case, the two orators' speech overlaps as each engages in his own monologue.

When an individual speaks in this way, much of what he says is actually the product of a collective discourse; *warã* speakers either act as spokesmen for a group that has met in a closed gathering beforehand, or they incorporate asides into their speech. For example, even though Warodi rarely put in an appearance at the *warã*, his thoughts were carried forth and stated in the men's council primarily by his younger brothers, particularly by Sibupa, with whom he remained closest. Thus, although Warodi rarely appeared in the *warã* in person, he did participate in the men's council. His brother's statements reflected the discussions of a group that had met beforehand. And Sibupa was not solely accountable for his own speech.

Individual speakers who stand to address a group also incorporate a great deal of what is said by their neighbors into their delivery. In this way too, the content of an individual's speech is very much the result of collective discourse production. *Warā* discourse is a veritable melange of multiple voices, with repetition one of its principal features. A speaker may repeat portions of prior discussions that have taken place in the domestic sphere as well as relay the ongoing comments of multiple participants.

Consequently, when orating, a man remains very much in tune with other *warā* participants' responses and regularly incorporates the comments of those around him, often word for word, into his speech. A skilled speaker who is paying close attention to others' remarks may be able to integrate them while still maintaining the rhythm of his delivery. Younger men, and those who have little speaking facility, interrupt their speech more frequently to monitor asides, and they incorporate such remarks into their speech less fluidly. The orations of skilled speakers, by contrast, are a type of dialogic production that joins the comments of multiple speakers.

Because many speakers are involved and their speech often overlaps in complex ways (as many as fifty men might appear on a given evening in Pimentel Barbosa), tape-recording *warā* gatherings presented unique technical problems. I would have had to pin a lavalier microphone onto each man and monitor a mixer with up to fifty channels in order to record the intersecting patterns of interruption and commentary. I did not undertake such an ambitious project. My analyses of men's council discourse are based on many hours of observation, tape recordings made with omnidirectional microphones that picked up the comments of multiple speakers, and recordings of principal speakers in which a considerable amount of audience input is audible.

Whenever a number of mature men gather away from the *warā*, their discussions typically entail repeated utterances, overlapping speech, and the incorporation of interlocutors' statements. Elder women also interact in this way, although repetition is a less prominent feature of women's speech. The elders' discursive interactions in Warodi's dream narrative follow the pattern mature men use in the men's council. Example 1 shows how audience comments are picked up and incorporated into a principal speaker's address. Here Warodi incorporates Etẽpa's comment nearly word for word. In repeating his interlocutor's utterance, Warodi slightly varies the prompt through an alteration in the grammatical category known as aspect. Etẽpa adds the morpheme *mono*, a continuative aspectual marker, and thus changes the postpositional verb form to *waʔaba*.

Whereas in his first repetitions Warodi uses the unmarked continuative form *waʔwa*, after Etẽpa's second comment, Warodi changes to use the same form (*waʔaba mono*) that Etẽpa did. The example shows that Etẽpa anticipates the end of Warodi's sentence, and Warodi finishes the sentence as Etẽpa has formulated it.[45] Through these repetitions the two speakers' voices overlap and merge as they make the same referential statements.

In the transcription, a large bracket ([), indicates the point at which one utterance interrupts or overlaps another. A set of two periods (..) indicates a pause of less that one second; a set of three periods (...) denotes a longer pause. Repeated utterances by the same speaker are not indicated.

XAMPLE 1

Warodi: *wahu te hã . . da-tsi-tsãnawã hã . .*
           du tsi-tsɛdɛ tsimaʔwara dzawi te . . .
                apö . . da-tsi-waʔrãmi . . [*da-tsi-tso da-nɛ waʔwa*
Etẽpa: *da-tsi-tso da-nɛ waʔaba* [*mono hã . . .*
Warodi: *da-tsi-tso da-nɛ waʔwa*
Etẽpa: [*da-tsi-tso da-nɛ waʔaba*
Warodi: *wahu da-tsi-tsãnawã dzo . .*
       apö . . da-tsi-waʔrãmi . . da-tsi-tso da-nɛ waʔaba mono hã

Warodi: in the dry season .. his brother ..
           the grass's smoke rose straight up[46] and he missed him . . .
                again .. he returned .. [for him to walk together
Etẽpa: for him to continue [walking together . . .
Warodi: for him to walk together
Etẽpa: [for him to [continue] walking together
Warodi: for his brother in the dry season ..
       again .. he returned .. for him to continue walking together

Interlocutors show enthusiasm for and agreement with an orator's speech by making short affirmative utterances such as *ĩhẽ* (yes), *tanɛ* (like that), *ãnɛ* (like this), *taha* (that's it). Repetitions of a key word or phrase also indicate the interlocutors' engagement with the principal speaker. When especially enthusiastic, interlocutors add emphatic markers, such as *dza,* or make explosive, aspirated glottal releases. These may or may not have a distinct vowel quality and are depicted as *ʔʌʔ* or *ʔãʔ* in the transcriptions. In Example 2, Sibupa enthusiastically affirms Warodi's statements with short expletive utterances and affirmative phrases. He then repeats the last part of Warodi's utterance and even elaborates on Warodi's preceding statements:

EXAMPLE 2

Warodi: *niha hã*
    hã da-dzarõno hã
    hã ʔate da-hõimanaʔuʔö da-ñitsi waʔwa hã
    taha
    taha aʔute pɔtɔ wa da hã
      ma ɔtɔ da-tsi-tsirɔbɔ aba ni
Sibupa: *ʔãʔˀ*
    tane dza
    tane dza
    ʔãʔˀ
      da-tsi-tsirɔbɔ aba ni
    da-dzarõno hã
    da-dzarõno hã
      aʔuwẽ to dzɛ hã
      ma tsaʔrata aba ni durɛ

Warodi: well ah
    ah the *da-dzarõno* [afternoon song]
    ah they [the ancestors] gave the ancestor his name
    that one
    that one is for the time when babies are born
      then they put feather-down on their foreheads
Sibupa: ʔãʔˀ
    that's it
    that's it
    ʔãʔˀ
    [they put] feather-down on their foreheads
    the *da-dzarõno*
    the *da-dzarõno*
      is for the Xavante to celebrate with
      the ancestors thought carefully, then

    Frequently the principal speaker continues to make sounds while allowing the comments of others to rise above his own speech. At such times he may repeat short phrases or the final line of his last utterance. For example, in one stretch of discourse Warodi repeats *ãnɛ* (like this) or *ãnɛ rotsaʔrada hã* (like this, the thought) six times as others' voices, overlapping and intermingling, assume acoustic prominence. Interlocutors also engage with the principal speaker by making short utterances (such as *ʔãʔ, ʔʌʔ,* or *tanɛ)* in counterpoint. This interaction produces what I believe must be the "antiphonal" effect Maybury-Lewis described in his initial discussion of the men's council speech style.[47]

Neither the individual voices nor the utterances themselves are clearly differentiated in this speech interaction: overlapping obscures the definition of each individual's utterance. Men's council discourse thus contrasts with, for example, the Xokleng ceremonial recitation of the *Wãñẽklen* origin myth during the *ãgyĩn* ceremony for the dead. In the latter, two speakers shout the myth syllable by syllable in an echo sequence; the second speaker repeats the syllable shouted by the first.[48] Each syllable is clearly audible in the *Wãñẽklen* performance, whereas distinct utterances and voices are frequently indistinguishable in Xavante speech.

Participants also show their engagement in a man's speech by repeating parts or all of his remarks. Warodi and Sibupa frequently echo each other throughout the narrative, as shown in Example 3. Here, each works variations on a theme introduced by Sibupa, referring to the time before the creators introduced the Xavante to the foods they eat today. The repetitions show not only that the interlocutor is in agreement with the principal speaker but also that he is particularly engaged in the narrative.

EXAMPLE 3

Sibupa:	*wa wana hã ʔre-tsimiʔwara*
	wedewaiʔu tete ʔre-huri mono rɛrɛ hã
	⎡ *ãne*
Warodi:	⎣ *tsai õ rɛ hã*
Sibupa:	*ĩhɛ tsai õ rɛ*
Warodi:	*tsai õ rɛ*
Sibupa:	*abadze õ rɛ hã*

Sibupa:	[the Xavante] before us always lay together
	when they always ate larvae
	⎡ it was like that
Warodi:	⎣ before they had food
Sibupa:	yes, before they had food
Warodi:	before they had food
Sibupa:	before they had game

The pattern of repetition in mature men's speech is so prevalent that even members of the audience repeat their own aside affirmations in exchanges among themselves. A nice example is an aside exchange between Etẽpa and Eduardo, who state that Warodi is improving upon the tale of the ancestors in his dream narrative.

EXAMPLE 4

Eduardo:	*tare õhã tete ĩ-petse mono*
Etẽpa:	*ĩhɛ tete ĩ-petse mono*
Eduardo:	*ĩ-tsi-petse mono*
Etẽpa:	*ĩ-tsi-petse mono*
Eduardo:	*te ĩ-rowahutu mono*
Etẽpa:	*te ĩ-rowahutu mono*

Eduardo:	he just perfected what he saw in the dream
Etẽpa:	yes he perfected what he saw in the dream
Eduardo:	they [the ancestors] perfected themselves
Etẽpa:	they [the ancestors] perfected themselves
Eduardo:	he is remembering the story
Etẽpa:	he is remembering the story

Participants are free to question the principal speaker, request information, and respond out loud to rhetorical questions he has posed. Speeches are often interrupted when the speaker, noticing an aside, asks, "What?" or exchanges words with a member of the audience. A loud comment from a member of the audience is often itself a summary of a discussion among adjacent members of the audience. The spokesman from such a "conversational group" may even be prompted by his neighbors as he loudly addresses the principal speaker.

Speeches thus involve considerable give and take from the audience, and audience participation clearly influences the development of public addresses. In this process, the principal speaker becomes a mouthpiece for those who do not speak up. His individual voice is absorbed as his speech accumulates the voices of others.

Members of the audience can become so involved in a narrative that they contribute to its development. In this way, multiple speakers become collaborators, or co-performers, in the evolution of the discourse itself.[49] At times, members of the audience insert new information and may even take over the role of principal speaker, especially if they are close to him. Such exchanges take place most frequently among those who share their thoughts extensively, as do Warodi and Sibupa. Of all the interlocutors present at the dream-narrative gathering, Sibupa plays the most active participant role in the narrative development. At times it becomes unclear just who the principal speaker actually is.

Overlapping and simultaneous utterances are very prominent features of Xavante mature men's speech, and they become more pronounced as the speakers age and practice. Xavante do not perceive asides and comments to be interruptions or disruptive in any way. Rather they describe them as assistance, affirmations, and collaboration.

Xavante decision making takes place as multiple speakers simultaneously state and restate their positions until consensus is reached. When a difficult decision must be made, men's council meetings can last late into the night. If no resolution is achieved, the issue is taken up in subsequent meetings. Those who are unfamiliar with this interactional style, and are instead used to Western middle-class turn taking,[50] may find Xavante decision making an extremely frustrating experience. Boanergis, the FUNAI agent during my first visit, had one such experience when he wanted the elders to decide on a proposal he had made. After he had outlined his proposal and Roberto, who understood Portuguese, had translated it for the group, Boanergis expected what he described as a "more orderly" response to his question. He was aghast when five or six elders simultaneously burst out speaking as soon as they had understood the proposal. No one appeared to be in charge; no one appeared to control the decision-making process. Boanergis grew increasingly impatient and finally burst out, pointing to Aiʔrere, who he assumed was in charge, "That's enough! Just one person speak! What do *you* decide?"

When the men's council is settling disputes between members of opposed factions or when visitors come from other villages, two speakers may stand facing each other and speak simultaneously. This performance practice foregrounds the social personae of the speakers. In factional disputes, individuals stand as representatives of either the *poridzaʔõno* or the *öwawẽ* moiety. Similarly, when a visitor from another village addresses the men's council, he speaks not only as a guest but as a *poridzaʔõno* or an *öwawẽ*. In cases where someone must defend himself and stands to address the men's council, he faces a member of the opposite moiety. While these positions would seem to underscore oppositions between the two, the discourse pattern in fact pulls them together. The individual's voice does not stand on its own. The other man standing joins his voice with the principal speaker's, making short affirmative utterances and statements such as *tane, ãnɛ, ʔãʔ*, or *ʔʌʔ*. The audience also collaborates with similar comments and promptings. Rather than categorically emphasizing oppositions, the acoustic arrangement of utterances merges the opposing voices. The individual speaker does not, in fact, stand or speak on his own.

On the eve of their departure from Pimentel Barbosa, the elder of two guests who had spent a month visiting and participating in the activities of the host village thanked the community for its hospitality by addressing the men's council. When the speaker, Garcia, a member of the *öwawẽ* moiety and the *aiʔrere* age-set, rose to speak, Sibupa, who is a member of the *poridzaʔõno* moiety and an *aiʔrere* as well, also stood to respond.[51]

He stood as the elder representative of the *poridzaʔõno* moiety, not as a particularly interested individual party. In his speech, Garcia noted the differences between his village and that of his hosts and praised his hosts for preserving Xavante traditions, such as proper coiffure, *warã* meetings, and *ʔritaiʔwa* singing, that were falling into disuse in his own community. As Garcia spoke, Sibupa affirmed his statements with regular explosive glottal sounds and kept up a constant rumble. The two speakers then switched roles, and Sibupa wished his counterpart a safe trip and speedy return. Garcia participated in Sibupa's address by adding in affirmations.

In 1982 a dispute between members of opposed factions was handled in a similar way. The bride of a man in the *öwawẽ* moiety was charged with infidelity, and when the young husband came to address the men's council, Sibupa again stood as an elder *poridzaʔõno* representative. In this exchange, the younger man was not an adept speaker. Sibupa made continual utterances while the youth told his version of the story in conversational Xavante, but the young man did not reciprocate during Sibupa's speech. Sibupa's speech style emphasized his elder status and underscored the fact that he spoke as a representative of his faction, not as an individual party engaged in settling a dispute. The issue was resolved in subsequent discussions that involved the entire male community.

Men also come together in private domestic meetings as representatives of social groups, rather than as individuals, in order to settle disputes or problems privately and to avoid bringing their affairs up in the men's council. In these meetings they meet as *poridzaʔõno* and *öwawẽ* and as family heads. For example, when Agostim's daughter Cecita and Supto were involved in a marital dispute that threatened to disrupt relations between the two families, Agostim and Supto's classificatory father settled the matter in a private session with each other. In this meeting the fathers acted as spokesmen for their families as well as for their children, who had been unable to resolve the dispute independently. The two men set up the meeting indirectly, using small children as messengers, and in the meeting itself they avoided confronting each other as individuals. They were, in fact, friends; they belonged to the same age-set and had lived together in the bachelors' hut. The conventions of meetings between men enabled them to avoid engaging one another as individuals.

On the morning of the encounter, Agostim silently entered Supto's natal house without making any gesture of greeting. None of the household members acknowledged his entrance. He went directly to his host's sleeping mat and lay down on his back. He never summoned his son-in-law's father, but waited for others to carry the message that he'd arrived. Several minutes later, Supto's uncle and classificatory father, Barbosa, joined him, and the two lay talking very quietly for almost an hour. Neither looked at the other, just gazed at the ceiling.

Although Agostim and Barbosa both belonged to the mature men's age grade, I had never heard either one speak in the style used by the elders in the men's council. However, during this meeting they used this style, with its characteristic intonational rising at the ends of phrases and its pronounced glottalization. They spoke simultaneously, and each man's speech was itself repetitious. Each repeated the other's utterances or affirmed his speech with short phrases; the distinctiveness of their individual voices disappeared. When they had completed their discussion, Agostim stood up and left without comment. Each family head would privately relay the outcome of the meeting to his family.

In this meeting, the two men met as family heads. They discussed matters of interest to themselves as individuals but also to their families. The conventions of the speech suggested a balanced interaction between opposing equals. The simultaneous speech acoustically pulled them together. From a semiotic point of view, such as the one Urban proposes for ceremonial dialogues, their speech interaction can be interpreted as a sign vehicle.[52] Like other forms of ceremonial dialogue practiced elsewhere by Native South American groups,[53] Xavante mature men's discourse signals social cohesion. It models an ideal form of solidarity between individuals who are, in social terms, maximally distant.[54]

ĩ-hi mrɛmɛ

As men hone their speaking abilities, their speech becomes increasingly marked by the repetition of short phrases. Repetition combines with several other features to constitute a distinctive speech style used by elder men, one that helps distance a speaker from the content of his speech.[55] This style, which Xavante recognize as ĩ-hi mrɛmɛ (elders' speech), is practiced by elders in the men's council. Very elderly men, those who have sharpened their skills as ĩ-hi mrɛmɛ speakers, also employ it in many other situations when they wish to throw around the weight of their age and wisdom and to stress the importance of their speech. Elderly men use it privately with members of their faction, telling traditional tales, giving instructions to youths, and making ceremonial greetings. Warodi slipped into this style nearly every time he made a statement of more than two or three sentences. It is the hallmark of old age among Xavante men and is considered eloquent and enjoyable to listen to. This is the style Warodi used in developing the narrative of his dream.

Formally distinct from conversational Xavante, ĩ-hi mrɛmɛ is characterized by extensive repetition and parallelism, a unique voice quality, and a special intonation pattern. These features give it a distinctive acoustic shape. The orators manipulate linguistic texts to achieve systematic, indeed musiclike, sound patterns.[56] Phrases uttered in ĩ-hi mrɛmɛ tend to be short and formally bounded; they are spoken with greater pharyngeal constriction than is used in everyday speech. Glottal stops at the ends of phrases and distinct pharyngeal constriction, especially in syllables at the ends of phrases, effectively establish phrase boundaries. Speakers often release the phrase final glottal stops with explosive bursts of air.

Phrases in Warodi's dream narrative, as in all instances of *ĩ-hi mrɛmɛ,* are characterized by descending pitch and end with a slight rise instead of a decline as in everyday conversational speech. This slight rise is emphasized by the glottal stops and explosive releases that occur at the ends of phrases. Although it is impossible to identify acoustic pitch in rhetorical speech, the parallel structure of intonation contours in adjacent phrases produces an aural quality that is indeed "musiclike."[57] A musiclike quality thus results from the repetition of phrases and clauses with parallel intonation contours.

Orators may further emphasize phrase boundaries with the particle *te* or the explosive aspirated *t'* at the ends of phrases. Elders also frequently punctuate their phrases with imploded lateral clicks, a sound that is not part of the phonetic inventory of everyday speech. Neither the lateral click nor *te,* in this context, carries referential meaning; both are purely pragmatic markers of elders' speech. As speakers become more animated, their rate of delivery increases and the pharyngeal constriction, glottalization, and rising pitch at the ends of phrases are increasingly exaggerated. These features produce a regular, staccato, rhythmical effect that frames the musiclike intonation patterns and highlights the variation between juxtaposed parallel sets.

Phonetic variations as well as some words and phrases that rarely appear in, or are not part of, everyday speech occur in elders' speech. For example, the expression Warodi uses as he begins his dream narrative, *niha diretɛ,* meaning "leave things be" or "everything is fine," is used only by Xavante elders. Elders also employ a distinct form for negative marking. Rather than using the negative marker *õ di,* common to everyday speech, elders mark the negative with *wẽtɛnɛ.* When Lino translated some segments of Warodi's elder speech from the dream narrative into a form that he, a young man, would use, he substituted *õ di* for *wẽtɛnɛ.* Example 5 illustrates the contrast between Warodi's and Lino's formulations of the same statement; I have underlined the differences to make the contrasts easier to see. Notice also that Lino does not use extensive repetition.

EXAMPLE 5
Warodi: *wa-waprui-re hã*
            wa-waprui-re hã
            wa-noi-re hã
            wa-noi-re hã te ʔre-wa-dzadze waʔaba wẽtɛnɛ

Lino: *wa-tsi-höiba hã*
wa-noi-re hã te ?re-wa-dzadze mono õ di

our flesh
our younger brothers [our descendants] no longer believe in us

This example also illustrates Warodi's metaphorical use of the noun *wapru* (blood) to mean "flesh" or descendants.[58] The youth chooses a more common noun, *höiba*. Such metaphors are commonplace in elders' speech. For example, elder speakers may denote "child" by *?u* (liquid), or by the expression "creation from his [or her] skin [or body]," as Warodi did in a *warã* speech he made following the death of his younger brother's infant: *tε marĩ ma ĩ-no hö wi pɔtɔ uprotsi te* (I don't know what caused the death of my younger brother's infant; literally, the creation which came from my brother's skin).

Some lexical items undergo slight phonetic changes when used by elders speaking in the *ĩ-hi mrεmε* style. For example, Warodi transformed the word *ai?ute* (baby) to *a?ute* in *ĩ-hi mrεmε*. The alternate form is underlined in the example below, an excerpt from the dream narrative in which Warodi speaks of the *da-dzarõno* (afternoon song).

EXAMPLE 6
taha
taha a?ute pɔtɔ wa da hã
ma ɔtɔ da-tsi-tsirɔbɔ aba ni

that one
that one is for the time when babies are born
then they [the ancestors] put feather-down on their foreheads

Younger Xavante men are not always familiar with the words or expressions employed by their elders. They claim to pick these up gradually by listening to the elder men's narratives, particularly by paying attention to the elders' speech in the men's council or by lying next to their fathers to hear family tales. My younger assistants often could not gloss words used by the elders; they did, however, usually infer the meanings of phrases from the context. Occasionally young men misinterpret the elders' speech. One of my young assistants, for example, sometimes translated segments incorrectly because he failed to detect when Warodi had switched referents.

In working on translations of the dream narrative, my assistants complained that Warodi had left out words or particles necessary to make complete, comprehensible sentences. The frequent omission of person markers in Warodi's narrative may be a feature of elders' speech, but my assistants claimed that the absence of pronouns, in elicited sentences, was unacceptable. Interlocutors must intuitively fill in the gaps while listening to *ïhi mrɛmɛ*, since technically, according to my consultants, the omission of person markers is ungrammatical. In elders' speech, much semantic information is, indeed, filled in by members of the audience. When an individual does not understand, convention allows him to question the speaker.

Elder men, especially, invoke the creators, or *höimanaʔuʔö*, in their speeches, as Warodi does in the dream narrative. This is a rhetorical device that further distances a speaker from the content of his speech. A speaker may remove himself from the position he advocates by presenting it as a position assumed by the ancestors; a man becomes less accountable if he presents his argument in this way.[59] When an elder refers to the ancestors in speech, he may not clearly identify them. As in everyday speech, Xavante avoid using personal names in public speeches. Instead they use kin terms, Portuguese names, or descriptive terms. In his dream narrative, for example, Warodi referred to two of the creators as "the one whose foot was pierced by a stick" and "the one who made the sea." Anyone unfamiliar with the topic of discussion will be unable to read the cues essential to understanding the message.

While Xavante recognize that the way elders speak, *ï-hi mrɛmɛ*, differs from everyday conversational speech, they do not have a developed metadiscourse with which to describe its salient characteristics. Neither do they have ways to evaluate a speaker's performance in terms of its formal properties. Xavante are not metalinguistically conscious of the formal characteristics of *ï-hi mrɛmɛ*, but they are clearly aware of the style; novitiates, for instance, stage impressive imitations of the elders by speaking in short repeated phrases with pharyngeal constriction and intonational rising at the ends of phrases. Yet they do not have ways of talking about these discourse features.

Instead of formal features, age and factional allegiance are the criteria people use to evaluate speakers. When asked to identify outstanding speakers in Pimentel Barbosa, people generally indicated "the elders," and in particular, elders from their own faction. My younger assistants invariably suggested that the elders from their factions were the most eloquent and competent speakers. One assistant, who belonged to a faction that aspired to greater influence in the village, refused to work with me in translating the speeches or narratives of anyone who did not belong to his faction. He claimed that the elders of his faction spoke more eloquently than others with whom I'd worked; he felt that the elders of his faction were more worthy of having their speeches recorded and transcribed. Assistants who belonged to opposed factions held the same opinions of their own elders. No one seemed able to support his position except by referring to the age and wisdom of the speakers in question. The speakers' various abilities to manipulate formal features of the style were not at issue and, in fact, individuals avoided explicitly evaluating speakers in terms of their oratorical abilities.

Men rarely claim responsibility for speeches they have given in the *warã*. Similarly, participants decline to comment about the speeches of others. If asked to summarize or remark upon an individual's speech in a previous men's-council meeting, men often respond that they didn't hear it, don't remember it, or were asleep. They may suggest inquiring of the speaker himself, who, when asked, downplays his role in the proceedings. No one admits having paid attention to any one individual or having had a position of prominence at a meeting. Similarly, when asked about what is to be discussed at an upcoming evening assembly, Xavante men usually decline to comment. They respond to such inquiries by saying that they don't know, they'll see what happens. Of course, most men do have some idea of the topics to be discussed, but it would be pretentious for someone to state outright what might happen in a gathering that involves the entire male community. Even the men's-council initiator remains unassuming in this regard.

DEPERSONALIZED DISCOURSE IN THE *WARÃ*

During my first trips to the Xavante, my attempts to make sense of the men's-council discussions were consistently frustrated. In the *warã* itself, I usually sat next to someone who could gloss the basic themes of discussion. In this way, I could patch together a vague impression of the proceedings, and it was evident that the Xavante were not trying to withhold information from me. To fill in the gaps in my understanding I often sought out participants for further discussion the day after a meeting. To my dismay, my interlocutors dodged my questions or gave the briefest possible responses to my queries. I hadn't yet come to comprehend the Xavante's particular view of the relationships among discourse, the individual, and the collectivity. Unknowingly, I was operating under the same assumptions that Habermas outlines in his theory of communicative action, the very assumptions that underlie Western humanist philosophical theories of discourse and Habermas's notion of the liberal public sphere: I had maintained a *personalist* view of discursive practice,[60] uncritically linking discourse and intentionality to individual subjectivity. These assumptions promoted certain expectations about how a Xavante man who had spoken in the men's council would answer my questions after a *warã* meeting, expectations at odds with the Xavante emphasis on collaborative discourse production and depersonalized accountability.

Xavante pragmatically represent discourse as the product of multiple selves in *warã* discourse practice. In the *warã*, the physical and acoustic features of performance effectively dissociate individual speakers from their utterances. Discourse production and its correlate, accountability, are distributed among the participants. A Xavante orator is like the Bakhtinian prose author; he speaks *through* language, harnessing the expressive resources of the repertoire to objectivize language and distance himself from it. He appears to "merely ventriloquate,"[61] using eloquent repetitive and overlapping discourse to incorporate statements made by others either before or during his speech. A speaker thus represents discourse as an extra-individual production to promote cohesiveness among the members of a faction. When discourse is effectively executed, an individual achieves "negativity" and offsets his "notability" as a speaker.

Simultaneously, the organization of speech blends the voices of members of opposed factions to counteract the centrifugal forces of factionalism, reinforcing egalitarian relations among senior males and holding the community together. Since women and youths are institutionally excluded from the discussions, however, the same discursive practices continually reproduce and reinforce relations of domination along age and gender lines. Although the discursive forms pragmatically promote egalitarian relations among senior male participants, unequal access to the participatory franchise underscores a fundamental inequality in Xavante society, an inequality not unlike that of the liberal public sphere that Habermas describes. In eighteenth-century Europe, according to Habermas, public discourse localized power in the speaking public and motivated the transition from autocratic states to democratic ones; however, not all voices were heard as part of the speaking public. Similarly, not all members of Xavante society are included in the working polity. Women, excluded from direct participation in the *warã*, have no direct voice in the public sphere; they contribute indirectly, and their participation is even more depersonalized than that of the junior and less notable men.

In the *warã*, then, the locus of political action resides in emergent social interaction, not in any single agent as in the idealized model of Western democratic tradition. The discursive interaction between senior males in the *warã* blurs the boundary between voice and individual subjectivity, fuses individual perspectives, and erases the boundaries between an orator's speech and the speech of others. By formally representing discourse production as a collaborative rather than an individual endeavor—a hybridization of voices—*warã* discursive practice pragmatically embodies a conception of language and speech acts that was articulated by Soviet theorists such as Bakhtin, Vološinov, and Vygotsky and that has been emerging in recent critiques of speech-act theory.[62] From such a perspective, discourse, meaning, and intentionality are contextually situated and intersubjectively produced.

DEPERSONALIZING THE DREAM

Sibupa: okay
            okay let's listen for ourselves, like this
                listen for ourselves
Aiʔrere: before the whites they had this custom
                the custom
            for this you are telling their story to the end
            really they remember this in each generation
            ⎡ really
Sibupa: ⎣ yes
            ⎡ yes
Warodi: ⎣ yes that's it
            that they
                united their work
            then the ancestors first created the dog
            then ah
                they created whatever
            ah
            ah
            ah foods
                foods
            cara roots they created then
            then they created a different root
            ⎡ then
Sibupa: ⎣ they thought carefully about their work

Just as *warã* discursive interaction blurs the boundaries between an orator's speech and the speech of others, through their *warã*-like discursive interaction in the *marã* the elders' voices depersonalized the narrative account of Warodi's dream. After sharing his dream-songs, Warodi behaved like the *warã* initiator; he launched into an account of the dream in which he received his songs from the creators. Immediately, other elders began to contribute to his telling.

Even though Xavante conceptualize a dream to be the experience of an individual self—Warodi was the one who initially "experienced" the dream—its telling nevertheless became a cooperative endeavor. The dream narrative evolved through a polyvocal process of discursive production. The acoustic arrangement of speaking voices downplayed Warodi's prominence as the initiator, the original dreamer. Simultaneously, the polyvocal discursive production highlighted the narrative as a representation of shared experience.

By collaborating in the telling, the participants altered the nature of Warodi's dream experience beyond what their collective singing had already accomplished. As participants in the telling, the elders transformed *more* of Warodi's dream (or what was represented as a dream) into collective experience. In singing, the elders had already moved part of Warodi's dream from the arena of individual experience into the public domain. Following that, in their collaborative telling, they brought forth another dimension: they shared in the formulation of what Warodi presented as the creators' exegesis of the songs—by singing *da-ño?re*, the creators' gifts to the living, and remembering their lives, the Xavante will remain forever Xavante.

> ah Xavante
> to be always Xavante
> in order to live as Xavante always
>   according to their customs
>   according to their customs
>   i[t, the dream performance]
>   it is for that
>   it is for that

Moreover, in their telling the elders were actually *doing* what Warodi was proposing. In joining their voices to tell the dream of Warodi's encounter with the creators, they too were remembering (telling) of the creators' remarkable lives.[63] Together with Warodi they demonstrated the way for the Xavante to remain forever.

For his part, Warodi enabled the others to participate more profoundly than is usual in his inner experience by elaborating his dream in narrative form. By publicly sharing more of his inner self than is normally the case, Warodi added to the already considerable notability he had achieved by sharing three songs. Yet the narrative was constructed in a manner that counterbalanced this notability. By their overlapping voices, asides, affirmations, elaborations, questioning remarks, and even contradictions, the elders invoked the principle of anonymity to formally offset Warodi's distinction. Moreover, by participating in the telling of his dream, each became further involved in the public presentation of Warodi's experience. With each remark, the elders became increasingly invested in its message. Their collaboration ensured their individual commitment.

As I mentioned in Chapter 4, Warodi downplayed his personal notability by framing the exegesis of his songs as the ancestors' advice to the living. Presenting it as advice he received in a dream, he convincingly attributed the origin of his message to a source beyond his personal self. By ascribing the message to the ancestors, a higher authority, he further depersonalized his own contribution to the narrative account. The others understood his message in this way.

Etẽpa: this isn't from the earth
      this isn't
      this isn't the angels' speech
      this is the creators' speech, it is this
         that he
         that he is remembering
      it is not something ordinary
      he there [Warodi] every time he goes there to the sky
      he
      he hears the creators' speech
         when the ancestors are gathered
       that's what this is
Sibupa: it is always this way

At another point in the narrative, Wadzaʔe put it this way:

from there [the creators]
there
the counsel comes from there
the counsel comes from there to correct [the behavior of the living]

Representing himself as someone who received communications from the ancestors on behalf of the entire community, Warodi portrayed himself as a fully socialized individual. He spoke not on behalf of his individual self but on behalf of the creators in the interests of the broader community. With their own remarks, the other elders corroborated the image Warodi evoked.

because they care for us
because they care for us
    they are turning toward us [thinking of us]
    they are turning toward us
        for us to always remain forever Xavante
        for us to always remain

"LIKE THIS WE WILL RISE ABOVE THE OTHER COMMUNITIES"

As they became increasingly involved with the narrative and with forging an image of Pimentel Barbosa as a privileged community to which the creators had turned their attention, the elders began to move the narrative in new directions. From the outset the various speakers made it evident that a principal objective of the dream performance was, through performing *da-ño?re* and remembering the lives of the creators, to exemplify the ways in which the community would continue its physical and cultural survival. However, as the narrative progressed, the elders' comments revealed that they were staging the performance to advance the community's interests in other arenas as well.

Their numerous references to the significance of the youths' understanding, for example, fit within the trajectory of the narrative as Warodi began it. Statements such as "If the youth were all there was, they would already be whites" expose the elders' concern over the youths' ability to perpetuate the creators' memory and thereby guarantee the Xavante's cultural survival. Yet as the narrative progressed, it took on an explicitly political cast. Issues not directly related to the community's survival, either cultural or physical, began to surface in commentary that addressed Pimentel Barbosa's status in relation to other Xavante communities, and eventually even its position with regard to the external world. According to Etẽpa,

> of course
> it is always we [the elders]
> it is always we who enliven the celebrations
>   and [thus] surpass the other villages

Sibupa put it this way:

> so our ancestors
> our ancestors
>   through our lives they will be remembered
> like this we will bring down [rise above] the other villages
> we will let our stories be heard
> now we see with careful detail our ancestors' customs
>   see with careful detail
> that is the way it will be

Here the elders boast of the superior quality of their ceremonials, the celebrations through which the people of Pimentel Barbosa remember the lives of their ancestors and the creators. Within this context, the elders announce that the youths are to play a special role in this process of "bringing down the other villages" and "letting our stories be heard." As "descendants of the first creator" and "descendants of the first chief" (*ĩ-höʔa naʔrata*), the young have a special responsibility to extend the news of Pimentel Barbosa's privileged position to the world beyond. WadzaʔE stated this most clearly when he said, "When they understand it [that we are descendants of the first creators] they are going to tell the *waradzu* [Brazilians, whites]. Then it will be known by everyone."

When word gets out that the people of Pimentel Barbosa are the descendants of the first creators, the ones who made the world for the Xavante before they worked for any other group, then those of Pimentel Barbosa, the true descendants, will receive their due recognition. It will be known, as WadzaʔE says, that "that one, that Marure [Mario Juruna] is not the [descendant of the] first creator like he says."

With these explicit statements, particularly the reference to Mario Juruna, the elders tied the performance, and through it the memory of the creators, directly to the rivalry that raged between Pimentel Barbosa and other Xavante communities, specifically those of the São Marcos Reserve, home of Mario Juruna. In Pimentel Barbosa, people resented the fact that Xavante of other communities, and Mario Juruna in particular, had risen above them as pioneers of relations with Brazilian national society. By this time, in fact, Juruna had expanded his sphere of notoriety beyond Brazil's borders: in November 1980, he traveled to Rotterdam as president of the Fourth Russell Tribunal on indigenous rights in the Americas. WadzaʔE's comment directly exposed the resentment people of Pimentel Barbosa harbored toward Juruna.

In their collaboratively produced narrative of Warodi's dream, the elders from Pimentel Barbosa contextualized their political rivalries with other Xavante communities within the domain of relations to the first creators. They shifted the arena of intervillage competition from the immediate one of relations with FUNAI, the sphere in which they competed for material goods, as well as from the sphere of national and even international politics, to that of their relationships to the first creators. Stating that the descendants of the first creators were here, living in Pimentel Barbosa, the elders of Pimentel Barbosa affirmed their superiority over other Xavante peoples. Their comments acknowledge that other communities have temporarily achieved prominence over Pimentel Barbosa. Nevertheless, these are coupled with an explicit determination that they will regain their position of externally recognized superiority. Through this performance the elders were actively initiating steps toward their triumph. They designed the performance to demonstrate their privileged links to the first creators—demonstrate them to themselves, to the women, to the youths, and also to me.

Once they understood this message, the youths were charged with disseminating this truth about their heritage to Brazilians. But the young people were not the only ones through whom the community could spread the word of its status. I was also a likely candidate to publicize their cause.

As he was verbally instructing the youths about their body paint during preparations for the dream performance, Etẽpa pointed directly to me. He expressed an explicit vision regarding the nature of my potential contribution.

> you [youths] are going to paint with this
> now you all are the descendants of the first creator
> this fact
> this fact they [the youths who speak Portuguese] will teach to her
> if she understands what you [youths] say, it is to be published

Immediately Sibupa affirmed, "It is for that."

Without the ability to write themselves, my skill as a scribe opened up a new avenue for publicity and for "surpassing" other Xavante communities. From our discussions of my interest in committing their narratives "as they speak them" to writing, the elders had devised a plan to use my skills to their advantage. Claude Lévi-Strauss had encountered a Nambiquara leader some fifty years before who perceived writing not as a skill related to the acquisition of knowledge or to remembering or understanding but rather as a symbol "of increasing the authority and prestige of one individual—or function [chieftaincy]—at the expense of others."[64] The Xavante elders perceived my scribe's knowledge to be accompanied by a certain power. Their understanding differed, however, from that of the Nambiquara headman: they envisioned putting writing to use for the benefit of the entire community, not just for a single individual.

Furthermore, the Xavante elders perceived writing not only in terms of advancing the community's prestige and authority in relation to other Xavante communities, but also as a way to educate peoples of the world beyond Brazil's borders about their life and their relationship to the first creators. Being a foreigner who could write, I had the potential to reach an audience they could not otherwise imagine reaching themselves. With me as their mouthpiece, a mouthpiece that other Xavante communities did not have available to them, I could spread their message farther than any other Xavante community could do. For them, as for the Nambiquara leader, writing was undoubtedly a craft that could be employed to increase prestige. It was also a resource that could be harnessed to disseminate their knowledge to the external world.

Not only did the elders perceive that writing could be put to use to advance their position in the world, they also saw my tape recorder to be an instrument that could be put to work in a similar fashion. The tape, they knew, stored their songs and guarded their message.

Since the outset of the dream rehearsal, my tape recorder had been recording the sounds in the *marã* forest clearing, although it had been largely overlooked. Only once did someone suggest that this recording was inappropriate. When Eduardo realized the tape recorder had "listened" to him when he was goofing around, he chastised me for taping before the singing was polished: "Reñipre [Laura], Reñipre not now! Only there, [in] the plaza. In the plaza." Aside from this the elders paid it no heed. Since the beginning, when Warodi first began to teach his songs, it had recorded all the singing and all the discussion within the rehearsal. It recorded the narratives, the discussions of body paint, and the instructions the elders gave to the participants. From start to finish, it "listened" to the sounds in the *marã*. But, apart from Eduardo's comment, no one acknowledged it or seemed to care whether or not it was there.

Yet when the discussion turned to particulars of the performance, the elders suddenly remembered it. "Is the tape recorder here?" "Huh?" "The tape recorder!" As the time drew near for the participants to move to the *warã* for the public performance, the elders became preoccupied with the tape recorder and with the fact that the singing would be recorded. Sibupa urgently reminded Warodi about it when Warodi was making his final comments about the songs.

Warodi: of them
             you must think well of them in the sky
             you must think well of them there
                there in the sky, the always living, there
             they are all gathered there
             they are all gathered there
             these, the descendants
                the descendants of the first Xavante
                the descendants of the first Xavante visit us . . .
             they don't die
             they have many lives
             those descendants like us
                they keep living
             the always living keep living
             they keep living

those, they keep visiting us
   they keep visiting us
they are forever Xavante
they are forever Xavante they keep livi[ng]
the
the first ones keep visiting us
since there is no difference we feel badly
we hide ourselves
we hide ourselves like others and they feel sorry for us
   they feel sorry for us

Sibupa: [whispering, reminds Warodi of the tape recorder]
Warodi: that's it
Sibupa: the tape recorder
Warodi: huh?
Sibupa: the tape recorder [incomprehensible]
Warodi: what

with the tape recorder
sing loudly for the tape recorder
we were going to call you to sing loudly
   to sing loudly for the tape recorder

At this point, Warodi made the tape recorder into an incentive for beautiful (loud) performance. He invoked the tape recorder to encourage performers to produce an aesthetically pleasing performance.[65] The tape recorder was not used as a motive for staging the performance itself. However, since it was there, it became one more reason why the performers should do their best. Although there were no tape recorders in the community at the time, the elders knew I would share the recording with them. They knew that performers would be able to listen to the songs and remember the performance. Moreover, they knew that I would take the tape to the United States, "across the ocean," for still others to hear their singing and learn of the first creators. For this reason I was encouraged to play the tape in my country, but not to pass it around to other Xavante communities. Through me and the tape recording, Warodi could share the songs he received from the first creators with the world beyond. In the performance, he gave something of himself to the members of the community. And through me, the written word, and tape recordings of his songs, he could give something of himself to his relatives (*nare*) across the ocean. In this way others would really know that the descendants of the first creators were still living in Pimentel Barbosa. There, because they continue to remember the lives of the first creators, they will continue as Xavante forever.

6

Becoming a Creator

they
they gathered as always
they gathered as always
there, like this, they
  like this
    suggested
    suggested
they, for us
they, for us, suggested something according to their knowledge
I
I, in [the meeting]
I, in [the meeting]
  tried
  tried to fight
  tried to fight tried
    [for us] to remain always Xavante
    to remain always Xavante
    to forever live as Xavante always
    to forever live as Xavante always

For the exceptional dreamer, such as Warodi, dreams can be a setting in which an individual may actually meet the creators. Whereas a young man *receives* songs from the immortals in his dreams, Warodi, an elder, speaks of *interacting with* the immortals and the creators who made the Xavante's world: "In the meeting, I tried to fight for us to remain always Xavante."

Warodi portrays himself as one who has actually moved into the realm of the distinguished immortal creators. He speaks of his active participation with them in the dream's *warã*-like gathering. And as the narrative flows on, by manipulating formal devices in his speech Warodi aligns his identity with that of the originators of the Xavante world. Creatively blurring the distinction between the present and the mythological past, between self and other, Warodi becomes an immortal creator himself. In his speech and in his self he establishes connections between the past and the present, the living and the dead. These are means by which the Xavante, and Warodi himself after death, will continue.

ELDERS AS ANCESTORS

As an *ĩ-hi* elder, Warodi belongs to the final phase of the life cycle for the living. When he dies, he will enter the ultimate phase of the life cycle: he will become one of the immortals. In many ways, his *ĩ-hi* behavior, like that of other elders, suggests that he is already more like an immortal than he is like his living juniors. For example, Warodi no longer participates in ceremonial activities. Instead, along with the other elders who have passed through all phases of the *waiʔa* and initiation cycles, he enjoys the privilege of sitting on the periphery to watch over and supervise the younger participants and to delight in the youths' spectacularly aggressive dancing. And, as if the youths' collective *da-ñoʔre* performances were meant for them, only the eldest shout out *he pãrĩ!* or *he te pãrĩ!* (well done! or, bravo!) to express appreciation for the song performances. As an elder, Warodi lives in a liminal arena between the immortals and the living.[1]

As those who watch ceremonies without actively participating, elderly men do indeed behave like the ancestors. Depending on one's point of view and life-cycle status, elders and ancestors occupy parallel positions relative to ceremonial participants: one or the other provides the primary audience for ritual performances. The *ʔritaiʔwa* novitiates explain that their singing performances are *ĩ-hi date madöʔö da* (for the elders to see). Elders, on the other hand, claim that the immortals constitute the primary audience. On the occasion of the *ʔuʔu* ceremony, for example, Warodi explained to me that the singing, dancing, and merriment were *höimanaʔuʔö date madöʔö da* (for the immortal creators to see). Since neither the elders nor the immortals participate actively in ceremonials, the elders' behavior in this sense resembles that of the immortals. As the primary audience, each provides incentive for their juniors to continue the traditional customs, the behaviors that make them and their descendants Xavante.

Two other ceremonial practices suggest an elder's movement away from the divisive factionalism of the mature life-cycle phase toward incorporation into a broader collectivity that resembles that of the immortals. By acquiring more and more *da-ãmo* ceremonial friends, becoming increasingly enmeshed in friendship bonds that blur the distinctions between kin and affine, an elder becomes assimilated into a more inclusive social body.

Similarly, through the give and take of names over the course of a lifetime, a man links himself into increasingly broader networks. These two practices, as Aracy Lopes da Silva convincingly illustrates, promote unity among men who are otherwise structurally opposed.[2] They effectively mitigate against factional divisions and promote continuity between men in and through time.

Male naming practices, like the institution of formal friends, align members of opposed exogamous moieties in and over time.[3] Ideally, when he becomes a *ʔritaiʔwa* novitiate, a youth receives his first adult name from his mother's brother (*da-ñorebzu-ʔwa*); then, throughout his life, a man gives old names to new recipients and takes on new ones from senior donors. Via his adult names, the individual becomes part of a nominally defined male lineage that is distinct from his patrilineal descent. These names crosscut, or mitigate against, exogamous moiety divisions at the same time they contribute to a man's adult social identity. Simultaneously, the practice of name giving and receiving establishes continuity between younger males and their seniors over time: by acquiring names, a man promotes ties between himself and ascending generations of men who have previously held the same name. Likewise, by giving away his names, a man forges links between himself and generations to come. Passing on his names, a man ensures his social survival.[4] The continuity of his names protects his immortality.

Once a man reaches the *ĩ-hi* (elder) stage, according to Lopes da Silva, he no longer replaces the names he gives up with new ones: "A man ends his life as it began: without a name."[5] Nameless, a man loses his definition as a member of a distinct, name-possessing group. He becomes part of a generalized set of elders in which his identity is no longer nominally defined. Like an immortal, he is nameless.

At the point in the life cycle when an elder's individual social identity, encoded in names, formal friendships, and other ceremonial behavior, begins to resemble that of the ancestors, most men are simultaneously experiencing a significant change in economic status. As a man moves toward becoming one of the immortals, he is gradually losing control over the productive and reproductive resources of his household. His claim to these resources diminishes in direct proportion to his son-in-law's increasing domestic presence. This was certainly the case in Warodi's household: with three of Warodi's daughters as his wives, Agostim commanded more economic and reproductive resources than did Warodi. However, as his control of material resources and his access to labor eroded, Warodi increasingly drew upon his cultural capital. He harnessed his wisdom, knowledge of history and customs, and skills in expressive performance to sustain and even increase his prestige.

In the dream performance, Warodi drew upon this cultural capital in the context of publicly advancing the community's interests. In the process, while outwardly adhering to the principle of anonymity and downplaying his personal interests, Warodi actually advanced his own standing within the community and, even more than this, attempted to promote his own immortality. His speech connoted not just an "average" immortality—that of the undifferentiated *wadzapari?wa* (see Fig. 10)— but elevated him to the status of the distinguished immortal creators, the *höimana?u?ö*, the only individuated members of the immortal collectivity. Through stories that tell of their lives, songs that bring their voices into the present, and dramatizations such as the dream performance, these immortals, the creators, stand out as the ones whom Xavante remember most for their individual deeds and accomplishments.

WARODI: ELDER OR IMMORTAL?

(1)   the Xavante
       after they [the immortals] taught the Xavante
       after they taught
          they don't remember us anymore
          they don't remember us anymore
          they don't remember us anymore

(2)   those there
       those there our blood [our descendants]
          our blood
          our younger brothers
          our younger brothers
             they no longer believe in us

(3)   because they [the immortals]
       because they care for us [to protect us]
          they are turning to us [thinking of]
          they are turning to us
             always Xavante
             so that we may remain forever Xavante always
             so that we may remain forever

In these utterances, among the first he makes after the song rehearsal, Warodi speaks as if he knows the ancestors' minds. He speaks with conviction about the immortals' thoughts and actions while he presents himself as their spokesman to the living. Yet in this passage Warodi's use of person markers leaves his speaker's point of view ambiguous. On the one hand, he speaks as a living elder. On the other, he speaks as if he were an immortal himself.

In the first and last sentences of the excerpt, Warodi uses first-person markers to align himself with the living. In sentence (1), when he states that the immortals don't remember "us," "us" clearly refers to the living, and through his use of first-person marking, Warodi includes himself among them. Again, "us" refers to the living when Warodi says, "They are thinking of us," in sentence (3). As the transitive object of sentences that have the immortals as their agentive subject, "us" denotes the living. Xavante first-person markers (*wa*) are underlined in the interlinear transcription and free translation of part of sentence (3) below:

(3)   *wa-höiba dzawi te   wa- temε da-tsi-   pidzari aba*
       our-body protect to us toward they-refl.- turn   hon.

       aʔuwẽ uötsi ʔre-wa-höimana   mono da.
       Xavante always iterative-us-live/remain cont. in order to

       They [the immortals] are turning toward us [the living], to protect us, so that we may remain always Xavante forever.

However, in the second sentence—a parallel to the first—the precise referents of *wa* (object "us") and *wa* (possessive "our") are unclear:

(2)   *wa-waprui-re hã, wa-noi-re   hã*
       our-blood-dim. foc. our-younger brother-dim foc.

       te   ʔre-wa-dzadze   waʔaba wẽtenε
       they iterative-us-believe hon.   neg.

       Our blood [our descendants], our younger brothers, they no longer believe in us.

This statement can potentially be heard in two ways. In one interpretation, "us" and "our" refer to the living elders. Then, "our descendants" and "our younger brothers" denote the living youth: the metaphoric expression (*wapru*, blood), combined with the first-person plural possessive marker (*wa*), signifies "our blood," or "our descendants." This and the following phrase, "our younger brothers," indicate the living youth. Correspondingly, "us" (*wa*), the object pronoun in the phrase "they no longer believe in us," stands for the elders: the elders are the objects of the youths' disbelief. In this interpretation, the statement means that the living youths no longer believe in "us," the living elders.

But another interpretation is equally valid: "us" can also be taken to stand for the immortals. Then the expression "our blood" ("our descendants") and the phrase "our younger brothers" would metaphorically refer to the living—the elders as well as the youths. In this case, the utterance may be viewed as a statement spoken from the point of view of the immortals: "They [the living] no longer believe in us [the immortals]." Then it would explain the immortals' neglect for the living: since the descendants (the living) no longer believe in the ancestors, the immortals have forgotten them.

Through his use of first-person markers (as objects and possessives), Warodi, in this second reading, might be seen to position himself among the immortals. His subtle manipulation of grammatical form suggests that Warodi may be heard and understood as one of the immortals. The ambiguity of his opening remarks foreshadows a potential shift in the identity Warodi projects—a shift to which I will return later in this chapter.

Nevertheless, in most of the early part of the narrative Warodi presents himself as the ancestors' spokesman among the living. As one who has had the privilege of knowing the ancestors' thoughts, he now has the honor of sharing them with the living.

> because they care for us [or, to protect us]
> because they care for us
>> the thought
>> the thought
>> their thoughts
>>> they joined as al[ways]
>>> they joined as always [they joined their thoughts as always]
> I [share] these, like this
>> like this, according to their speech, for you to think about
>>> for you to think about

Warodi makes his position as an intermediary clear. He is the immortals' representative among the living. He brings their thoughts into this world.[6]

> their thoughts
>> in order for you to learn
>>> I called you
>>>> to think about their thoughts

To tell the others to interpret his speech as the immortals' counsel, Warodi uses metadiscursive phrases as framing devices throughout the narrative.[7] These rhetorical phrases remind his audience that he is *reporting* the speech and thoughts of the ancestors. For example, phrases such as *taha dzadawa* (that is their speech) and *ãnɛ ʔrotsaʔrada hã* (that is the thought, the ancestors' thought) indicate that the words Warodi has spoken are not his own. At the same time, these rhetorical devices point out Warodi's privileged position: of the living, he is the one who heard the immortals' discussion.

For instance, when Warodi reports how the immortals spoke of the songs and the songs' purposes, he frames his narrative as a firsthand account of their speech, saying, "This is their thought," "This is how they spoke," "This is how they spoke of the song," or "That's it, the speech." The ancestors first explained the log-racing song (*uiwede-ñoʔre*, a type of *da-praba*): it is a song that belongs to the *wamarĩ tede-ʔwa*, a lineage of peacemakers.[8] This song is for peace:

> this one
> that one
> ah
> the log-race song
> the log-race song
>> it is the blood
>> the blood jo[ining]
>> the blood joining song [the song that brings people together]
>> the blood
>> the blood joining song
> ah
> *like this they spoke of the song*
> *like this they spoke of the song*
> ah
> the ones who are intelligent, who always win in the ɔiʔɔ [9]
> the ones who are intelligent, who always win in the ɔiʔɔ
>> the owners of the *wamarĩ*
>> the owners of the *wamarĩ* always avoid spilling blood
>> always avoid spilling blood
> ʔʌʔ
> ah the owners of the *wamarĩ*
>> always avoid spilling blood
> the blood song
> the blood joining song
> the log-race song
> the log-race song

Repeating the phrase "they spoke like this," Warodi reiterates that he speaks of the song as the ancestors did in the dream. I have italicized these repeated phrases in the excerpt to highlight the way they frame Warodi's report as the immortals' speech.

Warodi goes on to explain that the second song, the *da-dzarōno*, is for the Xavante to sing when they celebrate births. In the dream, when the ancestors performed this song, they put feather-down on their heads:[10]

> well ah
> the *da-dzarōno*
> they th[ey]
>   gave the ancestor his name
> that one
> that one is for when babies are born.
> they put feather-down on their foreheads
>   put feather-down on their foreheads
> the *da-dzarōno*
> the *da-dzarōno*
>   is for the Xavante to celebrate with
> *they thought carefully then*

Continuing, Warodi explains that the third song, the *da-hipɔpɔ*, belonged to the creator who gave the Xavante their beautiful, brilliant long hair—the one who created the sea. According to Warodi, when the immortals spoke of this song in the dream, they said that singing it would make the performers healthy and fat; those who were sick would walk again. Again, italics highlight the metadiscursive phrases that frame Warodi's account as a firsthand report:

> then, that one
> also
> the *da-hipɔpɔ*
>   it's his, the one who had long hair
>   that one
> again
> again
> again
> again ah
>   after shaking the body [in the dance]
>   after shaking the body, again
>   again, those

in those who make noise singing
   singing
   singing
     it cures sickness
those who shake their bodies [in dance] afterwards will walk again
that's it
that's their word
that's the word
continuing with this
continuing
   you won't have sickness
   you won't have sickness
while you are well
while you are well
   continue the custom
   continue the custom
this is their speech
this is their speech
so
so they shake removing the sickness
so they shake removing the sickness
like this, again, when you are sick
   when you are sick
   again
     you will walk again
     you will walk again
again
again you will all be fat and healthy
   you will all be fat and healthy
ʔã̃ʔ'
this is their speech
this is their speech

In themselves the songs offer proof that Warodi has been in contact with the immortals. But Warodi goes beyond simply presenting himself as one who has witnessed the ancestors' performance, as young men do when they represent their dreams through *da-ño̧ʔre*. He claims actually to have participated in a reunion with the ancestors.

       I
      I, in [the meeting]
      I, in [the meeting]

tried
tried to fight
tried to fight tried
   to remain always Xavante
   to remain always Xavante
   to forever live as Xavante always
   to forever live as Xavante always

With this claim Warodi implies that he participated in the immortals' gathering in a way that sets him as one among equals. Just as a young man's active participation in evening men's-council reunions marks his definitive incorporation into adult society, Warodi stakes out similar status as an immortal. And his his objectives are those of the ancestors: he seeks to ensure that the Xavante will remain forever Xavante. By participating in their meetings and sharing their ambitions for the Xavante's future, Warodi begins to equate himself with the immortals.

A TELLER IN TIME

for the Xavante
for the Xavante
for us to continue living
for us to continue living
   according to what
   according to what the Xavante will continue?

that, that, according to their work
   according to their work
that, for the Xavante
   for the Xavante
      they, food
      first taught foods
      they first taught foods
with this
with this, they then
   they then gathered together
   gathered together
for the Xavante
for the Xavante they [taught]
   they [taught], according to their teachings
so
so

so their work [the creation]
so
   is the *cara* [a root]

Near the beginning of the narrative, Warodi expresses his doubts that the others know how the Xavante will be able to continue. Responding to the rhetorical question he poses—"According to what [following what model] will the Xavante continue?"—he responds: the Xavante will continue by following the immortals' work. Then, without further introduction, he breaks into a narrative that retells an episode of the creation.

Why does Warodi begin to tell a myth at this point? Why doesn't he just make the proposition, "We must remember the work of the first creators"?

By breaking into myth telling, Warodi models the very process of cultural continuity he wishes to uphold. Instead of simply talking about passing the story from one generation to the next, he actually *tells* the story itself. For the memory of the creators to continue and for Xavante to continue as Xavante, the *practice* of myth telling must continue. By launching into myth tellings, Warodi implements the practices he prescribes. In words and actions, Warodi and the elders model the practices by which the Xavante will continue forever Xavante.

This is not to say that the content of a myth is not itself important, for certainly the contents and designs of Xavante myths are unique. However, the point I wish to emphasize is that the *practice* of myth telling is critical to processes of cultural continuity. Memories of the past depend on behaviors in the present, as well as on those to come in the future: the past cannot be separated from behaviors that preserve it. In his tellings of the creators' lives, Warodi demonstrates that the future of the past lies in the way the creators are remembered in the present.

While myth telling enables memories of the creation to persist—indeed, to have a future—tellings also enable these memories to evolve over time. Since each new telling is a creative act, tellings provide a site for change, contestation, and adaptation. When Warodi tells of the one who made the sea and prescribes the ornaments to be worn by the young man who is to portray that character in the performance, Sibupa corrects him for misidentifying the creator as a pre-initiate *waptɛ*. That creator, Sibupa specifies, was not a *waptɛ*; he was an *aʔirepudu*, a member of the life-cycle phase that preceeds *waptɛ* status:

ah
well ah
ah
ah

ah it is not like that
that one, he
   he was always a young boy, an *aʔirepudu*
that one
that one
   ah, he was not a *waptɛ*
although [he was] not a *waptɛ*, he [lived in] the bachelors' hut
   the bachelors' hut

To identify the immortal creators who participated in the dream gathering, Warodi sprinkles his narrative with excerpts of stories about the creations of the always living *höimanaʔuʔö*. For example, instead of simply stating that the ancestor who gave the Xavante their long hair (and then created the sea) was present in the dream reunion, Warodi *tells* part of the story of that ancestor's creation.

also the one with long hair
the one with
   that one, all the Xavante
      he could have worked for all the Xavante
         but he gave long hair to one relative only

so that one, his work is different
so *waʔ[a]*
   wa[ʔa] waʔa [tree]
   waʔa bark
tha[t]
tha[t]
   only that
   only that he took
that *waʔa* bark
     waʔa
   a piece of the *waʔa* he took
     he took
     he took
it is this   .
it is this that makes hair

also
ah
that [tree] that stands on the bank of the river
   the *jatoba*

the bark of the *datoba* [said in Portuguese]
 he also augmented

also there, in the *cerrado,* where they always burned the *babaçu* nuts
 that
 that also
 that also he augmented.
 ʔʌ
like this
like this [their speech was like this]

These mythic episodes retell bits of the Xavante creation and model the way in which these memories will survive. Furthermore, these tellings point to past tellings. Each telling recalls those that have gone before it, and the fact that individual Xavante have told these stories in each preceding generation. Telling, as Aiʔrere says, places Warodi within a long chain of raconteurs who have perpetuated the memory of the Xavante's remarkable creators through time:

> before the whites they had this custom
> the custom
> for this you are telling their story to the end
> really, they remember this each generation
> really!

Aiʔrere's utterance is a metadiscursive comment; it is a commentary that talks *about* the statements Warodi is making in the narrative. Like Aiʔrere, Warodi and other participants intersperse such metanarrative comments about the tales or the protagonists in and between the myth excerpts Warodi sprinkles throughout the dream narrative. Just as metadiscursive framing devices elsewhere point out that Warodi's speech is an account of what the ancestors said about the songs, these comments bring the act of myth telling, as a discourse practice, into focus. Expressions such as *taha dzadawa* (that is the speech, or, that is the way they tell it) focus attention on the practice of passing on the creators' memories through acts of telling.

These metadiscursive comments act like quotation marks, framing Warodi's myth narrative as a quotation of other, previous myth tellings. The instances of myth telling that Warodi recontextualizes in his narrative are replicas of previous tellings in the same way that any given instance of myth telling is a replica of prior discourse that is passed from generation to generation. Saying such things as "their speech was like this," Warodi reminds his listeners that his telling is a repetition of past tellings, tellings that ultimately originated with the immortal creators themselves. Therefore, as a teller, Warodi stands for all those who have told the same tales in the past: he represents the collectivity of previous myth tellers, those who are now immortals.

MYTH TELLINGS AND CONTEXT

yes, that's it!
that, they
   united their work
then they first created the dog
then ah, then they created things
ah, foods
then they created the *cara* root
then they created the *cara* root . . .
the jaguar
they created the jaguar
then ah
ah
they created the *babaçu* nuts then
then they created the *macauba* coconuts
then
yes they created everything
then the bees, re[d]
ah
the red bees they created
then they created the dogfish
then he created the insects
then he created the ants
then
next
then they created the jabiru stork

In these few brief, poetic lines Warodi recalls, for the elders who listen to the dream narrative, the entire act of creation of two *wapte* known as *parinai?a*. He tells the story of their creation eloquently, but in an abbreviated form.

   How different this telling is from Warodi's telling of the same story that I recorded one afternoon in his home! As I lay by his side to listen, his little granddaughters came to hear too; they climbed on his legs, adoringly poked at his arms, and fidgeted with my microphone. When they interfered too much Warodi gently brushed aside their little fingers, ever intent on his telling.

To tell the tale, to simultaneously teach and entertain us, Warodi took on the voices of the various protagonists, fashioning the dramatic tension with their dialogue. As he slowly edged toward revealing the ancestors' next creation, the little ones squirmed with anticipation. When the jaguar entered the scene saying *bɔh, bɔh, bɔh* in his low breathy voice, the girls squealed with delight. But first, the *parinaiʔa* created the dog:

     now the two are *waptɛ*
     now they are on trek
     next, they stayed inside the small [trekking] houses
        and the two remained behind

(5)   "let's wait for them to go ahead; perhaps then we'll go behind"
     [whispered]

     "hey, now *ĩ-ãmo* [my ceremonial friend]!
     "what will we be *ĩ-ãmo*?
     "what will we be for real?"

     "let's be dogs!" [whispered]

(10)   "yes that's it! [whispered]
     "let's be dogs for real!"

     "hau hau hau" [breathy voice—the dogs barking]

     they are playing like dogs

     "hau hau hau" [breathy voice—the dogs barking]

(15)   the two are barking around the small trekking houses
     now they are following behind the trekkers
     the elders are in the file of trekkers
     the two are nudging up against their legs

     "son of a bitch!" [pharyngeal, laryngeal constriction, the elders talking]
(20)   "they always run too close!"

they never hit them, they say
the elders continue trekking, they say

again the dogs nudge up against their legs

"son of a bitch! they always run too close!"

(25)   I don't know how they named their idea [the dog] so quickly

"damned dogs! they always run too close!"

they hit their legs, they say
they take it out on the dogs
well, the dogs—KWI [sound of their jump and escape, voiceless]
(30)   they throw sticks at them
KRU [sticks flying through the air, voiceless]

they jump so easily, they say

they are at the front of the line of trekkers, they say
they are people

(35)   ah, they are at the next campsite
they are standing there
    [with] baskets hanging from their heads

"what? didn't you two remain behind?"
"how is it that you are appearing here?"
(40)   "how did you two get here?"

"we came passing the others"
"we came passing the others"

they told only this to their age-set companions, they say
"we came passing the others"

This passage gives a taste of what an immensely entertaining teller Warodi could be. With only a minimum of descriptive commentary, he dramatized the two *wapté*'s creation of the dog. Through visual imagery, sound ornamentation, and quoted speech, Warodi lavishly elaborated this episode.

The plot develops as Warodi takes on the voice of first one creator, then the other, and then the voices of the ordinary Xavante whom the creators encounter. This dialogue, coupled with progressive tense-aspect marking, gives the tale an immediacy: it is as if the actions are occurring in present time. Dialogue, sound effects, and progressive tense-aspect imbue the narrative with the apparent reality of theater. As Warodi's speech brings the narrated events into the here and now, "the audience is made to feel as if it is in the presence of a non-present dialogue."[11]

In this theatrical telling Warodi constructs the plot almost entirely through direct quotations: nineteen lines of this forty-four-line passage are direct quotations of the protagonists' speech.[12] Instead of framing the protagonists' speech with phrases such as "he said" or "the elders said"—anaphoric devices that cross-reference the quoted speech with a designated protagonist—by taking on the voice of the character Warodi momentarily suggests to his listeners that he has become that character. He indicates the shift in his identity through features of the performance such as voice quality and intonation. For example, in the preceding excerpt, Warodi indicates the voices of the *wapte* through whispered voice (lines 5–11). This voice quality fits the mood of secrecy Warodi attempts to convey as he dramatizes the two *wapte*'s scheming over their next creation. He speaks as if he were the protagonists himself.

Those of us listening are able to infer that Warodi is taking on voices that are not his own from the descriptive narrative that forms a backdrop to the direct quotations. We also infer Warodi's assumed identities through associations with the story-telling context. In this performance frame a special set of interpretive rules apply:[13] we are predisposed to hear Warodi's voice as the voice of others because the narrative takes place in what is, by definition, a special speech situation. It is a warm afternoon and Warodi is lying on his bed after having called me "to teach me about the immortal creators' work." Knowing how tales of the creation are told in these situations, the little girls and I anticipated the theatrics of Warodi's telling; we expect the drama and his various dramatis personae in this telling. Paying close attention, we understand the indexical shifts in pronominal reference; we know that the identities he assumes in direct quotation are not those of his everyday self. When Warodi says, "Hey, now *ĩ-ãmo* [my ceremonial friend]! What will we be *ĩ-ãmo*? What will we be for real?" we know he speaks theatrically as one of the *parinaiʔa* creators, not as Warodi, our father or grandfather. Our delight over Warodi's use of altered voices and sound effects probably even encouraged him to further embellish his telling. With these devices he enlivened his telling and made the characters for whom he spoke, for a fleeting moment, real.

The remaining lines of Warodi's theatrical narrative are descriptive statements, twenty-two of which are exegetical.[14] These statements describe various actions and tell us about the protagonists' identities. The opening four lines of the excerpt, for example, are of this type:

> now the two are *waptɛ*
> now they are on trek
> next, they stayed inside the small [trekking] houses
> and the two remained behind

Of the twenty-two exegetical lines, Warodi tags six with a quotative particle *ʔu*, which I have glossed as "they say." [15] This is a metadiscursive statement which suggests that others before Warodi have made the assertions he repeats: "They hit their legs, they say." With this quotative particle Warodi emphasizes that his words restate what others have said in the past. In a single uninflected morpheme he calls attention to the fact that he is repeating the words of his predecessors. As Benjamin Whorf noted of such quotative devices,[16] through his use of this particle, Warodi displaces his speech from his individual self and attributes his words to the collectivity of those who have told the tale before. His words are those of the immortals.

The dog, like all things the *parinaiʔa* created, resulted from the *waptɛ*'s ingenious transformations. But when Warodi told this tale to the elders, he never mentioned these miraculous transformations. No theatrical devices enlivened that telling. No voices or sound effects animated the characters to stimulate the listeners' imaginations. For the elders, Warodi condensed the miraculous creation of the dog into one brief sentence: "Then the ancestors first created the dog." He summarized the *waptɛ*'s entire creation in less time than it took him to elaborate a single episode in his entertaining theatrical telling.

The difference between these two tellings highlights some of the ways in which context and audience can influence the way a myth is told. Although we tend to think of a myth as somehow having an abstract existence apart from its tellings, in truth, a myth comes to life *through* its tellings. Tellings give birth to and continue the life of a myth, although the sediments of tellings settle into memory, creating the impression of an entity, "a myth." This sediment is the precipitate of actual instances of myth telling. Since one telling can be different from the next, the differences in tellings enable a myth to change over time. Each new telling has the potential to shift, however slightly, the sedimented sands of memory.

When Warodi's audience consisted of a group of small children and me, an anthropologist eager to learn, he designed his telling for entertainment and didactic purposes. Using the theatrics of voice and sound, Warodi drew us into the telling. He held our attention as he transported us into the time of the first creators. To teach us, he chose his way of telling well, for we listened intently, hanging on his every word.

In the dream narrative, on the other hand, when Warodi recounted the creation tales, he told them in a very different manner. Rather than conjuring the imagination and amplifying the smallest details in acoustically graphic form, Warodi made elliptical references to mythological protagonists, passed over many events, and left out many details. He glossed the events of the mythological past in a way that would have made the telling largely incomprehensible to a younger, less informed audience.

Because the audience for the dream narrative consisted of his peers, Warodi was able to tell the tales in this fragmented way. The men who listened to and even collaborated in or contested his telling were well familiar with the stories he told. Each one had certainly heard the stories many times. By now, each had confidently told the same stories to his own children and grandchildren in afternoon sessions much like the one I was part of in Warodi's home. Having heard these tales many times, each elder had built an interpretive frame which he was able to draw upon to comprehend the often oblique mythological references and unelaborated instances of myth telling Warodi compacted into his narrative. The members of this audience already knew that the *parinaiʔa* transformed themselves into the beings and foods they created. They knew that the metamorphosed *waptɛ* creators had frightened the Xavante in the process and that, out of fear, the Xavante had ultimately killed them. With the elders as his audience, Warodi could pass over the details that sparked the imaginations and gripped the attention of younger listeners.

Armed with interpretive frameworks built up during the course of a lifetime, the elders were fully capable of understanding Warodi's often elliptical references and fractioned tales. Members of this group of listeners were able to fill in the gaps in Warodi's narrative based on their history of exposure to more elaborated tellings. Warodi could safely infer that they would bring this knowledge to interpreting his allusions to mythic discourse. Sometimes members of the audience even filled in the gaps with asides: when Warodi was first telling that the immortal creators taught the Xavantes about food, Daru embellished the telling by remembering that before they had food, the Xavante lived off *buriti* wood and larvae.

Warodi: ah, the Xavante's food
              the Xavante's food
              the Xavante's food
                  they taught the food according to their wisdom
Daru: they saved themselves
                  with *buriti*
                  with larvae, we always ate this

What is most important about the myth tellings that Warodi embedded in his dream narrative is not the content of the stories themselves, for the members of this audience knew the tales well, but the act of telling itself. Warodi was not teaching the elders the same lesson he taught me and his grandchildren; communicating the content was not his primary concern. His principal message in the dream narrative was different—it had to do with *telling*. It was a message of action. In telling, Warodi showed the elders the way for the Xavante to continue forever by replicating the behavior of his forebears. He brought the behavior of the past into the present and demonstrated the way to the Xavante's future.

IN THE CREATORS' "I"

As the dream narrative progresses, Warodi becomes increasingly absorbed in the tellings and in his role as a perpetuator of continuity. He becomes involved in the lives of the creators about whom he speaks. At times he even enters into a state in which he collapses the distinction between his individual self and the selves of the creators. As he loses the perspective of his individual self, his self merges with the selves of the creators. Through his discourse, Warodi's self becomes an other. He becomes an immortal creator, an always living *höimanaʔuʔö*, one of the distinguished ancestors. Through pronouns and person markers he signals the transformation of his self. But as the narrative moves forward and Warodi embeds excerpts from the stories of the creation into his telling, the distinctions Warodi makes between himself and the creators' selves become less clear. Warodi becomes further and further removed from the present, from the situation of the telling, and from his identity as a living mortal. His complete immersion in the telling transports him into the mythic frame he has narratively created. As he stacks one mythic episode onto the next, the pronouns he uses to denote the immortals—initially third-person "they" or "he"—become "we" or "I." The shift in pronominal reference occurs as Warodi loses his sense of his autonomous self. When he is completely absorbed into the frame of the narrative, he moves into a state in which he experiences himself as a creator. The first-person pronouns he uses in his speech express his subjective sense of himself as a creator.

Traditionally, linguists have thought of first-person pronouns as the nodal points in grammar that link a speaker's self, the contextually situated self of the everyday world, to the abstract distributional system of language.[17] This is so because the first-person pronoun is an element of language that is inherently context bound. It is a linguistic sign that can only be interpreted through processes of contextual association; as Michael Silverstein puts it, it is an indexical referential sign.[18] To interpret the referent of a first-person pronoun, listeners must know a speaker's identity. For example, if I say, "I am going to the store," I am using the pronoun "I" to refer to myself. But if you say "I," "I" stands for a different self—you instead of me. First-person pronouns, like other words that belong to the grammatical category known as deictics, provide a bridge between discourse and the actual context of speech. Because their meaning shifts according to context, members of this grammatical category are also referred to as "shifters."[19] A listener can only know what a deictic stands for by knowing something about its context. In the case of first-person pronouns, this means knowing the speaker's identity—and "I" is conventionally understood to stand for the speaker's everyday self.

In both his theatrical telling and his telling to the elders, however, Warodi uses first-person pronouns to denote other selves, selves that are not the self of his everyday social identity. The traditional linguistic model in which "I" is taken to stand for an ordinary self is not equipped to explain Warodi's use of multiple "I"s. How are we to understand and interpret Warodi's self in relation to the different "I"s that he quotes in these narratives?

Recent work focusing on actual instances of discourse has extended the previous conception of the interface between language and the self. In an analysis of quoted speech in Xokleng spoken texts, Greg Urban shows that speakers may use first-person pronouns to denote other selves, selves that are different from a speaker's everyday social identity.[20] In actual discourse speakers may use first-person pronouns, "I," to represent nonordinary or imaginary selves. When this occurs, "I" no longer points to the speaker's everyday self as in ordinary speech. Instead, it functions as a *non*-indexical referential signal; it points to other, nonordinary selves.

In Urban's scheme, the multiple and functionally distinct "I"s of nonindexical referential discourse range along a continuum, the poles of which are the everyday self and the ultimately social self. These different "I"s operate to express varying degrees of sociability in discourse, where sociability is understood as an identification with the points of view of another. In the most sociable state, what Urban calls the "projected I," a speaker moves into a state in which he perceives himself not just to speak as, but to *be*, an other.

When a speaker takes on the "projected I" he becomes so completely absorbed in his imitation of others that he may actually enter into a state in which he subjectively perceives himself as embodying the character or characters he represents. The speaker's theatrical representation merges with his everyday self and the speaker subjectively takes on the identity of another. Through his discourse he comes to embody the other. He not only represents but *is* that distinct person.

According to Urban, the projected "I" occurs in highly marked speech situations where speakers repeat texts that are relatively fixed or even

memorized. In the case of Xokleng origin-myth telling, speakers repeat the
tale syllable by syllable and enter into a trancelike state by focusing in-
ward to remember the text. Rocking motions characteristic of the delivery
and the repetitive sound patterns of the discourse intensify the speaker's
focus on the text and promote entry into an altered, trancelike state.[21] In
this trancelike state, the speaker subjectively assumes the identity of another, the self of past speakers. As the speaker becomes the embodiment
of those who have spoken in the past, he brings their perspective into the
present.[22] Ultimately he represents the continuity of culture.

Warodi, in his theatrical myth telling to me and the children, temporarily assumed the voices of the various characters surrounding the
parinaiʔa's creation. However, in speaking with their voices, he did not
go so far as to lose himself in the others' personae. Features of the telling
and the context broke the momentum that might have enabled him to
move into an altered state in which he experienced himself as a creator.
He did not become a creator in his theatrical telling.

For that telling, Warodi lay on his back staring up at the ceiling, avoiding eye contact with his listeners. Aside from an occasional gesture in
which he rapidly moved his arm down from an extended position, he lay
still. As he focused his energy on the narrative, the melodic and repetitious
sound of his voice might have moved him close to trance and to projecting
himself into the identity of the creators. However, the very drama of his
telling impeded him from moving completely in this direction. The taking
on of voices—the voice of first one protagonist and then the other, and
then the voices of the elders who experienced the *parinaiʔa's* fantastic
transformations—checked the possibility of his identifying closely with
any one perspective. Moreover, Warodi's attention to features that made
the dialogue entertaining—voice quality, intonation, and sound effects—
demanded his attention to presentational form. Although for brief moments he shifted into the voice of one character or another, the drama kept
him in the present, in himself.

Warodi also retained his individual, present time perspective by making
a number of observations on the telling, as well as didactic comments. He
frequently broke out of his role as an entertaining teller to comment on
the events of the narrative. Periodically he interjected comments from the
point of view of his everyday self in order to direct the interpretations of
his audience. With these, Warodi maintained a grip on his everyday self.

For example, in line 24 of his theatrical telling, Warodi comments, from
the perspective of his everyday self, "I don't know how they named their
idea [dog] so quickly." In the next line he quotes the ordinary ancestors
saying, "Damned dogs! They always run too close!" His comment, designed to inspire his listeners' awe, reminds them that prior to the *wapte's*
creation, not only did the animal known as "dog" not exist, but the word

"dog" itself did not exist. It follows that the following quotation— "Damned dogs! They always run too close!"—must have been the ancestors' first utterance of the word *dogs*. Warodi's telling theatrically illustrates how the ancestors instantaneously named the new creation. In these two utterances Warodi shifts from the perspective of his everyday self to the perspective of the ancestors. Such shifting prevents him from achieving a complete identification with the point of view of any single mythological protagonist.

Yet in the nontheatrical dream narrative, Warodi transports himself into the creators' world. He becomes enmeshed with the personae of the creators about whom he speaks. The selves of the others, the creators, displace his individual self, and Warodi becomes one of them. Through pronouns and person marking he reveals the extent of his immersion in their other world.

Warodi recounts excerpts from three stories about the different authors of the Xavante creation when he tells about the creators who gave the three songs he received in his dream. These are the stories of the two *waptɛ parinaiʔa* who made foods, animals, and insects; the *öwawĕ-ʔwa* who made the sea and the white people and who gave the Xavante their long beautiful hair; and "the one whose foot was pierced by a stick" (*wedehu date da-waʔre*), who augmented the Xavante population. As he tells of the first creation, the story of the *parinaiʔa's* creation, Warodi retains his perspective as his everyday individual self. Using third-person pronouns to refer to the creators, he keeps his self distinct from the creators about whom he speaks. He continually refers to the two *waptɛ* creators as "they": "*They* thought carefully about their work, *they* taught the Xavante's foods according to *their* wisdom." Later, as Warodi amplifies details of their creation, he still speaks using third-person pronouns. I have italicized the pronouns and possessives in this English excerpt to highlight Warodi's use of third person.

> the jaguar
> the jaguar *they* created
> then ah
> ah
> *babaçu* nuts *they* created then
> then the *macauba* nut *they* created
> then
> yes *they* created everything

As he moves into the second tale, Warodi continues to speak from the perspective of the present, from his own point of view. Speaking about the *wapte* who created the sea and the whites, he tells the episode in which the creator gives hair to his brother using the bark of the *waʔa* palm tree. As he speaks, he continues to use third person, referring to the mythological protagonist with the third-person honorific pronoun *date* (he).

As Warodi becomes increasingly involved in explaining how the creator made long hair, he switches deictics (pronouns, clitic person markers, possessives, and postpositions) from third person to first person. From referring to the protagonist as a separate other (he), Warodi changes to speak in the first person. He speaks as if he were the creator himself.

Warodi:	*dure date ĩ-da-dzɛrɛ-pa hã*
	date ĩ-da-dzɛrɛ-pa hã
	tahã date aʔuwẽ ubure
	ubure aʔuwẽ na date ĩ-romhuri mono rɛnɛ
(5)	*mitsi date da-tsitsanawã tsɛrɛ-pa waʔaba dza hã*
	to tahã da-ñimi-romhuri aimawi
	to wa
	wa waʔa
	waʔa hö
(10)	*ta[ha]*
	ta[ha]
	taha tsi
	taha tsi [ma] wadzere ni
	taha waʔa hö hã
(15)	*waʔa*
	waʔõno hã⌈wadzere ni
Sibupa:	⌊*taha wa-ñimi-romhuri dzɛ*
Warodi:	*wadzere ni*
	wadzere ni
(20)	*tahata*
	tahata da-dzere dzɛ
	dure
	niha
	to ãha pa-na ʔre-tsimatsa
Sibupa:	*aʔõ*
Warodi:	*aʔõ hã*
	datoba hö hã
	dure ãma waptom ni
	dure ã romna hã ñorõ dzö tsata dzɛ ʔre-tsimatsa

(30) *taha*
⌈ *taha durε*
Sibupa: ⌊ *da-dzεrε dzε*
Warodi: *taha durε āma waptom ni*
      ahāta?
(35)   *ī-ñimi-romhuri dzεp te?*
      ⌈ *ī-ñimi-romhuri dzεp te?*
Daru: ⌊ *ī-tsadaze tede hā*
Warodi: *ahāta*
      āhāta
(40) *āhāta ī-ñimi-romhuri dzεp te?*
      āhāta aʔuwē dzεrεpa-dzε
          aʔuwē dzεrεpa-dzε
      ?ʌ?

      āne
(45) ⌈ *āne*
Etēpa: ⌊ *to*
      to
      to dadzu-wede watsre bö te to a-tsötö na
          a-tsötö na dza hā
(50)   *ī-da-dzadawa āma wadzεre pe to*
Sibupa: *wa hā, ī-ñimi-romhuri dzεp te*

Warodi: also the one with the long hair
       the one with the long hair
       that one, he for all Xavante
          for all Xavante he could have worked
(5)   but he gave long hair to one relative only ah

       so that one, his work is different
       so the *wa?*
       the *wa waʔa*
          waʔa bark
(10)   tha[t]
       tha[t]
       only that
       only that he took
          that *waʔa* bark
(15)   *waʔa*
       a piece of the *waʔa* ⌈ he took
Sibupa: ⌊ this is for our work

Warodi: <u>he</u> took
                 <u>he</u> took

(20)   it is this
        it is this that makes hair
        also
        ah
        that [tree] that stands on the bank of the river
Sibupa: the *jatoba*
Warodi: the *jatoba*
        the bark of the *datoba*
            also <u>he</u> augmented
        also there, in the *cerrado,* where they always burned the *babaçu* nuts
(30)   that
   ⎡ that also
Sibupa: ⎣ it makes hair
Warodi: that also <u>he</u> augmented
        this here
(35)   is <u>my</u> real work
   ⎡ is <u>my</u> true work
Daru: ⎣ its smell is sweet and strong
Warodi: this here
        this here
(40)   this here is for <u>my</u> real work
        this here is for the Xavante's long hair
            for the Xavante's long hair
        ʔʌʔ

        like this
(45)   ⎡ like this
Etẽpa: ⎣ so
        so
        so your family works with the tree powder, so in your sleep
            so in your sleep
(50)   their speech is complete
Sibupa: <u>me</u>, this is for <u>my</u> true work

    Warodi's use of first person signals that he has taken on the mythologi-
cal protagonist's point of view. We can see this shift by examining his use
of person markers in the excerpted Xavante text and its English translation. Notice that Warodi uses third-person honorific pronouns and person
markers (*date, da*), possessives (*da-*),[23] and postpositions (*waʔaba, ni*)

from the outset of the telling through line 33. Then, on line 35, he changes to first person and continues to use first-person marking (possessive *ĩ-*) until the end of the episode, when he moves into recounting the third story, the tale of the boy whose foot was pierced by a stick. In the excerpt in both Xavante and English I have underlined the relevant person markers to underscore the deictic shifts in Warodi's speech.

In his summary statement, lines 34–45, instead of saying <u>*da-ñimi-romhuri dzɛp te?*</u> (this is for *his* work),[24] Warodi replaces the third-person honorific possessive, *da-* (his), with the first-person possessive, *ĩ-* (my). He says <u>*ĩ-ñimi-romhuri dzɛp te?*</u> (this is for *my* work). Wholly engrossed in the narrative at this point, Warodi merges his identity with that of the creator figure, and as Warodi becomes the ancestor, the creation becomes *his* work. Through the accumulation of tellings, Warodi's sense of his individual self is abolished and he is transported into the self of the other.[25] The change in person marking signals Warodi's shift into the perspective of the self of the creator.

The telling of the first tale—the creation of foods and animals—and then the recounting of the creation of long hair lay the groundwork that enables Warodi to move into a state in which he completely identifies with the creator. On line 35, Warodi moves out of his own self and assumes the perspective of the ancestor. He says, "This here is *my* true work." His switch to "I," where he predictably would have used "he," signals his merged identities.

As he leaves his individual self and becomes one with the creator, Warodi's speech is rapid and excited, his delivery accelerated, and his voice breathy. He drops almost to a whisper. In his excitement Warodi has difficulty getting his mouth to form some words; he fumbles with *taha-tsi* (only this) in lines 10–12. Having now told two creation tales, he has worked himself into a state in which he assumes the identity of the creator; by the end of the passage he speaks as if he were the creator figure himself. In making this shift toward embedding himself within the self of the ancestor, Warodi makes the transition from his everyday individual self into a highly socialized state, a state in which he is a creator himself. He stands at the pinnacle of the male life cycle, the epitome of the Xavante social self. Warodi has become an immortal creator.

Sibupa actually joins Warodi's projection into the creator's self in an aside (line 17). Saying, "This is for *our* work," Sibupa speaks as if he also were the creator. Sibupa, however, uses the plural possessive form *wa-* (we) and therefore links himself to Warodi. Warodi's incantatory narrative has swept up a member of the audience with its metamorphosing magic. However, when Warodi projects himself into the ancestral identity, he speaks in first person: "This is for *my* true work." Sibupa then echoes this perspective in line 51, the final line of the excerpt: "*Me*, this is for *my* true work." The narrative transforms both Warodi and Sibupa into creators. Their metamorphoses anticipate the transformation of all the others who, singing and dancing in the central plaza, will become the immortals of Warodi's dream.

After telling the second tale, about the origin of the Xavante's long hair, Warodi moves into a telling of yet another creator figure, the *ʔritaiʔwa* novitiate (*wedehu date da-waʔre*) who feigned injury to stay behind a group of trekkers and then magically augmented the population.

> tawamhã õhã
>> bödödi na da-waʔre hã da-ñimi-romhuri dzɛ hã
>>> da-ñimi-romhuri dzɛ hã
>> tahata
> (5) tahata
>> tahata pibu prãi nɛ õmhã taha
>> taha pibu prãi nɛ õṁhã taha
>> tahata
>> tahata
> (10) tahata ī̠-
>>> ī̠-ñimi-romhuri dzɛʔ
>>> ī̠-ñimi-romhuri dzɛʔ
>> ī̠-
>> ī̠-tsi-waprotsi
> (15) ī̠-tsi-waprotsi
>>> ī̠-ʔãre baba-re
>>> ī̠-ʔãre baba-re ʔre-ī̠-höimana mo
>>> ī̠-höimana mono
>> āhāta
> (20) āhāta
>> āhāta aʔuwẽ hã
>>> aʔuwẽ hã
>>> a[ʔuwẽ]
>>> aʔuwẽ
> (25) aʔuwẽ pɔtɔ dzɛb daʔ
>> āhāta aʔuwẽ pɔtɔ dzɛb daʔ

> so then, he
>> the one who pierced himself on the trail, his work
>>> his work
>> this one here
> (5) this one here
>> this one here I know very well, this one

this one I know very well, this one
this here
this here
(10)   this here is <u>my</u>
            is <u>my</u> work
            is <u>my</u> work
            [by] <u>my</u>
            by <u>myself</u>
(15)   by <u>myself</u>
            with <u>my</u> brother-in-law
            <u>I</u> lived with <u>my</u> brother-in-law
            <u>I</u> lived
            this here
(20)   this here
            this here, Xavante
            Xavante
            Xa[vante]
            Xavante
(25)   is to create Xavante
            this here is to create Xavante

He indicates his shift to another tale saying, "That one, the one who
pierced himself on the trail. His work, this one here, I know this one here
very well" (lines 1–8). Immediately thereafter Warodi conflates his identity with that of the creator, speaking in first person as if he were that
ancestor himself. With only the slightest interruption, Warodi carries his
identification with the creator of the previous myth-excerpt into the next.
    Warodi sustains the state of ancestral identity that he achieved through
the previous myth tellings throughout this brief telling. Whereas he narrated most of the first two tales in third-person descriptive narrative, in
telling this third tale he develops the story entirely from the point of view
of the creator; using first-person quoted speech, he projects himself into
the creator's identity. Beginning on line 8, Warodi says *tahata ũ-ñimi-
romhuri dzɛ* (this here is *my* true work). He continues, speaking clearly
from the creator's point of view: "By myself, by myself, I lived with my
brother-in-law." In his final lines when he says "This here is to create Xavante," Warodi is the creator speaking. Fully projected into the creator's
point of view, Warodi has become that original creator telling the story of
his creation.
    Not performing to entertain, using no quotatives to indicate that his
words repeat what others have said before, Warodi leaps away from the
present reality and becomes immersed in the world of the "always living"

immortal creators. As Warodi becomes the *höimanaʔuʔö* creator himself, it is as if he is telling the creation tale for the first time. He is the creator speaking about *his* work. Embodying the original teller, Warodi's telling represents the ultimate act of cultural transmission. He is the ultimate embodiment of cultural continuity.

In the next passage of his narrative, the passage that follows his telling about augmenting the population and the creation of long hair, Warodi takes a step further. He moves outside the frame of myth telling and continues to present himself as one with the always living creators. He includes himself as an immortal, not in a myth telling but in the narrative of his own dream.

    tahata
    tahata
    tahata da-dzɛrɛ-pa dzɛ
      da-dzɛrɛ-pa dzɛ
(5) *aiwaptsiʔ*
    aiptsi wa wa-ñipʔradaʔ
    aiwaptsi wa wa-ñipʔradaʔ
    aiwaptsiʔ
    aiwaptsi wa wa-ñipʔradaʔ'
(10) *ãne*
    ãne
    wa ãma
    wa ãma ʔre-rotsaʔrata petse aba mono
    wa ãma ʔre-rotsaʔrata petse aba mono
(15) *ʔãʔ*
    wa
    wa
    wa ɔtɔ wa-tsi-höiba ubumro ni
    wa ɔtɔ wa-tsi-höiba ubumro ni
(20) *ãhãta te ɛnɛ dza*
    ãwa
    ãwa mate da-tsi-höiba ubumroi waʔaba ni
    ãwa mate da-tsi-höiba ubumroi waʔaba ni
    ãhãta te ɛnɛ dza
(25) ⌈*romhöʔu wētɛpre*
Daru: ⌊*ma waʔuĩrĩ*
    mate wadzaʔrutu
Warodi: *romhöʔu wētɛpre*

    that there
    that there

that there is for long hair
for long hair
(5)   join
we joined our hands
we joined our hands
join
we joined our hands
(10)   like this
like this
of us
you must always think of us
you must always think of us
(15)   ʔã̃ʔ
we

we

now we are together
now we are together
(20)   over there stands the rock
over there
over there they gathered together
over there they gathered together
over there stands the rock
(25)   ⌈ it's not far away
Daru: ⌊ they are surrounding us
they are many
Warodi: it's not far

In speech that is not a quotation of the relatively fixed creation myths
but rather a report on the dream gathering, Warodi speaks of the immortals and himself as "we" (wa). He says, "We joined our hands like this"
(lines 5–11). He thus embeds himself within the immortal collectivity. In
his next statement he takes an even further step to differentiate himself
from the living. Speaking from the perspective of the immortals, he gives
a direction to the living, whom he addresses as "you." He says, "You [the
living] must always think of us [the immortals] like this [in myth telling]"
(lines 12–14). He differentiates himself from the living by referring to his
living interlocutors with the second-person pronoun "you." Thus distin-
guishing himself from the living, he includes himself as one of the immortals. His next statement, "We are now together" (lines 15–19), further
underscores his inclusion in the group of immortals.

In these lines Warodi does not assume the self of the ancestor through
quoted speech. Rather, he speaks from the point of his everyday self. That

self is now one of the ancestors. Gradually, through a process of narrative accumulation, as he stacks one tale upon the next, Warodi's self is absorbed into the lives of the creators.[26] The narrative has transported him into the creators' identity and abolished his own sense of self as an ordinary mortal. Warodi has reached a climax where his own self is merged with the selves of the creators. He has achieved the ultimate social self: his self has become indistinguishable from the selves of the creators. Moreover, as Warodi's world becomes their world, he brings the creators into the present. His telling demonstrates that the immortals continue to live in the present. Now, firmly embedded in the lives of the creators, his own immortality inhabits the very discourse practices he models.

7

Performing the Dream

As the sun rose higher in the sky, bathing the *marã* forest clearing in light, the *ʔritaiʔwa* novitiates finished removing the brush and enlarging the *marã* space. The clearing was now ready for the next phase of ceremonial preparations, when the participants would decorate themselves with body paint, and was large enough to receive the women for the final phase of the rehearsal. The fire had died to a few smoking embers, leaving plenty of charcoal to be used for black body paint. Bundles of precious, moist red *urucum* lay wrapped in inner palm bark waiting to be unraveled, mixed with the saliva of chewed *babaçu* nuts, and anointed to bodies slick with *babaçu* oil. By this time Warodi had shared with the elders what the creators in his dream had told him of the songs. He had recounted that the creators gave the songs to the living so that the living would think of them, and he had broken into tellings of the creators' lives.[1] In these tellings, he modeled the way for the Xavante, as well as the immortals, to continue forever.

Through the accumulated tellings, Warodi, along with his closest brother, Sibupa, had transported himself into the immortals' world. Now it was time to prepare the others—first the elders and youths, then the women—for their metamorphoses. Continuing the dream narrative as he directed the final preparations for the participants' body ornamentation, Warodi moved the others a step closer to becoming the immortals of his dream.

Warodi: they conversed
     they conversed
      in the reunion
       about the body paint, the
      in the reunion
       about the body paint in order to be seen
     they painted their backs and stomachs red
     they painted their backs and stomachs red

Etẽpa:	you [youths] are going to paint yourselves the same way
Warodi:	so then you, on our side [the elders], ⌈paint like warriors, like this
Sibupa:	⌊all of us
Daru:	so then, like warriors
Warodi:	⌈ yes warriors
Sibupa:	⌊ we are them
	we are them
Warodi:	they painted themselves very carefully
Sibupa:	we are them [whispering]
	them

Step by step, Warodi was orchestrating a performance event which, in its rehearsal as well as in its final enactment, replicated the immortals' behavior in his dream. Like the immortals, the living elders discussed their body decorations. And like the immortals, they discussed the songs. Next, applying body paint that mirrored the paint the immortals wore in the dream, the other elders began to transport themselves into the netherworld. They too began to think of themselves as immortals as they began to embody them in corporeal form. "We are them," Sibupa stated on behalf of the elders. A few moments later, amidst joking, admiring comments, and boasts that their paint looked better than the youths', Eduardo followed Sibupa's lead: "Our paint is the real thing!" As preparations for the final enactment proceeded, the line between the world of the immortals and the world of the living progressively blurred.

The men were nearly ready to receive the women, to teach them the songs and relay the immortals' message to the living. But before the women came to join the men, all the men, young and old, sang the songs again.

Abdzukã:	for the women
	for the women
	I'm going to call the women right away!
[Many voices overlap, incomprehensible]	
Sibupa:	to make the circle big
	right here
	right here for us to learn right away
Aiʔrere:	well
	after we learn [sing], we'll leave [for the women] right away
Sibupa:	yes
	they [the elders] will run right away
Aiʔrere:	they will run, it's the [young] men who screw up [it is the youth who need to practice]

Warodi: *hai morire morire* [begins to sing first song again]
Sibupa: sing everybody!
[All men practice the three songs]

In this rehearsal, the younger men joined their voices to sing with the elders, who had already practiced the songs three times before Warodi embarked into the dream narrative. Because the songs came from the creators, their repetition intensified the atmosphere in which participants felt the immortals' presence through sound. Singing the creators' songs again, the men harnessed the force of repetition to add to the immortals' accumulating presence among the living.[2]

At this point, the elders began to prepare the three young men who had been selected to embody the *höimanaʔuʔö*, the "always living" immortal creators (Fig. 15). As the preparations began to transform those around him into the creators of his dream, Warodi harmoniously integrated the present and the time of the creators' work in himself and in his speech. Warodi was simultaneously present in the immediate situation and absorbed in the mythological past of the creators' world. For Warodi, the two worlds, the two times did not conflict.[3]

For example, when he gave the instructions to initiate the bodily transformation of his son-in-law Bomfim into the *wapte* who created the sea, Warodi slipped briefly into telling an episode from the creator's life (lines 17–29, below). At the precise moment that Warodi directed the body-painting activities—activities oriented toward the immediate present—the mythological past flowed through him. Speaking of Bomfim as "*my* son-in-law," Warodi indicated Bomfim's relationship to his everyday self (lines 1–2). Then, after saying, "Let him paint himself as the *wapte*," Warodi lapsed into the telling. In nearly the same breath that he spoke of the brother's returning to look for the creator, he spoke of Bomfim's shooting firecrackers (lines 34–35), an action in the immediate present. He directed Bomfim to rub himself with *babaçu* oil, to appear as the *wapte* creator, and to be photographed (lines 36–41).

     ah, my son-in-law
     my son-in-law
       will be the *wapte*
     he [will be the] *wapte* who made the sea
(5) let
     le[t]
     let him clean himself up
       clean up

15. Warodi fitting the *buriti* fiber robe to his brother's son, who will become one of the creators in the dream performance of August 8, 1984. (Photo by Laura Graham, 1984.)

                let him clean up
(10)   after that let him paint himself
                    paint himself then
                    paint himself then
                        ah as the *waptɛ*
                        waptɛ
(15)   *waptɛ* he ah
                        waptɛ
                [in] the dry season
                the dry season
                the dry season
(20)   his brother
                his brother
                the grass
                the grass's smoke rose straight up and again he missed him
                again he returned
(25)   he returned
                    for him to walk together
                    for him to walk together
                    for his brother in the dry season
                he returned for his brother to continue walking together
(30)   he, that one, will paint himself as that *waptɛ*
                so
                so with a *buriti* headband
                    with a *buriti* headband he will paint
                he will paint to shoot firecrackers
(35)   to shoot firecrackers he will paint
                then, first
                    to be photographed
                    he will first
                    first he will rub himself with *babaçu* oil
(40)   rub with *babaçu* oil . . .
                then he will paint himself as the *waptɛ*

With this brief slip into the mythological past Warodi linked the young
man, through his body paint, to the creator's identity. However, instead
of simply saying, "You are to appear as the *waptɛ* who created the sea,"
speaking directly to Bomfim's intellect and prescribing how he should
think of himself, Warodi recalled a poignant episode from the creator's
life, telling of the time the abandoned creator's brother came to look for
him. Warodi's telling gracefully spoke to Bomfim's unconscious, to his
emotions, just at the moment Bomfim was to be decorated as another.

Certainly for Bomfim, this telling evoked feelings and memories of times when he had heard the tale in the past. Decorated with this body paint, paint that recalled the memory of the creator as well as the memory of past tellings, Bomfim was encouraged to do more than *think* of himself as another. Warodi's brief telling prompted Bomfim to *feel* himself as the creator. He was the *waptɛ* who made the sea.

To complete the image of the creators in Warodi's dream, the elders painted a red swatch of *urucum* across each creator's eyes. They then wrapped a jet black collar of charcoal paint around the neck of each. Next, each creator donned his woven fiber mask and headdress. With red eyes, necks black as coal, and flowing robes of *buriti* fiber, the creators became jabiru storks. As jabiru, they appeared in the form in which the creators present themselves to the living.

Once the elders had tied a headband on each to signal his *waptɛ* status, the creators' metamorphoses were complete. However, whereas the usual *waptɛ* headband is made of *buriti* fiber, on this day white crepe-paper headbands—imprinted with the message "Bebe Guarana" ("Drink Guarana")[4]—graced the forehead of each creator. No conflict existed between this commercial advertisement and the creators' image. Rather, the juxtaposition heightened the sense of blending. The two worlds, the two times were converging as the time for the performance grew near.

The women began to arrive in the *mará* forest clearing as the men were singing the songs yet another time. When they had assembled, Warodi taught the songs once again. The women joined their voices to sing with the men, and this repetition was the last one before the final performance.

Warodi:	have you learned it?
	all right, think about the song
Woman:	it's difficult
	it's very difficult
Another woman:	it's the same song [that the men sang] . . .
Warodi:	their thoughts
	in order for you to learn
	I called you
	to think about their thoughts

Again Warodi told his dream. Again he embellished his narrative with fragmentary myth tellings. Then the women painted themselves (Fig. 16) and the performers, both men and women, made their final preparations to sing and dance the immortals into the present. Warodi, in whom the two worlds had already converged, was the only performer who did not paint himself. As the others made last-minute touch-ups to their

16. Women applying body paint in preparation for performance. (Photo by Laura Graham, 1984.)

body paint and trimmed their coiffures just so, their shouts, urgent commands, and hasty responses intensified the atmosphere of anticipation. The performance—the climax of their efforts—was about to begin.

Etẽpa:	hurry! put *urucum* on my forehead!
	cut my hair! hurry!
	cut it right to here! hurry!
Warodi:	okay, this
	this is the jabiru stork's song
	the jabiru stork's song
Etẽpa:	⌈ [I shared this song for you] to know it
	⌊ I'm going to use *urucum* until my bones fall apart!
Sibupa:	⌈ I have a ball of *urucum* with me
	⌊ come on stand up!
Warodi:	just a minute!
woman:	⌈ just a minute
	⌊ all the men are leaving [for the *warã* central plaza]
	they should stay!
	maybe the younger ones are also [leaving]
	come stand here *tsadaʔro!* . . .
Sasão:	come on all you men! get up!
Sibupa:	hurry up! I'm making charcoal for myself!
Etẽpa:	I'm going to make charcoal for myself quickly!
	when I paint myself the smell of *urucum* is strong!
	this is for really black charcoal for me!
	for really black charcoal for me!
Sibupa:	⌈ it's
	⌊ come on everybody!
Joana:	this charcoal is itchy
	where's the charcoal?
Aiʔrere:	here, give me a firecracker to shoot!
Solange:	he
	he brought it
BANG! BANG! BANG-BANG!	
Irene:	WOW! that firecracker is really for spooking!

Amidst the crackling blast of firecrackers—noisemakers the *ʔritaiʔwa* novitiates had picked up from a local vendor to add their part to this innovative ceremony—the performers departed for the *warã* central plaza. "Is there more?" I shouted. Although Sibupa and Warodi had expressed their concern that the performance be tape-recorded, in their enthusiasm they had neglected to tell me that the performance in the *warã* was about

17. The dream performance in the village center is a crystallization of metamorphoses. The three creator figures—in the form of jabiru storks—flap their wings as if in flight. (Photo by Laura Graham, 1984.)

to start. "Just a minute!" I scrambled to collect my tape recorder, microphone, and camera and dashed toward the central plaza. I arrived in the *warã* and hurriedly set my tape recorder on a bench and positioned the microphone.

Solemnly the performers filed into the central plaza, where they formed a circle around the creators (Fig. 17). Instead of integrating the women and the men, as they do in most collective *da-ño?re* performances that are for fun, the senior men arranged for the young men to stand next to them. This arrangement impressed upon the somewhat skeptical adolescent *?ritai?wa* that this performance was not just for fun, nor was it something to be made fun of. The performers were enacting the creators but, as Etẽpa exclaimed in response to the fears of one novitiate, no one was going to be turned into a toad to replicate the unlucky fate of the one who made the sea's malevolent companion. This performance was serious. In it, the people of Pimentel Barbosa demonstrated their privileged connection to the first creators. They illustrated their superiority over other Xavante villages and the fact that "every time he [Warodi] goes to the sky, he hears the creators' speech, when the immortals are gathered."

A few moments passed as the performers positioned themselves (Figs. 18, 19). Wind rustled through the palm-fiber masks. Feet shuffled. Following

18. Women and men dance in adjacent sections rather than integrated by sex as in other mixed-gender *daño?re* performances. (Photo by Laura Graham, 1984.)

19. Warodi, in whom the two worlds had already converged, was the only performer who did not paint. From left to right the dancers are: Eduardo, A?ãma, Ai?rere, Warodi, Sibupa, and Agostim. (Photo by Laura Graham, 1984.)

Warodi's lead, the performers clasped hands and closed the circle around the creators.

Silence.

Then Warodi cleared his throat. He was ready to begin.

As the others joined their voices to sing with Warodi, they began to fill the *warã* with sound. It was the sound of the creators' songs, the sound of the immortals singing. Bodies, decorated as the immortals, began to move. They were the immortals in motion. Now the jabiru storks, the creators, waved their arms; they flapped their wings as Warodi had seen the creators fly in his dream. In sound, movement, and bodily image, through the smells of *urucum* and the palm fiber of the creators' costumes, the performers brought the immortals into the world of the living. They blurred the line between the living and the dead, and both the far past of the creators and the recent past of previous tellings merged into the present. The performers became the Xavante who never die.

> these the descendants of the first Xavante . . .
> they don't die
> they have many lives
> those descendants, like us
>   they keep living
> they continue living always
> they continue living
> those, they keep visiting us
> they keep visiting us
> they are forever Xavante
> they are forever Xavante, they keep livi[ng]
>   they keep living

Preparations for the performance had lasted most of the day, from 8:00 A.M. until just before 4:00 P.M., when the participants left for the *warã*. The lengthy preparations were an integral part of the whole; they laid the groundwork and provided time for the participants to shift, however briefly, into the immortals' world. In the *warã*, the performers sang each of the three songs once through and then began to disperse. Almost as quickly as it had begun, the performance itself was over. In their singing and dancing, through sound, bodies, and movement, the performers brought the immortals into the world of the living.

Afterward, a number of performers lingered in the plaza, not yet ready to wash off their body paint. Defying Etẽpa's boast that I would use up all the film on him, because he was so handsome, I obliged many requests for photographs from other attractive performers. Roberto, proud to have been one of the creators on this special occasion, was among those to make such a request. He asked me to photograph him with his wife so that later he would be able to show his children how he looked when he had been one of the "always living" creators. Each time I took a photo, I asked about the performance. "*E tiha õhã? E tiha da-tɔ hã?* (What was that? What was that celebration?)" "*Dzaʔuʔe*" (jabiru stork), I heard, "like Warodi saw in his dream." Or, as Agostim had told me before, "*Höimanaʔuʔö* (the always living, the creators)." No one offered more enlightening responses than these.

Led by Warodi, I had accompanied the performance from the first moments of its rehearsal to the final act in the *warã*. Yet I had understood very little of what I'd seen. I knew that this was not an ordinary performance, that it was not part of any ceremonial cycle. A number of unusual characteristics marked it as exceptional. Among these was the fact that Warodi and the other retired elders, including Sibupa, Etẽpa, Aiʔrere, and Daru, had joined in as active participants. It was extraordinary to see these elders decorate themselves and then sing and dance. Moreover, unlike in the mixed-gender *da-ñoʔre* performances I had seen in Pimentel Barbosa, this time the women and men who performed were not integrated in the circle; they sang and danced in gender-defined sections. And since this event was not part of any ceremonial cycle, performers had some flexibility for individual expression in their bodily decorations; several elder participants wore body decorations that pertained to other ceremonials or sported designs that expressed the individual's creative whim. Daru, for example, painted his hair like an Indian from the nearby Xingu Park, and a number of women painted themselves as if for the women's naming ceremony. These individuals had taken designs out of their usual contexts and had played with them. At the same time that they expressed a serious message, the performers also had fun. Indeed, the Xavante word for ceremonial, *da-tɔ*, means play.[5]

I also knew that for Warodi, as for many people, my return to the village had been something to celebrate; I was flattered that they had staged such an elaborate festivity to welcome my return. Undoubtedly this was an opportunity for them to show off, to display a spectacle, particularly since I could photograph and tape-record the event. Many people expected me to give them copies of the photographs I took, as I had done before. And because this was a year without scheduled ceremonial activity, most of those who remained in the village appreciated the opportunity to dance and entertain themselves.

Unbeknownst to me, however, in addition to welcoming my return, Warodi and the elders who collaborated with him had something more in

mind. They had designed this special theatrical performance to take advantage of my technological expertise with camera, tape recorder, and
writing to maximize the community's benefit from my presence. Warodi,
sensitive to the fact that I, unlike many of his regional neighbors, was
sympathetic to the Xavante, appreciated my interest in expressive culture.
Using his knowledge about me, he had envisioned a spectacle that would
capture my attention, that would motivate me to photograph and tape-
record images and speech that he deemed especially important. Thus, he
visualized the creators in their costumes to be photographed.

> then first
>   to be photographed
> he will first
>   first he will rub himself with *babaçu* oil
>   rub himself with *babaçu* oil
> then he will paint himself as the *waptɛ*
>   as the *waptɛ* he will paint himself

Warodi also urged the performers to "sing loudly" for the tape recorder:

> sing loudly for the tape recorder
> we were going to call you to sing loudly
>   to sing loudly for the tape recorder

Later, when I returned the images to the performers, they would remember the performance and see themselves as creators. They would
remember that they were the true descendants of the first creators. When
they heard the songs played back from the tape recorder, they would hear
the creators' songs. They would remember Warodi and the creators' gifts
to the living.

Perhaps most important, I—who came from across the ocean (*ö poʔre
dzaʔra ʔu*)—was "to publish it" if I could understand what I had seen.
Etẽpa, in his comment to the youths, had made this patently clear.

> now you all
>   are the descendants of the first creator
> this, they [will] teach it to her
> if she understands what you [Warodi] say, it is to be published

But what was the "it" that I was supposed to understand?

Knowing that at the time, my linguistic ability in Xavante was limited, Warodi and the elders chose to dramatize the dream to give its images a physical form. They thought of their dramatization in a way that is reminiscent of the French surrealist Artaud's thinking about the theater, in which language is less important than images.[6] This dramatization, they thought, would communicate its message most effectively through visual and other nonlinguistic media. Its visual and acoustic images, physical forms, and movement would make the message readily accessible to me. Moreover, the theatrical display would make a powerful, tangible impression on me, as well as on the youths and women. They designed the performance in a way that would enable me to *see, hear,* and *feel* their message.

But even after I had seen and heard the performance, even after I had been impressed by its powerful images, the meaning of those images— which Warodi had hoped would become transparent—remained opaque to me. Although I could see the actors dressed in woven palm-fiber costumes, beautifully decorated with red and black body paint, I had scarcely a notion of what Warodi wished to communicate. At the time, the images and sounds were, for me, little more than exotic and spectacular entertainment.

However, for Warodi and the other performers—who, for a brief period, became immortals in the present—the meanings of the performance resonated through the singing, dancing, and visual imagery. Clearly, those who had responded to my queries about the costumed figures with answers like "They are *dzaʔuʔe*" (jabiru stork, also *tsibaʔa*) and "They are *höimanaʔuʔö*" had infused these images with meanings. Where did this meaning reside? For me, the key to understanding the performance was missing.

A few days later, still baffled, I met with Etẽpa's son, Suptɔ, who had kindly offered to help me. Knowing that Warodi was anxious for me to understand, I confided, "*Dzahadu te waihuʔu õ di* (I still don't understand). It was his dream, right?" "Yes. It's like this." Then, instead of explaining that the figures were the authors of the Xavante creation and that Warodi had communicated with them in his dream, Suptɔ told me that the costumed figures were *höimanaʔuʔö* (always living). He then began to tell me of the creators' lives and deeds. Suptɔ, however, an adolescent *ʔritaiʔwa* at the time, was uncertain about many aspects of his telling. Several times he interrupted his narrative to make inquiries of his elders. Ultimately his explanation left me almost as confused as when we began our conversation. But then, to sum up, he explained, "*Höimanaʔuʔö* is like the Christians' God, like Jesus Christ. But he was Xavante first." Although I failed to grasp at the time that the concept of *höimanaʔuʔö* embraced several creators who, according to the tellings, were each responsible for different aspects of the Xavante's world, I understood that the costumed figures represented some kind of supernatural beings.

I returned to Warodi, delighted to report that I had understood at least something of the dream performance. Even though I was unclear on the concept, I exclaimed: "They, the *dzaʔuʔe* (the figures who were costumed as jabiru storks) are *höimanaʔuʔö!*" "*Ĩhe* (yes)," Warodi replied, and straightaway he launched into a telling that recounted the miraculous events of each creator's life. That day, as on subsequent days over the next three years, whenever I asked Warodi about *höimanaʔuʔö*, he broke into a telling that recounted part of the Xavante creation. Without any other exegesis, Warodi packaged his explanations in the form of myth tellings. Telling tales of the creators' lives, he evoked the inception of the Xavante's world.

I began to understand that *tellings* provided the key to unraveling the meanings embedded in the performance. The performance presupposed these tellings, the very discourse that Warodi had so kindly meant to spare me. He thought that he could *show*, instead of tell, the ancestors who made the creation. But in fact tellings were necessary to establish the link between the images of the performance and the mythological protagonists that the actors represented. For example, even though the principal actors resembled pre-initiate *waptɛ* in their body paint and headbands, without reference to mythological tellings they might have been recognized as just any *waptɛ*. Their reddened eyes, black necks, and palm-fiber costumes might have caused some observers to think of them as jabiru storks by virtue of iconicity, but it could only be known from a telling that the creators, once *waptɛ*, now appear in this form. The entire performance rested upon the narratives that tell the stories of the creators' lives.

Every Xavante is more or less familiar with these creators through his or her exposure to these narratives. For the participants, a history of tellings mediated between the images of the dream performance and their interpretations.[7] This was a history that I did not have. But once I had heard Warodi tell the tale of the one who made the sea, I was not surprised that one youth had feared he might turn into a toad. In the telling, that creator gave long black hair to his generous friend. Then he turned to the greedy one and transformed him into a toad:

> well, he took his companion by the hand
> and chose a spot in the water for him to sit

TU TU TU [a noise on his head]

his hair is growing
he is incredible

TU TU TU
his hair is incredible
it is lo-o-o-ng hair!

ah!
it is finished

the greedy one is standing at his side
suddenly he grabbed him

the glue is heating up
he made a noise on his head

TU TU TU
it [the glue] was already hot

TU TU TU
the noise went like this

TU TU TU
he put it in the nape of his neck

he shivered
shouted

Rɔ BU BU BU [noise of the surging water]
he threw him toward the water
he wiggled in the water

BU BU BU

he wriggled
he became a toad
he never came again
he never returned home

he became a toad
only his intimate companion got long hair [8]

With references to tellings, Warodi had joined the "*waptɛ*" of the drama to the *waptɛ* who created the Xavante's world.[9] Just mentioning "the *waptɛ* who created the sea" or speaking of "the one whose foot was pierced by a stick" stimulated him to launch into a myth narrative. For him as well as for his Xavante listeners, the fragmented myth tellings within the dream narrative recalled past tellings, tellings like the one excerpted above, that had sedimented into memory. These memories enabled each performer to infuse the costumed figures with meaning. The sounds of their voices, the movements of their dancing bodies recalled the memory of the immortal creators who, as Warodi told in his dream narrative, had given him their songs. As they sang and danced the songs with the creators in mind, the performers brought them into the present. The sounds, movements, and bodily images offered sensible proof that the creators continued living.

Actions such as these—actions that recall the memory of their lives and creations—enable the creators to continue living. Their immortality resides in the practices that keep memories of their lives and creations alive. Most Xavante can expect to be remembered as individuals for about two generations—for as long as those who knew them continue to evoke specific memories of their lives. As the details of an individual's life begin to merge into memories of other lives, she or he moves into the undifferentiated collectivity of immortals, the *wadzapariʔwa*, who form the final age grade of the life cycle. But because Xavante remember the individual lives and accomplishments of the creators in tellings that are passed from generation to generation, these immortals have an individualized immortality, an immortality that is greater than that of all others. The creators have a distinguished immortality because Xavante remember their lives above all others. Moreover, the creators' immortality increases each time Xavante tell the tales of their lives. Since the living bring forth and augment the creators' memory, they are the ones who give the "always living" *höimanaʔuʔö* the gift of individuated eternal life.

Later, as I worked on the translation of Warodi's narrative and grappled with his unexpected use of first-person pronouns in the embedded myth tellings, I began to understand the implications of Warodi's complete identification with the creators' point of view. Insofar as Warodi projected himself into the creators' identity and caused others to perceive him— perhaps even unconsciously—as a creator, Warodi moved that much closer to achieving his own distinguished immortality. By blurring the distinction between his self and the selves of the creators, Warodi merged his identity into theirs. With his identity conflated with that of the creators, each time Xavante remember the creators' lives, they also remember Warodi. Having projected himself into the identity of the "always living" *höimanaʔuʔö*, Warodi represented himself to be among the prestigious immortals even before his own death.[10] Demonstrating the way for the immortal creators to continue living in the dream performance, Warodi set forth the way to his own distinguished immortality.

At the same time, because Warodi's own immortality inhabits the discursive practice of myth telling, the very behavior that will enable him to continue "always living" is the same one that enables the Xavante to continue as Xavante themselves. It is through myth telling that Xavante reaffirm their connection to the first creators, the ones who worked for the Xavante before they worked for any other group. Perhaps most importantly, since the practice of myth telling passes from one generation to the next, in a dynamic way it embodies the very continuity of culture. Details of a story's content may change over time, but so long as Xavante continue to *tell* the tales that link them to the past and to the celebrated first creators, they expressively recreate the continuity of this uniquely Xavante cultural practice. And in their agent-centered myth tellings, narrators model a pattern of action in the world; this is the model for action that Xavante have transported into their dealings with the outside world. It lends them a sense of agency, which they bring to their dealings with outsiders, and the determination to continue as Xavante forever.

By embedding his personal quest for a distinguished immortality within the very practices that ensure the future of them all, Warodi celebrated community values together with his personal interests. In tellings, Warodi modeled the way for the Xavante to continue forever; he promoted his own interests as he simultaneously promoted the interests of others. The very same discursive practices that guarantee the Xavante's cultural survival are those that will give Warodi, as a creator, the gift of a distinguished immortality.

As I pondered the magnificent complexity of the dream performance after I came to understand it better, Warodi's commitment to staging this event during my visit began to come into sharper focus. Warodi could harness the technical skills I possessed in media not available to the Xavante, as well as my interest in documenting expressive performance, to assist him in his pursuit of a distinguished immortality. To facilitate my understanding, he designed the performance to present an image of the immortals that I could see and hear, as well one that I could document with my camera and tape recorder. Warodi knew that if I could understand what I'd seen, I had the ability to write it down. Moreover, as Etẽpa remarked, I had the potential to publish what I had learned, to make it into a book.

The forms of documentation I possessed have enabled Warodi to transmit his message to the world beyond Pimentel Barbosa, to reach new audiences. Others, like you, now see the photographs of the Xavante creators and know at least something of their lives, as Warodi has told them. Through the tape recordings of his narrative and the translations some young Xavante and I have made of them, new audiences—audiences that Warodi could not directly address—can learn that the Xavante immortals continue living. They continue living through tellings, as Xavante hear them, or as they are translated and written down for others to read. Now, as I write this, nearly ten years since the Xavante of Pimentel Barbosa performed his dream, Warodi is remembered for his life and deeds by those who knew him as a husband, father, grandfather, and caring man. Although he passed away in January 1988, in people's memories Warodi continues living. And insofar as his memory is recorded in the pages of this book, he has achieved a greater immortality. Warodi—the man who told the tales of the creators' lives, who staged the dream, whose self became one with the creators—inhabits the words printed here. To read or think of the Xavante creators is to remember Warodi. Each thought of Warodi's life, each recollection of his words, adds to his memory. Each addition moves him a step closer to greater immortality. And so long as living Xavante, you, or I remember him, Warodi continues "always living."

Epilogue

I n February 1988, just two months after I had returned to the United States and only a month since Warodi's death, I was surprised to re-ceive a letter from Warodi's nephew Cipassé. He told me of the sad-ness that had pervaded the community in the aftermath of his uncle's death, and in his final paragraphs he described his wish to establish an archive of materials documenting Xavante life. Cipassé envisioned a col-lection that would be *for* Xavante; it would bring together materials that outside researchers had published about them, especially writings about Pimentel Barbosa. He closed with a request that I send him copies of the tape recordings I had made of Warodi's speech.

I was both pleased and perplexed by Cipassé's request. During the more than six years that I had worked with the people of Pimentel Barbosa, no one except Warodi and Sibupa had paid much attention to the tape re-cordings of narratives and speech that I made. In contrast to their seem-ingly insatiable appetite for recordings of *da-ñoʔre*, only once did anyone ask me to play back a narrative. Still, Cipassé's request was gratifying; it indicated that he found merit in a project that involved documentation of expressive culture. Moreover, it offered me an opportunity to return some-thing to the community for its hospitality. In the process, I could contrib-ute to the life of Warodi's memory. I set to copying the tapes immediately and then sent them off to Cipassé.

When I returned to Pimentel Barbosa in June 1991, I was eager to learn about the archive and where the community had housed the tapes. Blank stares and shrugged shoulders met my inquiries. Supto, who still lived in Agostim's house and who was now *cacique*, replied, "Archive? Cassette tapes of your father's speech? We don't know anything about it." No one seemed to know or care what had become of the tapes I'd sent to Cipassé. "I still have the originals," I mentioned, "in case you ever want copies at some future time." Meanwhile, I made a mental note to ask Cipassé what he had done with the tapes when he returned to the village from Goiânia.

In the two and a half years since my last visit, a great deal had changed.

Strife over leadership and management of resources had divided the people since Warodi's death. Only two months before, in April 1991, Milton—Warodi's successor as *cacique*—along with eighty-one members of his faction, had left to join those at Caçula (see Map 3). In the wake of Milton's departure, the senior men had appointed Suptɔ, still a reasonably young man from the *tsadaʔro* age-set, to the *cacique* position. They named Paulo, a young man who, like Suptɔ, had worked very closely with me, to be his assistant. And even though Cipassé did not occupy an officially acknowledged leadership post, members of the community recognized him for his ambitious leadership in external affairs. These young men, my peers, now occupied important leadership positions.

Of all the changes I encountered, I least expected to find Cipassé's younger brother Riridu (pronounced [hiridu]) in a position of spiritual prominence. In 1987, during the time I worked in Goiânia, Riridu had accompanied his father on several trips to visit Cipassé, and I had come to know him quite well. He greatly admired his older brother and aspired to be just like him, learning Portuguese and attending school in Goiânia. To Riridu's great disappointment, an arrangement never worked out.

When he was in the city, Riridu spent most of his time with me. A preinitiate *wapte* at the time—about twelve years old—he was full of wonder and amazement over all the new things he was seeing in the world. Nothing about him struck me as particularly out of the ordinary for a Xavante boy his age; neither did he seem especially spiritual.

By 1991, Riridu had completely transformed himself. Instead of the eager boy I'd known, I met a somewhat arrogant young man who comported himself with a worldly air. It astounded me to see him, an adolescent *ʔritaiʔwa*, unhesitatingly give advice to his seniors as well as to his peers, and soberly offer earnest counsel to the *cacique*, Suptɔ, one of his most ardent supporters. Defying behavioral restrictions observed by other, deferential *ʔritaiʔwa*, Riridu strode about the village by day and slept through his cohort's *da-ñoʔre* performances by night. He had even managed to have his young wife move into the house he shared with Cipassé. By virtue of this arrangement Riridu bypassed his uxorilocal obligations and exempted himself from exhibiting appropriate deferential behaviors toward his in-laws in their home. Both Riridu's demeanor and his position were extraordinary for a *ʔritaiʔwa*.

According to his followers, Riridu had begun to reveal his "spiritual powers" just after the village fissioned. Since then, while gossip and fears of sorcery continued to plague the community, he had been active as a peacemaker and spiritual counselor. On June 11, my third full day in the village, in an unusual and strangely spectacular performance, I witnessed Riridu manifest his recently revealed spiritual gifts.

Just before sunrise, the senior men summoned the entire village to the central plaza. Men, women, children, and youths gathered in the morning stillness. Suddenly a single, high-pitched call pierced the silence. It appeared to come from the gallery forest near the river, from the area where ceremonial preparations take place. Another call issued from the forest. I felt suspense mounting. Then, silhouetted against the rising sun, a male figure emerged into the village clearing. Slowly, with deliberate movements, he approached the *warã*. With the rosy orange light illuminating the sky behind him, his features were indistinguishable. Nevertheless I could see that, except for a scant breechcloth, he was naked. Slowly, dramatically, he advanced toward the gathering. I saw then that it was Riridu. It astonished me to see the entire village assembled to witness the performance of a single individual. Once I realized that people had gathered to watch a *ʔritaiʔwa*, I was truly astounded.

In one hand Riridu carried a stick; in the other he clasped a tiny bow and a single, long arrow. All of these, as well as his breechcloth, were painted a deep red with *urucum*. His taut body was painted jet black with charcoal. Red areas—his forehead, a swatch around his mouth, and the square on his stomach—contrasted intensely against the solid mass of blackness. Erect, with bent knees and outstretched arms, Riridu moved dramatically. From time to time he made abrupt, karate-like moves. This impressive spectacle, in which his individual prominence was striking, was like nothing I'd ever seen in Pimentel Barbosa. It was like no other performance I'd ever seen or read about.

As Riridu began to speak, I was surprised at the eloquent manner in which he addressed the gathering. Unlike other youths his age, he spoke fluidly, in short phrases and with a great deal of repetition. In many respects his speech resembled that of an elder. He told the story of his life and of his persecution by members of his cohort when he was a pre-initiate *wapte*. Then, one by one, several members of the audience came forth to speak, to accuse or defend Riridu on charges of wrongdoing. When no others stepped forward, Riridu made a final speech. Adding to the drama of his address, he stared toward the heavens, crouched, and slowly twisted his body. As he gracefully moved his torso, he swung the tiny bow and long arrow in a wide arc above his head. Then, having finished his speech, he receded back into the forest.

Events that had taken place the preceding day precipitated Riridu's performance. That afternoon, an elder who had been among those who relocated to Caçula visited Pimentel Barbosa to challenge members of the community with allegations that stemmed from disturbing rumors. In a confrontational meeting that lasted more than three hours, the elder publicly accused Riridu of having an incestuous amorous affair. That night, according to his supporters, Riridu exercised his exceptional spiritual faculties. "He has the power to meet with spirits," Suptɔ explained. Later,

Paulo elaborated, "Riridu transmits the word of Warodi as well as Suptɔ's father, Etẽpa [who died in 1984]. It was they who painted him. He didn't paint himself. They gave him the tiny bow, the long arrow, and the *wamãri*, wood of peace." In this "trial of sorts," as Suptɔ put it, Riridu publicly confronted his opponents and cleared his name.

The jealous husband and members of his family maintained, on the other hand, that Riridu and his powers were a farce. Clearly these differing explanations revealed that factional rivalries continued to convulse the community—indeed, they played themselves out in Riridu's performance. With majority backing, Riridu forced the jealous husband and his supporters to vent their charges publicly.

Riridu's performance, his personal transformation, and the reports of his meetings with Warodi and Etẽpa captivated my interest. What resources had Riridu, a *ʔritaiʔwa*, mustered in order to represent himself as an emissary from Warodi? Along with learning what had become of the cassette tapes of Warodi's speech, learning more about Riridu became a priority for me that summer.

Meanwhile, I began to work on the summer's projects. In addition to continuing my ongoing study of discourse practice, the Xavante and I initiated a video project that involved instructing several people to use a video camera and to operate playback equipment. After the community's leaders and I discussed some initial practical matters concerning the video project, we needed to pick up the equipment in Barra do Garças, where I had left it after lugging it from São Paulo. Several days after Riridu's performance, Suptɔ, Jé Paulo (the truck driver), Riridu, and I piled into the community's pickup and set off.

As we drove along the dusty road toward Xavantina and then on to Barra do Garças, Riridu kept playing one song over and over again on his portable boom-box. It sounded exactly like songs from the Southern Gê Kaingang Indians that I had heard in the collection of Greg Urban, who had made recordings of Kaingang singing. Riridu told me that he had recorded the song in May at a gathering of Brazilian Indians in the Xavante community of São Marcos. Riridu softly sang along with the tape during nearly the entire trip to Barra do Garças, but I didn't think much about it at the time.

We spent a day in Barra do Garças making final purchases for the video project. Following Suptɔ's wish, we videotaped ourselves as we did our errands. At one point I noticed Riridu talking with a kiosk vendor in the plaza as he admired a watch display. When he rejoined the three of us, I noticed that he had bought a nice watch. We had lunch and packed the truck.

Night descended as we drove northward. Again Riridu played the song

I recognized as Kaingang, or very similar to the Kaingang style. He sang along with the tape softly as he played the song through once. Then he turned off the tape recorder and sang the song again, this time loudly. I recognized the pattern by which Xavante men learn songs. Riridu had now mastered it and, having put Xavante text to it, had appropriated it as his own.

At about 11:00 P.M. we turned off the dirt highway into the reserve, the last stretch of our trip. The truck bumped along the road. Abruptly Riridu commanded Jé Paulo to stop. As we came to a halt, Jé Paulo cut the engine. Without comment, Riridu, followed by Suptɔ, got out of the cab; Jé Paulo and I remained inside.

In the black night all I could see was Riridu's white T-shirt. I saw the T-shirt make sudden, karate-like moves. Then Riridu gave a sharp, high-pitched cry. Soon he began to talk, very softly, as if he were having a conversation with someone I couldn't see. He paused, as if listening to another's remarks. Suptɔ remained silent, listening. It was difficult for me to make out what Riridu said. I heard him speak of gathering the women for a meeting in which Riridu would give a speech. I overheard Riridu say, as if repeating someone else, that I would photograph the women "slowly," as they learned the hedza hymn. Precipitously, Riridu made more karate-like moves. Then he dramatically sank to a crouched position and held his arms outstretched for at least thirty seconds. His arms then fell to his side. He was silent, exhausted.

When Riridu and Suptɔ got back into the cab I sensed that it was not an appropriate time to ask questions. Despite a burning curiosity to know more about what had just happened, I remained silent the rest of the way to the village as Suptɔ and Riridu discussed arrangements for a gathering. Riridu was the first to get out of the cab when we reached the village. As we made our way in front of the ring of houses, Suptɔ turned toward me to explain. "My father came to that place. Riridu was talking with him." He went on to tell me that even though the idea for a gathering had come from both Warodi and Suptɔ's father, Etẽpa, only Etẽpa had come to transmit the message. "We couldn't see him. They only appear to Riridu."

Over the next few days Riridu presided over several assemblies. According to Suptɔ, Riridu convened these exceptional meetings according to orders he had received from Warodi and Etẽpa, who were leaders "in the other world." In the assemblies, Riridu extracted public confessions from individuals in order to—as Suptɔ, Paulo, and many others said—"clear the atmosphere and to put an end to the gossip." Each time they held one of these meetings, before Riridu emerged from the forest, Suptɔ commenced the proceedings by explaining that Riridu's power came from the immortal wadzapari?wa who lived in the sierra nearby and watched over the community. He clarified that Riridu transmitted the counsel of the "always living" *höimana?u?ö*. Some members of the community privately confided to me their opinions that Riridu was a charlatan. Those who held this opinion belonged to a minority faction, however, as indicated by the fact that Riridu was able to stage his performances publicly, in meetings attended by the entire community, without encountering public protest.

As part of his performance Riridu told the story of his life—of how, because he had been chosen, he suffered an illness in his chest. Because he was different, he had endured his age-mates' persecution during his life in the bachelors' hut. As proof of his privileged communication with "the others from there," he revealed that his watch (the watch he'd gotten in Barra do Garças) was a gift from them.

> even though I suffer, I continue
> it is like this, I feel pain in my chest
> it is like this
> only in my chest, it will kill me straightaway
> it is like this
>
> now, for just a while, I am living in my older brother's house
>   so that I can hear their speech [the speech of the *höimana?u?ö*]
> they tell the news
> then, whenever I receive a message, I will leave
>
> also, this wristwatch, could it be from here?
> no, it is not from here
> no
> this watch came directly to me in Barra [do Garças]
> the watch is for me to understand what people are saying
> you all can see it cinched around my wrist
> like this I am going to lead the communities forward
> it was like this that I began
> now I am going to lead them forward

Riridu told his audience, as Warodi had before him, that the Xavante never die. Authoritatively he pronounced that the descendants of the first creators keep living. He then closed these meetings by teaching the song he had learned from the cassette tape on our trip to Barra do Garças (Fig. 20). He explained that because of his illness he could not participate in the activities of his age-mates; instead he sings with the others, the immortals. They gave him this song.

20. Riridu sings with the tape-recorded version of the *hedza* he "received" from the immortals in June 1991. He is teaching the song to the community in the *warã* central plaza. (Photo by Laura Graham, 1991.)

I wanted to participate [with my group], but I could not
now I am entering there
I am singing together with them
they offered one, like this, because the first Xavante were from here

Although *?ritai?wa* typically receive *da-ño?re*, and only a few elderly men receive *hedza*, Riridu represented "his" song as a *hedza*, a *hedza* that demonstrated his exceptional contact with the *höimana?u?ö*. Paulo made the connection even more explicit: Riridu had told him and others that the song was from Warodi. Riridu later told me that he hadn't, in fact, recorded it in São Marcos but during one of his meetings with Warodi.

It was beginning to dawn on me that Riridu, frustrated by his inability to act as an intermediary between the community and Brazilian national society like his older brother, was aggressively seeking to carve out a role for himself *within* the community. To establish himself as a spiritual counselor, he incorporated novelties such as karate—which he had learned from Cipassé in Goiânia—and watches into his use of conventional resources such as *hedza* and narrative. Sibupa, who had previously acted as a spiritual counselor, had left an opening when he had gone with Milton to Caçula. Since this role was usually filled by a learned elder, it surprised me that Riridu would even think of representing himself in this way.

When Paulo and I began to translate one of Riridu's speeches that I had tape-recorded, I began to notice that Riridu patterned much of his biographical narrative on themes typical of mythic discourse. For example, portraying himself as a persecuted *wapt&*, he recalled themes from narratives about the creators. One day Paulo made a remark that made the analogies to the mythological protagonists explicit. "Riridu is like 'the one who pierced his foot with a stick,'" he said. "He may hurt his body but he remains unharmed." He added, "Riridu is like the *parinai?a*, it all happened when he was a *wapt&*."

Whereas most *?ritai?wa* defer to their elders and exhibit little confidence concerning myth telling, in his life-narrative Riridu portrayed himself to be remarkably like the creators who had become so familiar to me through my study of Warodi's narratives. How was it, I wondered, that Riridu could feel so confident with material most men accumulated over a lifetime? How could it be that he, a *?ritai?wa*, had such familiarity with these themes that he could skillfully weave them into a biographical narrative?

Several days after Riridu's performances, Teresa Aparicio, a Spanish anthropologist working for the Danish International Work Group for Indigenous Affairs, arrived in Pimentel Barbosa. Cipassé and his wife, Severiá, who were in Goiânia, offered her the use of their house, which they shared with Riridu. One afternoon Teresa told me that late the night before she had heard Riridu talking to someone who spoke "in a different voice." She did not know the identity of Riridu's interlocutor but said the way he spoke reminded her of the speeches that Warodi and Sibupa had used when they greeted her. The voice spoke in short phrases with a lot of repetition. From her description I suspected that Riridu had met with an elder who had spoken in the ĩ-hi mrɛmɛ (elders' speech) style.

Our conversation took place over a cup of tea in Cipassé's house. Riridu was there resting, hidden behind a curtain of buriti fibers. During a pause in our discussion we heard a strange voice coming from the area of Riridu's bed. Since we thought that Riridu was alone, the voice surprised us. Mute, we listened. Teresa nodded. "That's it!" she exclaimed in a whisper. Instantly I recognized the speech as ĩ-hi mrɛmɛ. I listened for another moment, almost stunned by what I heard. I recognized the voice: it was Warodi's. He was telling a narrative, one that I had tape-recorded over five years before.

I excused myself from Teresa and went to Riridu. He lay on his back with his boom-box by his ear. Respectfully avoiding Warodi's name, I inquired, "E ĩ-mama watsuʔu (is that my father's story)? E ĩ-ñimi-wapari (is that my recording)?" "Ĩhe (yes)!" Riridu exclaimed excitedly as he sat up. A broad smile spread across his face. Despite my concern that Riridu might feel exposed, that he might try to hide the secret of his anomalous wisdom, he immediately reacted with elation. He was overjoyed to know that I had recognized Warodi's voice and Warodi's telling.

As I marveled over this discovery, I saw that Riridu was eager to show me something. He stood up and walked over to a bag that hung against the wall. He rummaged around in it for a moment and then returned to the sleeping mat with a handful of cassette tapes. I recognized these as the tapes I had sent to Cipassé for the archive. "I am studying them," he boasted proudly. "Where did you get them?" I inquired. "From Cipassé." Riridu had found an unanticipated use for the recordings I had made of Warodi.

When Warodi died, Riridu had just become a pre-initiate wapte. He did not have the opportunity to spend the long afternoons of his ʔritaiʔwa seclusion lying by Warodi's side, listening to his tales of the creation, hearing him tell that the Xavante—the descendants of the first creators—never die. But listening to the tapes, Riridu had absorbed much of Warodi's knowledge, and he apprehended Warodi's message that through telling, through remembering the lives of the creators, the Xavante will continue forever.

Riridu adapted the tapes differently than I, and perhaps Warodi, might have imagined. In the guise of promoting community welfare, and certainly to promote his own interests, he reworked Warodi's telling into his own public addresses. Adapted and reformulated, Warodi's message continues to be heard in Pimentel Barbosa, and through "Riridu's" song, Warodi's voice continues to resound in the realm of the living.

Appendix: Musical Transcriptions

T. M. Scruggs

All musical transcriptions are approximations of actual sound. The ones in this book are provided to give the reader a general idea of the characteristics of the compositions discussed in the text.

Transcriptions of the three *da-ño?re* (1–3) in this appendix show the principal sections that make up each song. The *hedza* (4), as well as the *da-ño?re* in Figure 12, can be shown in their entirety because their formal structures allow for a more compact rendering. The formal structures of the three *da-ño?re* in the appendix follow a basic arch form. In all three the first part (shown in the transcriptions) or a portion of it is repeated in the middle of the song at a higher pitch, forming the "keystone" of the arch pattern. A repetition of the initial material, slightly varied in each case, constitutes the final part of the song. The *hedza* (4) does not follow this arch pattern, no doubt because the *hedza* form is derived from Western missionary hymns. This may also explain why its structure more conveniently fits a format that can utilize several of the symbols in Western notation that relate to formal structure. The notation *D.S. senza repetizione* literally refers one back to the symbol (D.S., *dal segno*) at the beginning of the fifth system and instructs one to not take the repeat the last time. Instead, one moves directly to the coda, the last measure of the transcription, to complete the song.

The basic pulse is notated as a quarter note. All four songs are nearly identical in tempo, except for the *uiwede-ño?re* (2). An *uiwede-ño?re* is a type of *da-praba*, and *da-praba* have characteristically fast tempos relative to other types of *da-ño?re* (see Chapter 4). At the beginning of each *da-*

ñoʔre an explicit, regular metric phrasing is established that is maintained throughout the song. The principal exceptions to this are phrases that extend beyond a division of four beats per phrase, notated as 6/4 meter, in the *da-dzarõno* (1) and the *marawaʔwa* (3), and the shorter phrases, shown as measures of 2/4, that serve as musical tags in the *marawaʔwa* (3). In the *hedza* (4) the measures of 5/4 and 2/4 meter could stem from the original meter of the Kaingang song on which it is based, or they could have developed from constraints suggested by the lyrics.

In all these songs, as is discussed in Chapter 4, one singer initiates the singing and introduces new sections by himself, with the rest of the singers falling in to form a monophonic chorus. The notes marked as less definite are due, at least in part, to the fact they are at the lowest part of the singers' range, where it is more difficult to produce a distinct pitch. With two exceptions, the transcriptions reflect the actual pitches, as indicated by the key signatures. The first exception occurs in the *da-dzarõno* (1), where the melodic range incrementally expands throughout the composition. The transcription shows the basic melodic material that constitutes the first section. The pitches are initially sung as notated, and the range spans a perfect fifth. In the middle section (not shown) the first section is sung a minor second higher, but the highest note rises a major second and the lowest note actually drops a minor second, making the melodic range a minor seventh. In the last part of the song (also not shown), the reprise of most of the same material presented in the first section, the highest note drops a minor second and the melodic range correspondingly contracts to a major sixth. The second exception takes place in the *marawaʔwa* (3). The pitch shown as the note F at the beginning of the song gradually rises throughout the piece. By the end of the composition it has risen to F-sharp, a minor second above its initial pitch. Because this pitch remains between the principal outer pitches of a lower D and higher A, the overall effect to Western ears is a gradual change from minor to major tonality (D minor to D major). Of course, it is extremely unlikely that this change has any relation to Western functional tonality. Aside from these exceptions, the pitches in all the songs adhere closely to the notes of a standard Western scale.

Microtonal rising, the gradual rise in pitch throughout a song, appears to be characteristic of keening and singing among Gê peoples, as discussed elsewhere by Laura Graham and Anthony Seeger. Although these transcriptions do not show this characteristic within each individual song, when viewed as separate parts of a single performance the three *da-ñoʔre* that Warodi sang in succession show a similar trait. Warodi began the *da-dzarõno* (1) on C, the *uiwede-ñoʔre* (2) on C-sharp, and the *marawaʔwa* (3) on D, which by the end of the performance constitutes a stepwise rising of a major second.

The duration of the songs and the transcribed portions are listed below:

1.	*Da-dzarõno*	Transcribed section	0:58
		Total length of song	2:29
2.	*Uiwede-ño?re*	Transcribed section	0:37
		Total length of song	1:48
3.	*Marawa?wa*	Transcribed section	1:08
		Total length of song	2:17
4.	*Hedza*	Total length of song	1:32

A. Warodi's Dream Songs

1. *Da-dzarõno*; given by *öwawẽ-ʔwa* (the one who made the sea).

wa u - du õ re wa u - du õ re

wa u - du õ re wa u - du õ re

wa u - du õ re wa u - du õ hõ

wḗ wḗ hḗ

2. *Uiwede-ño?re (da-praba)*; given by "the one whose foot was pierced by a stick."

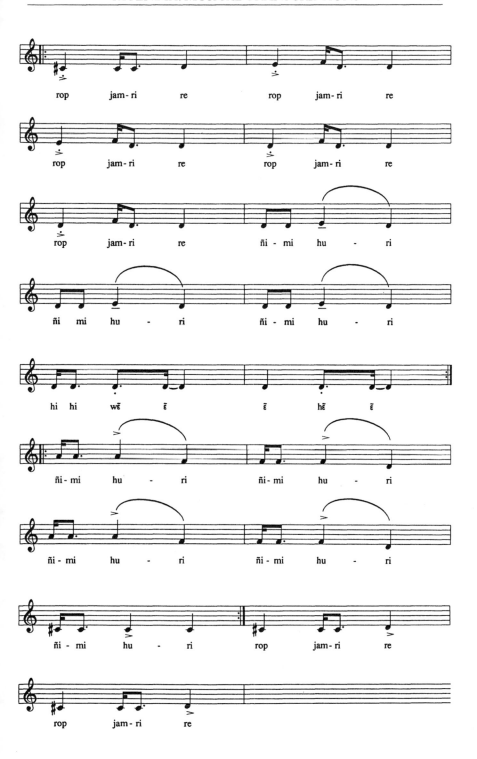

3. *Marawaʔwa (da-hipɔpɔ)*; given by the *parinaiʔa* jabiru storks.

B. Riridu's song

4. *Hedza*; given by Warodi.

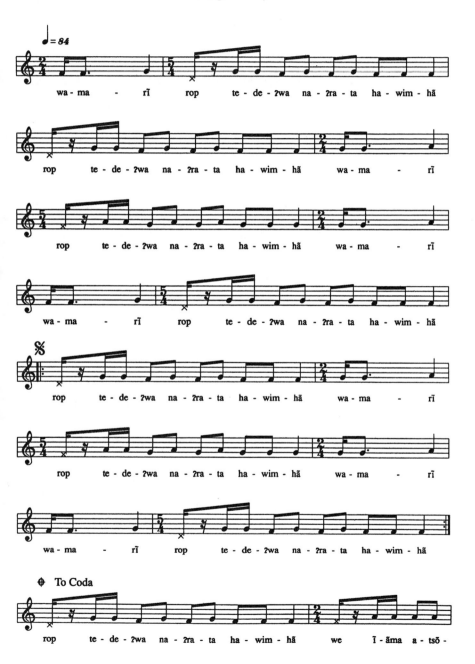

pre dza - ?ra a - ba we ī - ăma a - tsŏ -

pre dza - ?ra a - ba wa - ma - rī

rop te - de - ?wa na - ?ra - ta ha - wim - hã wa - ma - rī

D.S. senza repetizione

wa - ma - rī rop te - de - ?wa na - ?ra - ta ha - wim - hã

⊕ Coda

rop te - de - ?wa na - ?ra - ta ha - wim - hã

Riridu's *hedza*

wamarĩ
rop tede-?wa na?rata hawimhã
rop tede-?wa na?rata hawimhã wamarĩ
we ĩ-dãma atsõpre dza?ra aba
we ĩ-dãma atsõpre dza?ra aba wamarĩ
rop tede-?wa na?rata hawimhã wamarĩ wamarĩ
rop tede-?wa na?rata hawimhã

the *wamarĩ* [wood of peace]
came from the Lord of the world
the *wamarĩ* came from the Lord of the world
to seve as an example for you all
to serve as an example for you all *wamarĩ*
the *wamarĩ* came from the Lord of the world
came from the Lord of the world

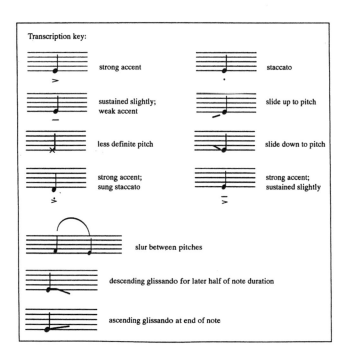

Transcription key:

strong accent

staccato

sustained slightly; weak accent

slide up to pitch

less definite pitch

slide down to pitch

strong accent; sung staccato

strong accent; sustained slightly

slur between pitches

descending glissando for later half of note duration

ascending glissando at end of note

Notes

CHAPTER 1

1. Following the Xavante practice of referring to this community by its Portuguese name in speech to outsiders, I refer to the village as Pimentel Barbosa. Similarly, I use people's Portuguese or Xavante names according to the way they choose to be known to outsiders. To avoid invoking names of the deceased, as is the Xavante custom, I refer to those who have died in the interval between my research and the publication of this book by age-set affiliation, except in the case of Warodi and his father, Apöwẽ, who have exceptional status.

2. Because the dream narrative is collaboratively constructed through the contributions of multiple voices, it is polyvocal in the Bakhtinian sense.

3. Xavante translate the term for non-Indians, *waradzu*, to Portuguese *brancos* (whites); the category includes peoples of African and Asian descent.

4. Only three individuals from the young men's age grade were available at the time of the performance. Because the elders did not consider it appropriate for adolescents or younger boys to play the creators' roles, one of the creators, "the one whose foot was pierced by a stick," was not represented. The young men who acted the creators' parts all happened to be from Warodi's extended family.

5. Bauman (n.d.) and Schechner (1985).

6. See Herdt (1987:79).

7. Barbara Tedlock suggests this shift in her excellent overview of Western scholarly approaches to dreams (1987a:20–30).

8. This includes a large number of scholars, too many to list, whose work builds on the insights of John Gumperz and Dell Hymes in the tradition of the ethnography of speaking (Bauman and Sherzer 1989; Gumperz and Hymes 1964; Hymes 1974; Sherzer 1983), ethnopoetics (Hymes 1975, 1977, 1981); (D. Tedlock 1977, 1983), performance (for example, Bauman 1977; Brenneis 1978, 1986, 1987a; Briggs 1988; Caton 1990; Duranti 1986, 1988; Kuipers 1990), and more recent discourse-centered approaches (E. Basso, ed. 1990; Ochs 1988; Sherzer 1987; Urban 1991); as well as those who work in the tradition of the sociology of language using ethnomethodological approaches (Goodwin 1981; Goodwin and Goodwin 1992; Sacks, Schegloff, and Jefferson 1974; Schegloff 1972).

9. See Urban (1991:1).

10. See Silverstein (1976b); Urban (1991); also Singer (1984); Errington (1985).

11. According to Peirce (1931–58) three basic types of relationships may obtain between a sign and its object. When the relationship is one of physical similarity, the sign is said to be iconic. The sign is indexical if the relationship is one of spatio-temporal contiguity. When the connection between the sign and its object is based on a mental rule, then the sign is symbolic.

12. See, for example, Feld (1984); Roseman (1991).

13. See Schutz (1962) for a discussion of multiple social realities.

14. See Connerton (1989); Lipsitz (1990); Stoller (1992a, n.d.); Terdiman (1985).

15. See Schechner (1985:36).

16. Bauman (n.d.); also Kuipers (1990); Urban (n.d.).

17. See Bauman (n.d.: 1, ms.).

18. Vološinov (1973).

19. See, for example, Abu-Lughod (1986); Feld (1990); Lutz (1988); Narayan (1989); Stoller (1989).

20. See Maybury-Lewis (1974:253–254).

21. Issues of Xavante claims to land are discussed further in Chapter 2.

22. Warodi; David and Pia Maybury-Lewis, personal communications.

23. See for example, Da Matta (1982); Henry (1941); Seeger (1987); Urban (1991).

24. David Maybury-Lewis (1974) first mapped the major features of the Xavante's complex system of social organization, and Aracy Lopes da Silva (1986) further refined an anthropological understanding of Xavante social organization in her focused study of Xavante naming and the system of formal friends. Other studies that have contributed to knowledge about the Xavante are works by Oswaldo Ravagnani (1978), Nancy Flowers (1983), and Regina Müller (1976). Several descriptive studies have been completed by Salesian missionaries who worked among the Xavante (Giaccaria and Heide 1972, 1975a, 1975b; Guariglia 1973) and who have themselves been the subjects of anthropological study (Menezes 1985). A team from the Summer Institute of Linguistics also did initial work in descriptive linguistics (McLeod and Mitchell 1977) and has produced a Xavante dictionary (Hall, McLeod, and Mitchell 1987).

25. Studies carried out within the comparative framework of the Harvard Central Brazil project organized by David Maybury-Lewis demonstrated how each Gê society manifests distinct variations on the complex theme of intersecting dual systems. See papers in Maybury-Lewis (1979); also Bamberger (1967); Crocker (1985); Da Matta (1982); Lave (1967); Melatti (1970); Turner (1966). Subsequent studies among the Gê have further illustrated the principle of variation—for instance, in naming and ceremonial friendship systems (Carneiro da Cunha 1978; Ladeira 1982; Lea 1986; Lopes da Silva 1986).

26. See for example, Aytai (1985); Seeger (1979, 1980, 1987); Urban (1984, 1985a, 1991).

27. Kirin Narayan (1993:678) urges anthropologists to move beyond dichotomies of insider-outsider and examine how we are situated in relation to the people we study.

28. See Graham (1983).

29. See Sherzer and Urban (1986); also Hymes (1977); Sherzer (1979).

30. Cipassé and Jurandir are among the few Xavante who have completed secondary school. Owing to family obligations that necessitated his return to São Marcos, and to FUNAI personnel's unwillingness to adapt his work schedule to his course schedule, Lino has not yet completed the requirements for his secondary school degree.

31. Warner (1990).

32. See, for example, Culler (1975); Fish (1980); Rabinowitz (1987); Tompkins (1980).

33. See Stoller (1994; also 1992b).

CHAPTER 2

1. Out of fear of their miraculous powers, the Xavante killed the creators.

2. Maybury-Lewis (1974:48).

3. Etẽpa speaking of his sons and nephews in preparation for the dream performance.

4. For discussions of agent centricity in myth, see, for example, Hill, ed. (1988); also Urban (1991:29–57).

5. See Bauman and Briggs (1990).

6. Lopes da Silva (1992:362); Maybury-Lewis (1974:1). These earlier works note that colonial documents first locate the Xavante in "what is now the northern part of the state of Goiás." This region is now within a new state, Tocantins, which was created shortly after the passage of the 1988 constitution.

7. Maybury-Lewis (1974:2); Nimuendajú (1942:3–4).

8. Maybury-Lewis (1974:2).

9. Ravagnani (1978).

10. Lopes da Silva (1992:365).

11. Those interested in a more detailed summary of Xavante history may wish to consult Lopes da Silva's excellent account (1992), as well as works by Ravagnani (1978, 1987). See also Chaim (1974, 1983); Flowers (1983:67–145); Lazarin (1985); Lopes (1988); Maybury-Lewis (1974). Much of the information presented in this section is culled from these sources.

12. See also Giaccaria and Heide (1972:13n); Flowers (1983); Lopes da Silva (1992:362).

13. The name öwawẽ-ʔwa translates, according to Xavante assistants who glossed it this way, to "the one who made the sea." It can be morphologically segmented as follows: öwawẽ (sea, which can be further segmented as ö [water] and wawẽ [large]), and -ʔwa, agentive, "one who does or makes."

14. On the Pombaline legislation, see Chaim (1983:75–95); Carneiro da Cunha (1987:58–63), Karasch (1992), Perrone (1992).

15. For more information on Carretão, see Lazarin (1985). On the aldeamentos, see Ravagnani (1978:36); Chaim (1983:99–152); Lopes da Silva (1992:363–364).

16. Lopes da Silva (1992:364).

17. Lopes da Silva (1992:265).

18. Also see Giaccaria and Heide (1972:23); Lopes da Silva (1992:365, 1984); Lopes (1988:37 n. 21).

19. See, for example, E. Basso (1985); Hill (1988); R. Rosaldo (1980); Stoller (1989); Turner (1988). Ellen Basso's (1985) work on narrative as symbolic expression is particularly significant in this regard. She argues that discourse-focused analysis can result in more precise understanding of how events are interpreted within a causal framework. No easy contrast can be drawn between history and myth because all narratives are constructed by means of discourse elements and verbal images that are symbolic and imply others within a general worldview.

20. Ravagnani (1978:132).

21. Xavante working with Lopes da Silva identified this village as *ĩ-tsõrepre* (transcribed *ĩ-sõrepré*), a pronunciation which includes the third-person marker *ĩ*. I record the village's name as *tsõrepre*, henceforth Tsõrepre, following the usage in Pimentel Barbosa. Either pronunciation would be recognizable to Xavante speakers from any of the present communities.

22. See Giaccaria and Heide (1972:37); Lopes da Silva (1992:365–366).

23. Initiated at Tsõrepre were the age-sets *hötörã, aiʔrere, etẽpa, tirowa, nodzöʔu*. Warodi's father Apöwẽ was himself initiated with the *nodzöʔu* at this location.

24. Lopes da Silva (1992:367).

25. See Duroure and Carletti (1936); Lopes da Silva (1992:367); Maybury-Lewis (1974:3).

26. See Maybury-Lewis (1974:3).

27. Warodi's narration.

28. Warodi's narration.

29. It was also officially named the Rio das Mortes Indigenous Post.

30. Before moving to Pimentel Barbosa, they first settled in Baheira (from Portuguese *baheira*, "dam"), which was located directly across the river from Wededze. Several families claim to have maintained gardens at a place known as Ö tõ, also across the river from Wededze, even before the move to Baheira occurred. Although Maybury-Lewis (1974:28–29) observed during his 1962 visit that a number of Xavante from Wededze had relocated across the Rio das Mortes to Ö tõ, Xavante state that Baheira, not Ö tõ, was the site of their village. It is possible, however, that the name Baheira is now used to refer to the community Maybury-Lewis knew as Ö tõ.

31. See, for example, Maybury-Lewis (1974:21); Lopes da Silva (1992:369).

32. Maybury-Lewis (1974:6).

33. See Lopes da Silva (1986:30–44). This contrasts with the groupings Maybury-Lewis identified for the immediate postcontact period. He distinguished between two groups of Xavante, the Eastern and Western, principally on the basis of geographical location but also because of differences in some details of their social organization, such as the order of age-sets (Maybury-Lewis 1974:13–30, 161, 338).

34. See Lopes da Silva (1986) for a more detailed review of the histories of the second and third groups.

35. Menezes's work (1985) focuses specifically on the São Marcos Xavante and questions of missionary influence.

36. See also Maybury-Lewis's discussion of government neglect in land surveys (1974:8–9).

37. Fernando Schiavinni, personal communication.

38. Fernando Schiavinni, personal communication.

39. See CEDI (1991:510).

40. *Folha de São Paulo* 12/4/89, cited in CEDI (1991:510).

41. *Correio Braziliense* 11/2/90, cited in CEDI (1991:510).

42. Leeuwenberg (1991:4).

43. Leeuwenberg (1991:7).

44. Leeuwenberg (1991:22).

45. In the case of the bridal hunt, *da-batsa*, the pattern of distribution varies from the typical pattern. The groom gives his offering to the bride's mother, who in turn gives it to her brother, the bride's name giver (*tsorebzu-ʔwa*), who prepares her *tsorebzu* necklace and applies the body paint for her participation in the *adaba* wedding ceremony. The name giver turns the meat over to his wife or wives, who oversee its distribution.

46. I calculated conversions for the 1981–1982 fiscal year by taking an average of the quarterly exchange rates, assuming that the fiscal year runs from July 1981 to June 1982; using the *International Financial Statistics* (International Monetary Fund 1986), this figure is 128.975 cruzeiros/dollar. It is possible that the fiscal year for this budget ran from September 1981 to August 1982. In that case the quarterly average would be 151.475, making the U.S. figure $16,313.20.

47. Source: Ministry of the Interior, FUNAI Assessoria de Planejamento e Coordenação, Project Parabubure I, PI Kuluene. I was not able to obtain data for other reserves.

48. Lopes (1988:103–105).

49. For further discussion of Juruna, see Juruna with Hohlfeldt and Hoffman (1982).

50. Lopes da Silva (1992:376).

51. Lopes da Silva (1992:376).

52. In East Africa, where rice cultivation has supplanted the traditional cultivation of millet, similar nutritional problems have resulted (Paul Stoller, personal communication).

53. This information comes from Dr. Horácio Friedman of the University of Brasília, via Nancy Flowers (personal communication); see also Friedman et al. (1992).

54. Maybury-Lewis (1974:172–213).

55. Lopes da Silva (1986:49).

56. Reliable demographic data are unavailable subsequent to the 1984 census, after which many FUNAI posts were left either partially or totally unstaffed.

57. Missionary assistance in the area of health care, as well as in education, generally surpasses that of FUNAI. Since the mid-1980s, medical assistance in the Xavante areas has declined at an alarming rate.

58. See Graham (1987).

59. See Ramos (1988); Turner (1988).

60. *Correio Braziliense* 9/20/87.

61. CEDI (1991:511).

62. See *Folha de São Paulo* 1/30/90; *O Globo* 9/14/91.

63. Other Xavante leaders have also traveled abroad. In addition to Pastor Filipe and Romero from Kuluene, who traveled to the United States with church sponsorship, Benedito from Sangradouro has been to Japan campaigning for indigenous eco-rights (Miamoto 1990).

CHAPTER 3

1. See Gregor (1977) and Seeger (1987).

2. I take the notion of a twenty-four-hour cycle of sound, or soundscape, from the work of Steve Feld (1987, 1990:267) and his recording, *Voices in the Forest* (1988b).

3. The Xavante provide a counterexample to Turner's observation concerning the differential contributions of men's and women's labor to interfamilial levels of distribution in Gê societies (see Turner 1979a, especially pp. 154–155). In contrast to the pattern Turner describes, in which men contribute to interfamilial networks of distribution while women do not, Xavante women regularly distribute food to affines and, through ceremonial distributions, contribute food to others beyond their immediate kin and affines.

4. Austin (1962).

5. See Maybury-Lewis (1974).

6. See Radcliffe-Brown (1940).

7. Dixon (1979); see also Haviland (1979a, 1979b).

8. Turner (1979a, pp. 157–161 especially; also 1979b).

9. *Reme?õ* is the name the elders gave me when I returned to the village after being expelled. It means "don't let her go" or "don't throw her out" (*reme*, "to throw away, to throw out," *õ*, negative marker). I also continued to be called by the name I had received in Kuluene, *Reñipre* (red-headed parrot).

10. Given that person marking is an arena of the grammar that is particularly weighted in terms of its semantic load (person-marking particles indicate person and number as well as aspect and clause type [independent/dependent, affirmative/negative]), it is not surprising that it is singled out to perform a pragmatic function as well. Moreover, as Silverstein (1976b)—building on the observations of Roman Jakobson (1957)—points out, the inherently context-bound nature of person marking as a grammatical category suitably lends itself to functioning as a social index.

Honorific marking is a widespread linguistic pattern typically found in ranked or hierarchical societies (for example, Duranti 1992; Errington 1985; Luong 1984); but as Irvine points out (1992), the kinds of rank and power that are marked through honorifics vary from one system to another. Honorific marking has not been known to exist among lowland Amerindian groups. Honorifics, however, have been reported for Nahuatl by Jane Hill and Kenneth Hill (1978, 1980; also Buchler 1967; Buchler and Freeze 1966). The presence of an honorific system in a relatively acephalous society such as the Xavante is therefore unusual; however, it may be a phenomenon that is found in other societies (William Crocker, personal communication; Seeger 1981:125).

11. For more detailed information on Xavante honorifics, see Graham (1990).

12. Each of these song types is appropriate for different ceremonial events, and particular variants combine with different times of the year, either the rainy season or the dry season. The correlation between season, ceremonial life, and distinct types of song performance is a notable feature of singing in Gê societies, as has already been noted for the Xavante by Aytai (1985) and by Seeger for the Suyá (1981:71).

Readers interested in further descriptive discussion and classification of *da-ño?re* may wish to consult Aytai's pioneering study of Xavante music. In addition to classifying *da-ño?re* into the three types according to time of day, his classificatory scheme divides *da-ño?re* into various activities—for instance, songs related to economic activity, war, or other situational contexts. While the correlation between *da-ño?re* and type of activity is a significant observation, Aytai overlooks the fact that Xavante classify all of these activity-related songs within the three basic types.

Giaccaria and Heide (1972) and Maybury-Lewis (1974) also briefly mention *da-ño?re* in their ethnographic descriptions of Xavante social life. Subsequent research (Aytai 1985; Graham 1984, 1986) has elaborated and in some instances refined information offered in these initial discussions.

13. Among the Kaluli, singing can also move others to lament (Feld 1990).

14. See Urban (1988).

15. For discussion of the organization of social space in Gê societies, see, for example, Seeger (1981); also Carneiro da Cunha (1978); Da Matta (1982); Graham (1984, 1986).

16. Urban (1988, 1991); Briggs (1992a).

17. Data available on wailing in Xavante and other societies suggest an implicational universal that "in societies where ceremonial forms of keening are a male form of expression, they are also a mode of expression available to women" (Graham 1984:164, 1986:87).

18. See Sacks, Schegloff, and Jefferson (1974).

19. The intervocalic uvular fricative [ʁ], an allophonic free-variant for the alveolar tap /r/, is found in the speech of both men and women. However, in the Pimentel Barbosa Reserve, it appears more frequently in the speech of some women than it does in the speech of most men. Xavante from other reserves note this variant as a characteristic of Pimentel Barbosa speech, and they often use it when mocking the Pimentel Barbosa Xavante. It is doubtful that this could be interpreted as a status form or norm of prestige that reflects, in speech pragmatics, women's social consciousness (Labov 1966; Trudgill 1972) since it is infrequently found in the speech of influential individuals in Pimentel Barbosa or in the speech of Xavante from other reserves. In any case, there is no great prestige differential between individuals, although there is considerable rivalry between factions and among villages.

20. Women have their own distinctive dance movements in *da-ño?re* performance that differentiates their dance from that of men. Women stand with their legs locked tightly together and shuffle slightly forward and backward with each rhythmic beat. These movements are the same for all *da-ño?re*, so that unlike men's, women's movements do not differentiate between the three basic *da-ño?re* types.

21. According to senior men, distinctive calls are used in hunting to signal the spotting or downing of different species of game. Given the chaos of burning savannah, running, and general shouting during the trips I accompanied, I was not able to verify this. However, in story-telling, elder men imitate hunting calls which vary for different animals.

22. Discussion of these ceremonial offices can be found in Maybury-Lewis's description of the *tirowa* age-set's initiation (1974:115–137; also Giaccaria and Heide 1972:139, 162, 165). For further discussion of ceremonials surrounding the initiation, see Maybury-Lewis (1974:248–254).

23. *Aʔãma*, ceremonial parents to the collectivity of pre-initiates, appear to be a refraction of the Northern Gê pattern of ceremonial parents (Carneiro da Cunha 1978; Da Matta 1982; see Lopes da Silva 1986 for a comparative profile). The role also embodies aspects of clowning, a phenomenon prevalent in Northern Ge groups (see, for example, Nimuendajú 1967:30; also Seeger 1981:114–115), which is manifested through use of a linguistic variant known as *aʔãma mrɛmɛ* (*aʔãma* speech). *Aʔãma* speech consists of lexical substitution (see Graham 1990:107–111, n.d.; also Giaccaria and Heide 1972:141–143). The two linguistic variants *aʔãma mrɛmɛ* and the honorific system are inversely related with respect to variation of formal elements of the linguistic system.

24. For several months prior to the actual bestowal of names, the women to be named engage in sexual relations with their potential namers, men who are classificatory husbands. Then, in a ceremony in which the men enter the name receivers' homes to sing, the women are told several names their namers have dreamed; a woman must choose one of these. In 1986 I witnessed the public dimension of the ceremony's first phase, when women enter the men's council and choose their evening partners. Giaccaria and Heide (1972:221–235) describe the women's naming ceremony, omitting discussion of the extramarital liaisons. Mission villages were the first to abandon this ceremony, and it is likely that missionaries discouraged its practice. The women's naming ceremony is the only occasion I know of in which male singers actually enter individual houses to sing. In this respect it is reminiscent of the Suyá (Northern Gê) pattern of *ngere* singing (Seeger 1979).

25. Warodi and other Xavante call me *tsoimba*, an address term which is used for married girls without children.

26. Girls are considered to be members of the same age-set as boys their age; no ceremony, however, marks their formation.

27. *Wa-ñi-wĩm-hö* and *õ-ñi-wĩm-hö* are relational terms used to distinguish between agamous moieties only. The term *wa-ñi-wĩm-hö* is not used, as Maybury-Lewis mistakenly notes, with reference to exogamous moiety distinctions (1974: 167, for example). The terms *tsiʔre-ʔwa* (other) and *wa-tsiʔre-ʔwa* (our) label exogamous moiety distinctions. *Tsiʔre-ʔwa* can also be used to refer to members of the opposite agamous moiety.

28. In other societies such as the East African Mursi, age-sets operate in a similar fashion. According to David Turton (1978), Mursi society has continuously transformed its relationships to peoples and land in the process of northward migrations from southern Sudan into the Ethiopian highland. Its age-sets, Turton argues, have enabled Mursi to conceptualize themselves as an enduring social

group despite the metamorphoses activated by their migrations. The age-sets "shield the Mursi from the realization that their society is, by its very nature, ephemeral" (1978:128).

29. Seeger (1981:112).

30. See Turner (1979a) and Seeger (1981) for discussion of the differential nature of men's and women's participation in extradomestic corporate entities in Gê society.

31. Xavante translate ʔritaiʔwa as adolescent. I suspect that the label denotes the close association between members of this age grade and the prescription to remain at home, because the word can be morphologically segmented as follows: ʔri, (house); tai (?, untranslated); -ʔwa (agentive).

32. Maybury-Lewis (1974:148).

33. Seeger (1981:66).

34. For discussion of body ornamentation, see Müller (1976, 1992); Seeger (1975, 1981); Turner (1993); Vidal (1992). Seeger (1981) includes an excellent discussion of social space; see also Lévi-Strauss (1967[1963]).

35. Although Xavante who spoke about the wadzapariʔwa sometimes glossed them as ʔaʔuwẽ (Xavante people) or "those who live in the sierra," the word may be morphologically segmented as follows: wa (us); tsapari (to wait for); -ʔwa (agentive), suggesting that it may denote "those who wait for us."

36. Carneiro da Cunha (1978).

37. The only possible exception to this gendered division is Star Woman. However, in Xavante tellings of Star Woman, the protagonist is a male höimanaʔuʔö creator (see Graham 1983; Wilbert 1978:194-216).

CHAPTER 4

1. For discussion of the waiʔa, see Giaccaria and Heide (1972:181-210); Maybury-Lewis (1974:255-269); also Valadão (n.d.).

2. In 1982 Warodi and members of his family dramatized the Star Woman story. I analyze and discuss this performance elsewhere (Graham 1983).

3. When I understood the performance practice of repeating da-ñoʔre, I often intentionally recorded multiple repetitions of the same song. These recordings provide interesting information about the process of song learning; they reveal, for example, where people tend to make mistakes as part of the learning process. When I didn't realize what I was doing, and the Xavante knew I didn't, my hosts found my making multiple recordings extremely humorous.

4. Unlike the Kaluli, the Xavante neither compose nor engage in vocal performance to blend with natural sounds (see Feld 1987, 1988a).

5. From the Portuguese sonho (dream).

6. Maybury-Lewis (1974:105-106).

7. Residents of the bachelors' hut are known as hö-ʔwa in Xavante. The term is a complex noun, from hö (bachelors' hut) and -ʔwa (agentive).

8. Waptɛ pre-initiates as well as novitiate ʔritaiʔwa are supposed to show respect, particularly to women, by not looking at them.

9. I was unable to determine by what criteria a house was designated to have da-ñoʔre performed on its patio. I could detect no obvious pattern. It did not ap-

pear that the prestige of the household head was considered important. In Pimentel Barbosa, for example, dancers stopped at the house of a man who was generally considered to have a mental disability. In a few *da-ñoʔre* performances, such as the *da-ñoʔre* performed by the mature men prior to a ritual hunt, the dancers performed on the patios of houses where men did not usually perform. It may be that certain ceremonial songs are performed at houses that are not routinely on the itinerary of *waptɛ* or *ʔritaiʔwa* performances.

10. Jakobson (1960) was the first to systematically define the phenomenon of parallelism—repetition with variation—as a fundamental aesthetic of verbal art (see Caton 1987). In this discussion I include strict repetition as a type of parallelism, thereby differing somewhat from Jakobson's usage of the term as repetition with variation. For discussion of straight repetition as a form of parallelism, see Urban (1991, especially Chapter 5).

11. A few exceptional women claim to have dreamed *da-ñoʔre* during their youth.

12. As this remark suggests, it is also the case that Xavante tell dreams among intimates. During my field research I was present on several occasions when dream narratives were told informally within the household. A young man may share an account of his dream vision with his wife or other intimate friend but not with the age-set cohort as a whole. The relationship between tellings among intimates and public performance awaits future study.

13. It is a biological fact that all human beings dream and that the physiological activity experienced by the person "having the dream" is a uniquely individual experience which, to be shared, must be put into some culturally interpretable semiotic form (for a review of laboratory research on dreaming, see B. Tedlock (1987a:12–20). Nevertheless, it is conceivable, at least in theory, that through discourse the experience of a dream could be construed as involving more than one individual. To the best of my knowledge, no ethnographic accounts exist to date which suggest evidence of cultural representations of dreaming as shared experience. Even were such documentation found, reports would necessarily have to be considered at the level of metapragmatics. As it is presently understood, the phenomenon of dreaming occurs within an individual organism and may be considered as an *endo-semiotic* experience (Sebeok 1978).

14. See Herdt (1987); also Mannheim (1987).

15. Dorothy Eggan's pioneering remarks concerning the creative relationship between dreams and folklore (or "cultural provision"), although not focused on discursive practice or semiotic processes per se, prefigure a specific focus on the creative relationship between the expression of subjective experience and publicly circulating discursive practice (see Eggan 1955, 1966; also 1961).

16. See Vološinov (1973).

17. See Vološinov (1973:90).

18. See Price-Williams (1987).

19. Seeger reports a similar connection between "hearing" songs and sex among the Suyá (1981:108).

20. Only men from the *öwawẽ* moiety who belong to the *waiʔa dzöretsi-ʔwa* grade have the ability to dream *waiʔa-ñoʔre*.

21. Little boys, even toddlers, may be encouraged to join in some *da-ñoʔre*

performances. They are not expected, however, to make it through an entire set of singing around the village; their participation is considered amusing and entertaining. Nevertheless, the experience plays an important role in the youngsters' internalization of the form. It effectively extends the period of active internalization of the *da-ñoʔre* form beyond the *waptɛ* phase.

22. Members of the sponsor group may participate with their sponsored group even after the *waptɛ* have become *ʔritaiʔwa*. This is the case, for example, after the *uiwede* log races. The *tsimñohu* of novitiate *ʔritaiʔwa* show up less frequently for nocturnal performances, but occasionally when a man feels nostalgic, he may put in an appearance. In these instances the *ʔritaiʔwa* defer to their senior and perform his song rather than one of their own.

23. There are a few exceptions to this general rule. A number of songs that are specifically linked to certain ceremonies, such as the *uʔu*, are replicated as closely as possible in each performance.

24. See Seeger (1979).

25. Schechner (1985, especially Chapter 1) argues that the power to abolish a sense of individuality accumulates through repetition in performance.

26. According to Marina Roseman (1991, pp. 105–118 especially), features of Temiar dream-song performance operate in similar ways. Specifically, phrasal overlap and repetition act as leveling devices; they collapse the distinction between the roles of leader (spirit medium) and chorus (also see Feld 1984; Roseman 1984).

27. For discussion of Xavante body decoration, see Müller (1976, 1992).

28. See E. Basso (1985:6).

29. Instances in which a song's dreamer does not initiate performance are when the dreamer is dead or when a sponsored group sings the songs of its sponsors in performance without the sponsors.

30. See Urban (1986a).

31. See Graham (1984, 1986).

32. Also see Aytai (1985:55).

33. Also see Aytai (1985:79). For discussion of temporal and spatial parameters in music, see Zuckerkandl (1956) .

34. As Aytai (1985) has observed, it appears that some syllables and words occur with relative frequency in *da-ñoʔre* texts. Before conclusive statements can be made concerning possible regularities in *da-ñoʔre* texts, however, further investigation must be carried out. Regarding this particular text, the approximant [j] is an allophonic variant of the voiced affricate /dz/.

35. Forms of ceremonial dialogue, in contrast, formally demonstrate overt recognition of the "other" and, as Urban (1988) shows in the case of lowland South American societies, can be correlated with societies with permeable boundaries (see also Bowen 1989). The forms used in these societies contrast with those of societies which have relatively impermeable boundaries, where ceremonial wailing is practiced as a greeting form (see Urban 1986a).

36. See Hinton (1980).

37. The title *aihöbuni* is given at the time a group of boys is inducted into the bachelors' hut to one or more boys who are considered to be exceptionally mature and who belong to the *poridzaʔõno* exogamous moiety. *Aihöbuni* have their ears

pierced at this time, in contrast to the other members of their cohort, who have their ears pierced when they leave the bachelors' hut.

38. So far as I am able to distinguish, Xavante divide the continuum between waking and dreaming realities on the basis of sleep; I am not thus far aware of any notions of waking dreams. For discussion of the waking/sleeping dream continuum, see Price-Williams (1987).

39. Depending on the type of song he dreams, the individual will impart his composition to the members of his age-set at gatherings in the early morning, afternoon, or evening. Although I have never witnessed an instance in which a song was rejected, Aytai (1985:24–25) describes a ceremony in which elder men judge songs according to their merits for inclusion in important festivities. Although he does not specify which, if any, other formal elements may prompt a negative response, he notes that a weak voice or monotonous execution (which I take to mean lack of variation in volume) is likely to prejudice the elders against a song (1985:25). Aytai's experience that Xavante are unable to formulate the criteria for rejection accords with my own attempts to elicit aesthetic metacommentary. I have never witnessed the ceremony described by Aytai nor the rejection of a song and am therefore at present unable to further illuminate an understanding of Xavante aesthetics or criteria for acceptance of a song into a group repertoire.

40. See Urban (1988); also Briggs (1992a).

41. See Urban (1991:171).

42. See Urban (1991:171, 1986a); also E. Basso (1985).

43. I have also witnessed elders wailing in response to songs that were not composed by a relative but were performed by the age-set to which the individual belonged, when the relative was not present in the village. In such instances, the age-set's performance provoked the memory of the absent individual. Similar responses, where songs provoke others to weep, are described by Feld (1990) for the Kaluli.

44. See Urban (1988, 1991).

45. The only expressions of dissent came from adolescents, whom the elders chastise for their materialism, ignorance of Xavante customs, and affinity for the ways of the whites.

46. These deictic pronouns are discussed in Chapter 6.

47. It is unusual for the women to prepare for ceremonial participation in the *mará* forest clearing.

48. This is possibly a reference to the ancestral village of Tsõrepre.

CHAPTER 5

1. Babies who are born with light skin ("white babies") are considered to be beautiful and healthy; the expression does not refer to "white" as in "non-Xavante".

2. See Graham (1983). Such performances are not unheard of among Gê groups; the Apinajé, for example, engage in ritual performances that act out myths (Nimuendajú 1967:177).

3. The language ideology expressed in Western philosophy of language can by no means be taken to represent all Western ideologies of discourse.

4. Habermas (1984, 1987).

5. See Roger (1985:205).

6. Searle (1969:21).

7. See Searle (1969); also Gumperz and Hymes (1964); Hymes (1962).

8. For discussions of language, the law, and courtroom proceedings, see O'Barr (1982) and Philips (1984).

9. See, for example, Briggs (1992a, 1992b); Du Bois (1987); Duranti (1988); Hancher (1979); Keane (1991); M. Rosaldo (1982).

10. See Sacks, Schegloff, and Jefferson (1974); Schegloff and Sacks (1973); and more recently, among others, Goodwin (1981); Testa (1988).

11. See Keane (1991).

12. See Du Bois (1987) and Duranti (1988).

13. M. Rosaldo (1984).

14. Bakhtin (1981:292); see also Briggs (1992a, 1992b); Duranti (1988); Vološinov (1973).

15. Warner (1990).

16. For explicit statements on instances of discourse as semiotic phenomena, see Urban (1991) and Silverstein (1976b).

17. See for example, Abrahams (1970, 1983); Albert (1964); Caton (1986); French and Kernan (1981); Irvine (1989); Labov (1972); Strathern (1975).

18. See Comaroff (1975); Bauman and Sherzer (1989).

19. See Turton (1975).

20. See Bailey (1981); Bloch (1975); Salmond (1975).

21. See Lederman (1984); Myers (1986).

22. See Bauman (1970, 1983, 1989).

23. Bauman (1989:145).

24. Bauman (1989:153).

25. Warner (1990:42).

26. Warner (1990:39).

27. See, for example, Atkinson (1984); Brenneis (1984a, 1984b, 1987b); French and Kernan (1981); Keenan (1973); McKellin (1984); Murphy (1981); M. Rosaldo (1973, 1984); Sapir and Crocker (1977); Strathern (1975).

28. See, for example, Irvine (1989); Myers (1986).

29. Brenneis and Myers (1984); Myers (1986).

30. M. Rosaldo (1984:132).

31. Strathern (1975:193).

32. See Brenneis (1984b, 1986, 1987a, 1987b, 1988); also Duranti (1986, 1988); Feld (1988a).

33. Brenneis (1987a:242).

34. Brenneis (1987a:242).

35. Brenneis (1988:281).

36. See also Duranti (1988).

37. See Brenneis and Myers (1984).

38. The term *warã* refers both to the place where the meeting takes place—the village center—and the meeting itself.

39. One's body position at public meetings is significant to the Xavante. Ma-

ture men may lie down, whereas *waptε* (pre-initiates) and *ʔritaiʔwa* (novitiates) are supposed to sit up.

40. So that they can play soccer in the afternoon, novitiates are now exempted from a prohibition against entering the village center during the day.

41. Maybury-Lewis (1974:143).

42. See Warner (1990:73–96).

43. Maybury-Lewis (1974:146).

44. Maybury-Lewis (1974:143).

45. Etẽpa also adds a focusing device, *hã*, which does not alter the meaning.

46. Warodi uses this expression to indicate that it is the hunting season.

47. Maybury-Lewis (1974:144–146).

48. See Urban (1985a, 1986b).

49. See Brenneis (1978, 1986, 1987b); Duranti (1986, 1988).

50. See Sacks, Schegloff, and Jefferson (1974).

51. The fact that Sibupa is an *aiʔrere* appears to be a coincidence, since Sibupa frequently performed as an elder *poridzaʔõno* in dialogues with *öwawẽ* of various age-sets.

52. See Urban (1986b).

53. See Fock (1963); Rivière (1971); Sherzer (1983:72–109); Urban (1985a, 1986a).

54. See Urban (1986a).

55. Following Urban (1985a), I define speech style as a multifunctional, complex signal that can be distinguished as a "type," as opposed to actual instances or "tokens" of usage. As a multifunctional signal, a speech style can transmit semantico-referential meaning (Silverstein 1976b) as well as communicate via indexical and iconic sign modes.

56. See Graham (1984, 1986).

57. See List (1963).

58. According to a phonological rule, the noun *wapru* becomes *waprui* when followed by the morpheme *-re* (with).

59. See Myers (1986); also Bloch (1975).

60. See Holquist (1983).

61. Bakhtin (1981:299).

62. See Du Bois (1987); Duranti (1988); M. Rosaldo (1982).

63. Examples of narratives performatively accomplishing referentially stated objectives can be found in reported speech (see Janowitz 1985; Urban 1984).

64. Lévi-Strauss (1973 [1955]: 298).

65. It is interesting to compare the Xavante's use of tape-recording with that of the Yemeni tribesmen Steve Caton describes. According to Caton (1990:265), the tape recorders motivate new compositions of a certain genre (*qasidah*) which are valued for the final linguistic result or product of the act of composition; tape recorders also facilitate the sharing of compositions across distances (1990:62–65; 218–220). Among the Xavante, tape recorders themselves have not been taken up in a way that stimulates aesthetic production. However, many people enjoy listening to tape-recorded *da-ñoʔre* performances inside their homes—particularly amorous youths, as discussed in Chapter 3.

CHAPTER 6

1. Baxter and Almagor (1978) suggest that the spiritual prestige, or sacredness, of senior members is a characteristic of age-set societies.

2. See Lopes da Silva (1986).

3. Women's naming practices operate according to entirely different principles. Rather than emphasizing social ties and continuity over time, female names celebrate a woman's physical body in present time. See Lopes da Silva (1986) for further discussion of the differences between men's and women's naming.

4. This is a point Roberto Da Matta makes for Apinajé names (1982:75).

5. Lopes da Silva (1986:84).

6. Similar presentations are made by public dream sharers in many Amerindian societies (see, for example, Crocker 1985; Kracke 1987:33; B. Tedlock 1987b:115, 127).

7. Using the terminology of the ethnography of speaking, these metadiscursive phrases "key" portions of the narrative as the immortals' speech. The notion of "keying" (Hymes 1974) grows out of Goffman's discussion of frame (1974); see also Bateson (1955).

8. Literally, the owners or trustees of the *wamarĩ*, a type of wood that, when placed above a man's head at night, enables him to have clear and powerful dream communication with the immortal creators.

9. The *ɔiʔɔ* fight (see Maybury-Lewis 1974:107–108; 240–244; also Giaccaria and Heide 1972:133). In using this expression Warodi means those who are the strongest and the bravest.

10. Xavante use down from the vulture, *urubu rei*, for this decoration.

11. Urban (1989:44).

12. Lines 5–12, 14, 19–20, 24, 26, 38–42, and 44 are direct quotes. In the excerpt, spaces between lines differentiate speakers' voices and separate dialogue from descriptive statements.

13. See Goffman (1974).

14. Lines 1–4, 13, 15–18, 21–23, 25, 27–28, 30, 32–37, and 43 are descriptive or metanarrative statements.

15. See lines 21, 22, 27, 32, 33, and 43.

16. Whorf discusses the collectivizing properties of such quotative devices (1956:119).

17. See Benveniste (1971a, 1971b); also Singer (1984).

18. See Silverstein (1976b).

19. See Silverstein (1976b); also Jakobson (1957, 1971). For discussions of spatial deictics, see Hanks (1990).

20. Urban (1989).

21. Features of the speech style that promote entry into this trancelike state share similarities with musical features that Rouget identifies as typical to trance (1985).

22. While neither Xavante nor Xokleng tellers are possessed by individual or distinct spirits per se, the notion that an individual comes to embody another while in a trancelike state suggests some similarities with spirit possession else-

where. However, unlike trance situations in which others help to create the appropriate conditions for an individual's possession, among the Xokleng and Xavante, the appropriate conditions for trance are largely created through an individual's speech. For an overview of the anthropological literature on and approaches to spirit possession, see Stoller (1992a, pp. 54–60 especially).

23. The collective genitive marker *da-* is also used in honorific marking.

24. In non-honorific speech, "his work" would be *ĩ-tsimi-romhuri*.

25. See Schechner (1985:4–14).

26. See Schechner (1985).

CHAPTER 7

1. I take the notion of "breakthrough" into telling from Hymes's "Breakthrough into Performance" (1975:79–141).

2. See Schechner (1985, pp. 11–12 especially) for discussion of the power of repetition to accumulate performance energies and effect transformations (or "transportations"). See also Trisha Brown's discussion of the power of repetition in dance (1975:29, cited in Schechner 1985:11).

3. I thank T. M. Scruggs for pointing this out to me. Warodi's subjective state, in which he integrated the world of the creators with that of his present self, is qualitatively different from the state of spirit possession and what is known as shamanistic trance. In the former, a spirit presence displaces the medium's self-identity, whereas in the latter, the shaman incorporates into himself a spirit essence which displaces his own self. See Rouget (1985) for a comparison of these two types of trance.

4. Guarana Champagne is a Brazilian soda pop made from the bark of an Amazonian tree.

5. *Da-tɔ* (*da-*, collective genitive; *tɔ*, play or game) can be glossed as "play" or "game." The homonym, *da-tɔ* (*da-*, collective genitive; *tɔ*, eye), "a person's eye" or "eye," explains Maybury-Lewis's mistaken understanding that the Xavante name for ceremonies describes a thing to be looked at.

6. Artaud (1958).

7. Greg Urban and Janet Hendricks (1983) make this point in a discussion of the interpretation of abstract masks in Amazonia.

8. This passage is excerpted from one of Warodi's tellings of the creation of the sea and the whites, not from the dream narrative.

9. As Sibupa pointed out, in some tellings the mythological protagonists are not *waptɛ* but boys (*airepudu*) who act like *waptɛ*.

10. Because the creators the Xavante remember are all male, women can never achieve the status of *höimanaʔuʔö*. Even the protagonist in the tale of Star Woman, who bestowed heavenly gifts upon the earth, was a *waptɛ* (see Graham 1983).

References

Abrahams, Roger
1970   Patterns of Performance in the British West Indies. In *Afro-American Anthropology: Contemporary Perspectives*, N. Whitten and J. Szwed, eds., pp. 163–179. New York: Free Press.
1983   *The Man-of-Words in the West Indies: Performance and the Emergence of Creole Culture*. Baltimore: Johns Hopkins University Press.
Abu-Lughod, Lila
1986   *Veiled Sentiments: Honor and Poetry in a Bedouin Society*. Berkeley: University of California Press.
Albert, Ethel
1964   "Rhetoric," "Logic," and "Poetics" in Burundi: Culture Patterning of Speech Behavior. *American Anthropologist* 66(6):35–54.
Artaud, Antonin
1958   *The Theater and Its Double*. Translated by Mary Caroline Richards. New York: Grove Press.
Atkinson, Jane M.
1984   "Wrapped Words": Poetry and Politics among the Wana of Central Sulawese, Indonesia. In *Dangerous Words: Language and Politics in the Pacific*, D. L. Brenneis and F. R. Myers, eds., pp. 33–68. New York: New York University Press.
Austin, John
1962   *How To Do Things with Words*. Oxford: Clarendon Press.
Aytai, Desidério
1985   *O mundo sonoro Xavante*. Coleção Museu Paulista, Etnologia, vol. 5. São Paulo: Universidade de São Paulo.
Bailey, Frederick G.
1981   Dimensions of Rhetoric in Conditions of Uncertainty. In *Politically Speaking: Cross-Cultural Studies of Rhetoric*, R. Paine, ed., pp. 25–40. Philadelphia: Institute for the Study of Human Issues.
Bakhtin, Mikhail M.
1981   Discourse in the Novel. In *The Dialogic Imagination: Four Essays by M. M. Bakhtin*, Michael Holquist, ed., pp. 259–422. Translated by C. Emerson and M. Holquist. Austin: University of Texas Press.

Bamberger, Joan
1967   Environment and Cultural Classification: A Study of Northern Kayapó. Ph.D. dissertation, Harvard University.
Basso, Ellen
1985   *A Musical View of the Universe: Kalapalo Myth and Ritual Performances.* Philadelphia: University of Pennsylvania Press.
1990   Introduction: Discourse as an Integrating Concept in Anthropology and Folklore Research. In *Native Latin American Cultures through Their Discourse*, Ellen Basso, ed., pp. 3–10. Bloomington, Ind.: Special Publications of the Folklore Institute.
Basso, Ellen, ed.
1990   *Native Latin American Cultures through Their Discourse.* Bloomington, Ind.: Special Publications of the Folklore Institute.
Basso, Keith
1970   "To Give Up on Words": Silence in Western Apache Culture. *Southwestern Journal of Anthropology* 26:213–230.
Bateson, Gregory
1955   A Theory of Play and Fantasy. American Psychiatric Research Reports II, pp. 39–51. Reprinted in *Steps to an Ecology of Mind: Collected Essays in Anthropology.* San Francisco: Chandler Publishing Co., 1972.
Bauman, Richard
1970   Aspects of Quaker Rhetoric. *Quarterly Journal of Speech* 56:67–74.
1977   *Verbal Art as Performance.* Rowley, Mass.: Newbury House. Reprinted by Waveland Press, 1984.
1983   *Let Your Words Be Few: Symbolism of Speaking and Silence among Seventeenth-Century Quakers.* Cambridge: Cambridge University Press.
1989   Speaking in the Light: The Role of the Quaker Minister. In *Explorations in the Ethnography of Speaking*, second edition, R. Bauman and J. Sherzer, eds., pp. 144–160. Cambridge: Cambridge University Press.
n.d.   Transformation of the Word in the Production of Mexican Festival Drama. In *Natural Histories of Discourse*, G. Urban and M. Silverstein, eds. Chicago: University of Chicago Press, forthcoming.
Bauman, Richard, and Charles Briggs
1990   Poetics and Performance as Critical Perspectives on Language and Social Life. *Annual Review of Anthropology* 19:59–88.
Bauman, Richard, and Joel Sherzer, eds.
1989   *Explorations in the Ethnography of Speaking*, second edition. Cambridge: Cambridge University Press.
Baxter, Paul, and Uri Almagor
1978   Introduction. In *Age, Generation and Time: Some Features of East African Age Organizations*, Paul Baxter and Uri Almagor, eds., pp. 1–35. London: C. Hurst and Company.
Benveniste, Emile
1971a   The nature of pronouns. *Problems in General Linguistics*, translated by M. E. Meek, pp. 217–222. Miami: University of Miami Press. Originally published in *For Roman Jakobson*, M. Halle, H. G. Lunt, H. McLean, and C. H. van Schooneveld, eds., pp. 34–37. The Hague, 1956.

1971b Subjectivity in Language. *Problems in General Linguistics*, translated by M. E. Meek, pp. 223–230. Miami: University of Miami Press. Originally published as De la subjectivité dans le langage, *Journal de Psychologie* 55, July–September, 1958.

Bloch, Maurice

1975 Introduction. In *Political Language and Oratory in Traditional Society*, M. Bloch, ed., pp. 1–28. London: Academic Press.

Bowen, John

1989 Poetic Duels and Political Change in the Gayo Highlands of Sumatra. *American Anthropologist* 91(1):25–40.

Brenneis, Donald

1978 The Matter of Talk: Political Performances in Bhatgaon. *Language in Society* 7:159–170.

1984a Straight Talk and Sweet Talk: Political Discourse in an Occasionally Egalitarian Community. In *Dangerous Words: Language and Politics in the Pacific*, D. L. Brenneis and F. R. Myers, eds., pp. 69–84. New York: New York University Press.

1984b Grog and Gossip in Bhatgaon: Style and Substance in Fiji Indian Conversation. *American Ethnologist* 11:487–506.

1986 Shared Territory: Audience, Indirection, and Meaning. *Text* 6(3):339–347.

1987a Performing Passions: Aesthetics and Politics in an Occasionally Egalitarian Community. *American Ethnologist* 14:236–250.

1987b Talk and Transformation. *Man* 22:499–510.

1988 Telling Troubles: Narrative, Conflict and Experience. *Anthropological Linguistics* 30(3/4):279–291.

Brenneis, Donald, and Fred Myers, eds.

1984 Introduction. In *Dangerous Words: Language and Politics in the Pacific*, D. L. Brenneis and F. R. Myers, eds., pp. 1–29. New York: New York University Press.

Briggs, Charles L.

1988 *Competence in Performance: The Creativity of Tradition in Mexicano Verbal Art*. Philadelphia: University of Pennsylvania Press.

1992a "Since I Am a Woman, I Will Chastise My Relatives": Gender, Reported Speech, and the (Re)production of Social Relations in Warao Ritual Wailing. *American Ethnologist* 19(2):337–361.

1992b Linguistic Ideologies and the Naturalization of Power in Warao Discourse. *Pragmatics* 2(3):387–404.

Brown, Roger, and Albert Gilman

1960 The Pronouns of Power and Solidarity. In *Style in Language*, T. A. Sebeok, ed., pp. 253–276. Cambridge, Mass.: MIT Press.

Brown, Trisha

1975 Three Pieces. *Drama Review* 17(3):37–51.

Buchler, Ira

1967 The Analysis of Pronominal Systems: Nahuatl and Spanish. *Anthropological Linguistics* 9(5):37–43.

Buchler, Ira, and R. Freeze
1966   The Distinctive Features of Pronominal Systems. *Anthropological Linguistics* 8(8):78–105.

Carneiro da Cunha, Manuela
1978   *Os mortos e os outros.* São Paulo: Hucitec.
1987   Terra indígena: História da doutrina e da legislação. In *Os direitos do indio: Ensaios e documentos,* Manuela Carneiro da Cunha, ed., pp. 53–101. São Paulo: Editora Brasiliense.

Carneiro da Cunha, Manuela, ed.
1987   *Os direitos do indio: Ensaios e documentos.* São Paulo: Editora Brasiliense.

Caton, Steve
1986   Salam Tahiyah: Greetings from the Highlands of Yemen. *American Ethnologist* 13:290–308.
1987   Contributions of Roman Jakobson. *Annual Review of Anthropology* 16:223–260.
1990   *"Peaks of Yemen I Summon": Poetry as Cultural Practice in a North Yemeni Tribe.* Berkeley: University of California Press.

CEDI (Centro Ecumênico de Documentação e Informação)
1991   *Povos indígenas no Brasil 1987/88/89/90.* Aconteceu Especial 18, Carlos A. Ricardo, coordinator and general editor. São Paulo: CEDI.

Chaim, Marivone M.
1974   *Os aldeamentos indígenas na capitania de Goiáis: Sua importância na política de povoamento (1749–1811).* Goiânia: Oriente.
1983   *Os aldeamentos indígenas (Goiáis 1749–1811),* second edition. São Paulo: Nobel; Pró-Memória, Instituto Nacional do Livro.

Comaroff, John
1975   Talking Politics: Oratory and Authority in a Tswana Chiefdom. In *Political Language and Oratory in Traditional Society,* Maurice Bloch, ed., pp. 141–161. London: Academic Press.

Connerton, Paul
1989   *How Societies Remember.* Cambridge: Cambridge University Press.

Crocker, Jon C.
1985   *Vital Souls: Bororo Cosmology, Natural Symbolism, and Shamanism.* Tucson: University of Arizona Press.

Culler, Jonathan
1975   *Structuralist Poetics.* Ithaca, N.Y.: Cornell University Press.

Da Matta, Roberto
1982   *A Divided World: Apinayé Social Structure.* Translated by Alan Campbell. Cambridge, Mass.: Harvard University Press. Originally published in Portuguese under the title *Um mundo divido: A estrutura social dos índios Apinayé.* Petropolis: Vozes, 1976.

de Lery, Jean
1990   *History of a Voyage to the Land of Brazil.* Translated and Introduced by Janet Whatley. Berkeley and Los Angeles: University of California Press.

Dixon, R. M. W.

1972   *The Djirbal Language of North Queensland*. Cambridge: Cambridge University Press.

1979   Ergativity. *Language* 55(1):59–138.

Du Bois, John

1987   Meaning without Intention: Lessons from Divination. *Papers in Pragmatics* 1(2):80–122.

Duranti, Alessandro

1986   The Audience as Co-author. *Text* 6(3):239–247.

1988   Intentions, Language, and Social Action in a Samoan Context. *Journal of Pragmatics* 12:13–33.

1992   Language in Context and Language as Context: The Samoan Respect Vocabulary. In *Rethinking Context: Language as an Interactive Phenomenon*, A. Duranti and C. Goodwin, eds., pp. 79–99. Cambridge: Cambridge University Press.

Duroure, Jean, and Ernest Carletti

1936   *Sur la fleuve de la mort*. Paris: Emmanuel Vitte.

Eggan, Dorothy

1955   The Personal Use of Myth in Dreams. *Journal of American Folklore* 68 (270):445–453.

1961   Dream Analysis. In *Studying Personality Cross-Culturally*, Bert Kaplan, ed. Evanston, Ill.: Row, Peterson, and Company.

1966   Hopi Dreams in Cultural Perspective. In *The Dream and Human Societies*, G. E. Von Grunebaum and Roger Caillois, eds., pp. 237–265. Berkeley and Los Angeles: University of California Press; London: Cambridge University Press.

Errington, Joseph J.

1985   On the Nature of the Sociolinguistic Sign: Describing the Javanese Speech Levels. In *Semiotic Mediation: Sociocultural and Psychological Perspectives*, Elizabeth Mertz and Richard J. Parmentier, eds., pp. 287–310. New York: Academic Press.

Feld, Steven

1984   Sound Structure and Social Structure. *Ethnomusicology* 28(3):383–409.

1987   Dialogic Editing: Interpreting How Kaluli Read *Sound and Sentiment*. *Cultural Anthropology* 2(2):190–210.

1988a   Aesthetics as Iconicity of Style, or "Lift-Up-Over Sounding": Getting into the Kaluli Groove. *Yearbook for Traditional Music* 20:74–113.

1988b   Voices in the Forest: A Papua New Guinea Soundscape. *Yearbook for Traditional Music* vol. 20, part 2, side B.

1990   *Sound and Sentiment: Birds, Weeping, Poetics, and Song in Kaluli Expression*, second edition. Philadelphia: University of Pennsylvania Press.

Fish, Stanley

1980   *Is There a Text in This Class?* Cambridge, Mass.: Harvard University Press.

Flowers, Nancy
1983   Forager-Farmers: The Xavante Indians of Central Brazil. Ph.D. dissertation, City University of New York.

Fock, Neils
1963   *Waiwai: Religion and Society of an Amazonian Tribe.* Copenhagen: National Museum.

Folha de São Paulo
1990   Indios têm projeto para exportar frutas. January 30, section G-6.

French, Robert, and Keith T. Kernan
1981   Art and Artifice in Belizean Creole. *American Ethnologist* 8:238–258.

Friedman, Horácio, Carlos Coimbra, Jr., Rosicler Alvarez, Iphis Campbell, Luiz Diaz, Nancy Flowers, Ricardo Santos, Maria Bertoli, Glória Gama, and Monica Alcalá
1992   Pênfigo foliáceo endêmico (fogo selvagem) no grupo indígena Xavánte, Mato Grosso, Brasil (Endemic phemphigus foliaceus among the Xavánte Indians, State of Mato Grosso, Brazil). *Cadernos de Saúde Pública* 8(3): 331–334.

Giaccaria, B., and A. Heide
1972   *Xavante: Povo autêntico.* São Paulo: Dom Bosco.
1975a   *Jerônimo conta.* Campo Grande, Mato Grosso: Publicação no. 1 da Casa da Cultura.
1975b   *Jerônimo sonha.* Campo Grande, Mato Grosso: Publicação no. 2 da Casa da Cultura.

Goffman, Erving
1974   *Frame Analysis.* New York: Harper and Row.

Goodwin, Charles
1981   *Conversational Organization: Interaction between Speakers and Hearers.* New York: Academic Press.

Goodwin, Charles, and Marjorie H. Goodwin
1992   Assessments and the Construction of Context. In *Rethinking Context: Language as an Interactive Phenomenon,* A. Duranti and C. Goodwin, eds., pp. 151–189. Cambridge: Cambridge University Press.

Graham, Laura
1983   Performance Dynamics and Social Dimensions in Xavante Narrative: *Höimanaʔuʔö Wasuʔu.* M.A. thesis, University of Texas at Austin.
1984   Semanticity and Melody: Parameters of Contrast in Shavante Vocal Expression. *Latin American Music Review* 5(2):161–185.
1986   Three Modes of Shavante Vocal Expression: Wailing, Collective Singing, and Political Oratory. In *Native South American Discourse,* Joel Sherzer and Greg Urban, eds., pp. 83–118. Berlin: Mouton de Gruyter.
1987   Uma aldeia por um "projeto." *Povos indígenas no Brasil—85/86.* Aconteceu Especial 17, pp. 348–350. São Paulo: CEDI.
1990   *The Always Living: Discourse and the Male Lifecycle of the Xavante Indians.* Ph.D. dissertation, University of Texas at Austin.
n.d.   Putting the ʔaʔãma in context. Unpublished paper. Department of Anthropology, University of Texas at Austin.

Gregor, Thomas
1977 *Mehinaku: The Drama of Everyday Life in a Brazilian Indian Village.* Chicago: University of Chicago Press.
Guariglia, G.
1973 *Gli Xavante in fase acculturativa: Vita e pensiero.* Milan: Universitá Cattolica del Sacro Cuore.
Gumperz, John J., and Dell Hymes, eds.
1964 *The Ethnography of Communication.* Washington, D.C.: American Anthropological Association.
Habermas, Jürgen
1984 *The Theory of Communicative Action. Vol. 1: Reason and the Rationalization of Society.* Translated by T. McCarthy. Boston: Beacon Press.
1987 *The Theory of Communicative Action. Vol. 2: Lifeworld and System: A Critique of Functionalist Reason.* Translated by T. McCarthy. Boston: Beacon Press.
Hall, Joan, Ruth A. McLeod, and Valerie Mitchell
1987 *Pequeno dicionário: Xavánte-Portuguese/Portuguese-Xavánte.* Brasília: Summer Institute of Linguistics.
Hancher, Michael
1979 The Classification of Cooperative Illocutionary Acts. *Language in Society* 8:1–14.
Hanks, William
1990 *Referential Practice.* Chicago: University of Chicago Press.
Haviland, John
1979a How To Talk To Your Brother-in-Law in Guugu Yimidhirr. In *Languages and Their Speakers,* Timothy Shopen, ed., pp. 161–239. Cambridge, Mass.: Winthrop.
1979b Guugu Yimidhirr Brother-in-Law Language. *Language in Society* 8:365–393.
Henry, Jules
1941 *Jungle People: A Kaingáng Tribe of the Highlands of Brazil.* New York: Vintage Books.
Herdt, Gilbert
1987 Selfhood and Discourse in Sambia Dream Sharing. In *Dreaming: Anthropological and Psychological Interpretations,* Barbara Tedlock, ed., pp. 105–131. Cambridge: Cambridge University Press.
Hill, Jane H., and Kenneth C. Hill
1978 Honorific Usage in Modern Nahuatl: The Expression of Social Distance and Respect in the Nahuatl of the Malinche Volcano Area. *Language* 54(1):123–155.
1980 Mixed Grammar, Purist Grammar, and Language Attitudes in Modern Nahuatl. *Language in Society* 9:321–348.
Hill, Jonathan D.
1988 Introduction. In *Rethinking History and Myth: Indigenous South American Perspectives on the Past,* Jonathan D. Hill, ed., pp. 1–17. Urbana and Champagne: University of Illinois Press.

Hill, Jonathan D., ed.
1988   *Rethinking History and Myth: Indigenous South American Perspectives on the Past*. Urbana and Champagne: University of Illinois Press.
Hinton, Leanne
1980   Vocables in Havasupai Song. In *Southwestern Indian Ritual Drama*, C. Frisbie, ed., pp. 83–118. Albuquerque: University of New Mexico Press.
Holquist, Michael
1983   The Politics of Representation. *Quarterly Newsletter of the Laboratory of Comparative Human Cognition* 5(1):2–9.
Hymes, Dell
1962   The Ethnography of Speaking. In *Anthropology and Human Behavior*, T. Gladwin and W. C. Sturtevant, eds., pp. 13–53. Washington, D.C.: Anthropological Society of Washington.
1974   *Foundations in Sociolinguistics: An Ethnographic Approach*. Philadelphia: University of Pennsylvania Press.
1975   Breakthrough into Performance. In *"In Vain I Tried To Tell You": Essays in Native American Ethnopoetics*. Philadelphia: University of Pennsylvania Press. Reprinted in *Folklore: Performance and Communication*, Dan Ben-Amos and Kenneth S. Goldstein, eds., pp. 11–74. The Hague: Mouton, 1981.
1977   Discovering Oral Performance and Measured Verse in American Indian Narrative. *New Literary History* 8:431–457.
1981   *"In Vain I Tried To Tell You": Essays in Native American Ethnopoetics*. Philadelphia: University of Pennsylvania Press.
International Monetary Fund
1986   *International Financial Statistics*. Washington, D.C.: International Monetary Fund.
Irvine, Judith
1989   Strategies of Status Manipulations in the Wolof Greeting. In *Explorations in the Ethnography of Speaking*, second edition. R. Bauman and J. Sherzer, eds., pp. 167–191. Cambridge: Cambridge University Press.
1992   Ideologies of Honorific Language. *Pragmatics* 2(3):251–262.
Jakobson, Roman
1957   *Shifters, Verbal Categories, and the Russian Verb*. Cambridge, Mass.: Harvard University Russian Language Project.
1960   Concluding Statement: Linguistics and Poetics. In *Style in Language*, Thomas A. Sebeok, ed., pp. 350–377. Cambridge, Mass.: MIT Press.
1971   *Selected Writings, Volume II*. The Hague: Mouton.
Janowitz, Naomi
1985   *The Poetics of Ascent: Theories of Language in a Rabbinic Ascent Text*. Albany: State University of New York Press.
Juruna, Mario, with Antonio Hohlfeldt and Assis Hoffman
1982   *O gravador do Juruna*. Porto Alegre: Mercado Aberto Editora e Propaganda Ltda.

Karasch, Mary

1992   Catequese e cativero: Política indigenista em Goiás 1780–1889. In *História dos índios no Brasil*, Manuela Carneiro da Cunha, ed., pp. 397–412. São Paulo: Editora Schwarcz Ltda.

Keane, Webb

1991   Delegated Voice: Ritual Speech, Risk, and the Making of Marriage Alliances in Anakalang. *American Ethnologist* 18:311–330.

Keenan, Elinor

1973   A Sliding Sense of Obligatoriness: The Polystructure of Malagasy Oratory. *Language in Society* 2:225–243.

Kracke, Waud

1987   Myths in Dreams, Thought in Images: An Amazonian Contribution to the Psychoanalytic Theory of Primary Process. In *Dreaming: Anthropological and Psychological Interpretations*, Barbara Tedlock, ed., pp. 31–54. Cambridge: Cambridge University Press.

Kuipers, Joel

1990   *Power in Performance: The Creation of Textual Authority in Weyewa Ritual Speech*. Philadelphia: University of Pennsylvania Press.

Labov, William

1966   The Social Stratification of English in New York City. Washington, D.C.: Center for Applied Linguistics. Reprinted, with some changes, under the title, The Social Stratification of (r) in New York City, in Labov, *Sociolinguistic Patterns*, pp. 43–69. Philadelphia: University of Pennsylvania Press, 1972.

1972   *Language in the Inner City: Studies in the Black English Vernacular*. Philadelphia: University of Pennsylvania Press.

Ladeira, Maria Elise

1982   A troca de nomes e a troca de cônjuges: Uma contribuição ao estudo de parentesco timbira. M.A. thesis, University of São Paulo.

Lave, Jean

1967   Social Taxonomy among the Krĩkati (Gê) of Central Brazil. Ph.D. dissertation, Harvard University.

Lazarin, Rita Heloisa de Almeida

1985   O aldeamento do Carretão: Duas histórias. M.A. thesis, Department of Anthropology, University of Brasília.

Lea, Vanessa

1986   Nomes e nekrets Kayapó, uma concepção de riqueza. Ph.D. dissertation, Museu Nacional/Federal University of Rio de Janeiro.

Lederman, Rena

1984   Who Speaks Here? Formality and the Politics of Gender in Mendi, Highland Papua New Guinea. In *Dangerous Words: Language and Politics in the Pacific*, Donald L. Brenneis and Fred R. Myers, eds., pp. 85–107. New York: New York University Press.

Leeuwenberg, Frans

1991   Ethno-zoological Analysis and Wildlife Management in the Xavante Territory, Pimentel Barbosa, Mato Grosso State (December 1990–November 1991). Report on first-year study commissioned by the Center for Indian Research and Training on Resource Management, Indian Research Center, Union of Indian Nations.

Lévi-Strauss, Claude

1955   *Tristes Tropiques*. Librarie Plon.

1956   Les organisations dualistes existent-elles? *Bijdragen tot de Taal-, Landen Volkenkunde* 112:99–128. Reprinted in Lévi-Strauss, *Anthropologie Structurale*. Paris: Librarie Plon, 1958. In English, it appeared under the title, Do dual organizations exist? *Structural Anthropology*, translated by Claire Jacobson and Brooke Grundfest Schoeph, pp. 128–160. Garden City, NY: Doubleday, 1963.

Lipsitz, George

1990   *Time Passages: Collective Memory and American Popular Culture*. Minneapolis: University of Minnesota Press.

List, George

1963   The Boundaries of Speech and Song. *Ethnomusicology* 7:1–16.

Lopes, Marta M.

1988   A resistência do índio ao extermíno: O caso dos Akwẽ-Xavante, 1967– 1980. M.A. thesis, Department of History, State University of São Paulo, Assis.

Lopes da Silva, Aracy

1986   *Nomes e amigos: Da prática Xavante a uma reflexão sobre os Jê*. São Paulo: Universidade de São Paulo.

1992   Dois séculos e meio de história Xavante. In *História dos índios no Brasil*, Manuela Carneiro da Cunha, ed., pp. 357–378. São Paulo: Editora Schwarcz Ltda.

Luong, Hy van

1984   "Brother" and "Uncle": Rules, Structural Contradictions, and Meaning in Vietnamese Kinship. *American Anthropologist* 86:290–314.

1987   Personal Pronouns and Plural Markers in Vietnamese Person Reference: An Analysis of Pragmatic Ambiguity and Native Models. *Anthropological Linguistics* 29:49–70.

Lutz, Catherine

1988   *Unnatural Emotions: Everyday Sentiments on a Micronesian Atol and Their Challenge to Western Theory*. Chicago: University of Chicago Press.

Mannheim, Bruce

1987   A Semiotic of Andean Dreams. In *Dreaming: Anthropological and Psychological Interpretations*, B. Tedlock, ed., pp. 132–153. Cambridge: Cambridge University Press.

Maybury-Lewis, David

1974   *Akwẽ-Shavante Society*, second edition. New York: Oxford University Press.

1979   *Dialectical Societies: The Gê and Bororo of Central Brazil*. Cambridge, Mass.: Harvard University Press.

McKellin, William H.

1984   Putting Down Roots: Information in the Language of Managalase Exchange. In *Dangerous Words: Language and Politics in the Pacific*, D. L.

Brenneis and F. R. Myers, eds., pp. 108–128. New York: New York University Press.

McLeod, Ruth, and Valerie Mitchell

1977   *Aspectos da língua Xavánte*. Translated by Mary I. Daniel. Brasília: Summer Institute of Linguistics.

Melatti, Julio C.

1970   O sistema social Krahó. Ph.D. dissertation, Universidade de São Paulo.

Menezes, Claudia

1985   Missionários e indios em Mato Grosso: Os Xavante de São Marcos. Ph.D. dissertation, Universidade de São Paulo.

Miamoto, Mitsugi

1990   Interview: Mr. Benjamin Wappria, the "Indio" Tribal Chief Who Is Appealing for the Protection of the Rainforest. *Asahi Journal*. Tokyo, Japan, July 23.

Müller, Regina

1976   A pintura do corpo e os ornamentos Xavante: Arte visual e communicação social. Master's thesis, UNICAMP, Campinas.

1992   Mensagens visuais na ornamentação corporal Xavante. In *Grafismo indígena*, Lux Vidal, ed., pp. 132–142. São Paulo: EDUSP, Studio Nobel Ltda.

Murphy, William P.

1981   The Rhetorical Management of Dangerous Knowledge in Kpelle Brokerage. *American Ethnologist* 8:667–685.

Myers, Fred

1986   Reflections on a Meeting: Structure, Language, and the Polity in a Small-Scale Society. *American Ethnologist* 13:430–447.

Narayan, Kirin

1989   *Storytellers, Saints, and Scoundrels: Folk Narrative in Hindu Religious Teaching*. Philadelphia: University of Pennsylvania Press.

1993   How Native is a "Native" Anthropologist? *American Anthropologist* 95 (3):671–686.

Nimuendajú, Curt

1942   *The Šerente*. Los Angeles: Frederick Webb Hodge Anniversary Publication Fund.

1967   *The Apinayé*. Robert H. Lowie and John M. Cooper, eds. Translated by Robert H. Lowie. Washington, D.C.: Catholic University Press. Originally published 1939.

O'Barr, William

1982   *Linguistic Evidence: Language, Power and Strategy in the Courtroom*. New York: Academic Press.

Ochs, Elinor

1988   *Culture and Language Development: Language Acquisition and Language Socialization in a Samoan Village*. Cambridge: Cambridge University Press.

O Globo

1991   Ecologia une ciência á tradičão indígena. Rio de Janeiro, September 14, p. 22.

Paine, Robert, ed.
1981 *Politically Speaking: Cross-cultural Studies of Rhetoric.* Philadelphia: Institute for the Study of Human Issues.

Peirce, Charles Sanders
1931– *Collected Papers.* Vols. 1–6, C. Hartshorne and P. Weiss, eds. Vols. 7–8,
1958 A. W. Burks, ed. Cambridge: Harvard University Press.

Perrone, Beatriz
1992 Indios livres e índios escravos: Os princípios da legislação indigenista do período colonial (séculos XVI a XVIII). In *História dos índios no Brasil,* Manuela Carneiro da Cunha, ed., pp. 115–132. São Paulo: Editora Schwarcz Ltda.

Philips, Susan
1984 Contextual Variation in Courtroom Language Use: Noun Phrases Referring to Crimes. *International Journal of the Sociology of Language* 49:29–50.

Price-Williams, Douglass
1987 The Waking Dream in Ethnographic Perspective. In *Dreaming: Anthropological and Psychological Interpretations,* B. Tedlock, ed., pp. 246–262. Cambridge: Cambridge University Press.

Rabinowitz, Peter
1987 *Before Reading.* Ithaca: Cornell University Press.

Radcliffe-Brown, A. R.
1940 On Joking Relationships. *Africa* 13(3)195–210. Reprinted in A. R. Radcliffe-Brown, *Structure and Function in Primitive Society: Essays and Addresses,* pp. 90–104. Glencoe, Ill.: Free Press, 1952.

Ramos, Alcida
1988 Indian Voices: Contact Experienced and Expressed. In *Rethinking History and Myth: Indigenous South American Perspectives on the Past,* Jonathan D. Hill, ed., pp. 214–234. Urbana and Champagne: University of Illinois Press.

Ravagnani, Osvaldo
1978 A experiência Xavante com o mundo dos brancos. Ph.D. dissertation, Fundação Escola de Sociologia e Política de São Paulo.
1987 Aldeiamentos oficias Goianos. Unpublished manuscript.

Rivière, Peter
1971 The Political Structure of the Trio Indians as Manifested in a System of Ceremonial Dialogue. In *The Translation of Culture,* T. O. Biedelman, ed., pp. 293–311. London: Travistock.

Roger, John J.
1985 On the Degeneration of the Public Sphere. *Political Studies* 33:203–217.

Rosaldo, Michelle
1973 "I Have Nothing to Hide": The Language of Ilongot Oratory. *Language in Society* 2:193–223.
1982 The Things We Do with Words: Ilongot Speech Acts and Speech Act Theory in Philosophy. *Language in Society* 11:203–237.
1984 Words That Are Moving: The Social Meanings of Ilongot Verbal Art. In

Dangerous Words: Language and Politics in the Pacific. D. L. Brenneis and F. R. Myers, eds., pp. 131–160. New York: New York University Press.

Rosaldo, Renato
1980   *Ilongot Headhunting 1883–1974: A Study in Society and History*. Stanford: Stanford University Press.

Roseman, Marina
1984   The Social Structuring of Sound: The Temiar of Peninsular Malaysia. *Ethnomusicology* 28(3):411–445.
1991   *Healing Sounds from the Malaysian Rainforest: Temiar Music and Medicine*. Berkeley: University of California Press.

Rouget, Gilbert
1985   *Music and Trance: A Theory of the Relations between Music and Possession*. Translated by Brunhilde Biebuyck. Chicago: University of Chicago Press.

Sacks, Harvey, Emanuel A. Schegloff, and Gail Jefferson
1974   A Simplest Systematics for the Organization of Turn-Taking Conversation. *Language* 50:696–735.

Salmond, Anne
1975   Mana Makes the Man: A Look at Maori Oratory and Politics. In *Political Language and Oratory in Traditional Society*, Maurice Bloch, ed., pp. 45–63. New York: Academic Press.

Sapir, David, and J. Christopher Crocker, eds.
1977   *The Social Uses of Metaphor: Essays on the Anthropology of Rhetoric*. Philadelphia: Institute for the Study of Human Issues.

Schechner, Richard
1985   *Between Theater and Anthropology*. Philadelphia: University of Pennsylvania Press.

Schegloff, Emanuel A.
1972   Sequencing in Conversational Openings. In *Directions in Sociolinguistics*, J. Gumperz, ed., pp. 346–380. New York: Holt, Rinehart and Winston.

Schegloff, Emanuel, and Harvey Sacks
1973   Opening Up Closings. *Semiotica* 8:289–327.

Schieffelin, Bambi
1986   The Acquisition of Kaluli. In *The Crosslinguistic Study of Language Acquisition*, D. Slobin, ed., pp. 525–595. Hillsdale, N.J.: Erlbaum.

Schutz, Alfred
1962   *Collected Papers, Volume I: The Problem of Social Reality*. The Hague: Marcus Nijhoff.

Searle, John R.
1969   *Speech Acts: An Essay in the Philosophy of Language*. Cambridge: Cambridge University Press.

Sebeok, Thomas
1978   Semiosis in Nature and Culture. In *The Sign and Its Masters*, T. Sebeok, ed., pp. 3–26. Austin: University of Texas Press.

Seeger, Anthony

1975   The Meaning of Body Ornaments: A Suyá Example. *Ethnology* 14:211–224.

1979   What Can We Learn When They Sing? Vocal Genres of the Suyá Indians of Central Brazil. *Ethnomusicology* 23:373–394.

1980   Sing for Your Sister: The Structure and Performance of Suyá *akia*. In *The Ethnography of Musical Performance*, M. Herdon and N. McLeod, eds., pp. 7–43. Norwood, Pa.: Norwood Editions.

1981   *Nature and Society in Central Brazil: The Suyá Indians of Mato Grosso.* Cambridge, Mass.: Harvard University Press.

1987   *Why Suyá Sing: A Musical Anthropology of an Amazonian People.* Cambridge: Cambridge University Press.

Sherzer, Joel

1979   Strategies in Text and Context: Cuna *kaa kwento*. *Journal of American Folklore* 92:145–163.

1983   *Kuna Ways of Speaking: An Ethnographic Perspective.* Austin: University of Texas Press.

1987   Poetic Structuring of Kuna Discourse: The Line. In *Native American Discourse: Poetics and Rhetoric*, J. Sherzer and A. C. Woodbury, eds., pp. 103–139. Cambridge: Cambridge University Press.

1989   *Namakke, Sunmakke, Kormakke*: Three Types of Cuna Speech Event. In *Explorations in the Ethnography of Speaking*, second edition, R. Bauman and J. Sherzer, eds., pp. 263–282. Cambridge: Cambridge University Press.

Sherzer, Joel, and Greg Urban

1986   Introduction. In *Native South American Discourse*, Joel Sherzer and Greg Urban, eds., pp. 1–14. Berlin: Mouton de Gruyter.

Sherzer, Joel, and Sammie Ann Wicks

1982   The Intersection of Language and Music in Kuna Discourse. *Latin American Music Review* 3:147–164.

Sherzer, Joel, and Anthony C. Woodbury, eds.

1987   *Native American Discourse: Poetics and Rhetoric.* Cambridge: Cambridge University Press.

Silverstein, Michael

1976a   Hierarchy of Features and Ergativity. In *Grammatical Categories in Australian Languages*, R. M. W. Dixon, ed., pp. 113–171. Australian Institute of Aboriginal Studies (Canberra), Linguistic Series no. 22. New Jersey: Humanities Press.

1976b   Shifters, Linguistic Categories, and Cultural Description. In *Meaning in Anthropology*, K. H. Basso and H. A. Selby, eds., pp. 11–56. Albuquerque: University of New Mexico Press.

Singer, Milton

1984   *Man's Glassy Essence: Explorations in Semiotic Anthropology.* Bloomington: Indiana University Press.

Staden, Hans

1929   *Hans Staden: The True History of His Captivity, 1557.* Translated and edited by Malcolm Letts. New York: Robert M. McBride and Company.

Stoller, Paul

1989 *Fusion of the Worlds: An Ethnography of Possession among the Songhay of Niger.* Chicago: University of Chicago Press.

1992a Embodying Cultural Memory in Songhay Spirit Possession. *Archives de Sciences Sociales des Religions* 79: 53–69.

1992b *The Cinematic Griot: The Ethnography of Jean Rouch.* Chicago and London: University of Chicago Press.

1994 Ethnographies as Texts/Ethnographers as Griots. *American Ethnologist* 21(2):353–356.

n.d. *Embodying Colonial Memory: Spirit Possession, Power and the Hauka in West Africa.* London: Routledge. Forthcoming.

Strathern, Andrew

1975 Veiled Speech in Mount Hagen. In *Political Language and Oratory in Traditional Society,* M. Bloch, ed., pp. 185–203. New York: Academic Press.

Tedlock, Barbara

1987a Dreaming and Dream Research. In *Dreaming: Anthropological and Psychological Interpretations,* Barbara Tedlock, ed., pp. 1–30. Cambridge: Cambridge University Press.

1987b Zuni and Quiché Dream Sharing and Interpreting. In *Dreaming: Anthropological and Psychological Interpretations,* Barbara Tedlock, ed., pp. 105–131. Cambridge: Cambridge University Press.

Tedlock, Dennis

1977 Toward Oral Poetics. *New Literary History* 8(3):507–519.

1983 *The Spoken Word and the Work of Interpretation.* Philadelphia: University of Pennsylvania Press.

Terdiman, Richard

1985 *Discourse/Counter-Discourse: The Theory and Practice of Symbolic Resistance in Nineteenth-Century France.* Ithaca, N.Y.: Cornell University Press.

Testa, Renata

1988 Interruptive Strategies in English and Italian Conversation: Smooth versus Contrastive Linguistic Preferences. *Multilingua* 7(3):285–312.

Tompkins, Jane, ed.

1980 *Reader-Response Criticism: From Formalism to Post-structuralism.* Baltimore: Johns Hopkins University Press.

Trudgill, Peter

1972 Sex, Covert Prestige, and Linguistic Change in the Urban British English of Norwich. *Language in Society* 1:179–195.

Turner, Terence

1966 Social Structure and Political Organization among the Northern Kayapo. Ph.D. dissertation, Harvard University.

1979a The Gê and Bororo Societies as Dialectical Systems: A General Model. In *Dialectical Societies: The Gê and Bororo of Central Brazil,* David Maybury-Lewis, ed., pp. 147–178. Cambridge, Mass.: Harvard University Press.

1979b Kinship, Household, and Community Structure among the Kayapó.

In *Dialectical Societies: The Gê and Bororo of Central Brazil*, David Maybury-Lewis, ed., pp. 179–217. Cambridge, Mass.: Harvard University Press.

1988 History, Myth, and Social Consciousness among the Kayapó of Central Brazil. In *Rethinking History and Myth: Indigenous South American Perspectives on the Past*, Jonathan D. Hill, ed., pp. 195–213. Urbana and Champagne: University of Illinois Press.

1993 The Social Skin. In *Reading the Social Body*, Catherine B. Burroughs and Jeffrey David Ehrenreich, eds., pp. 15–39. Iowa City: University of Iowa Press. Originally published 1979.

Turton, David

1975 The Relationship between Oratory and the Exercise of Influence among the Mursi. In *Political Language and Oratory in Traditional Society*, Maurice Bloch, ed., pp. 163–183. London: Academic Press.

1978 Territorial Organization and Age among the Mursi. In *Age, Generation, and Time: Some Features of East African Age Organizations*, P. T. W. Baxter and Uri Almagor, eds., pp. 95–130. London: C. Hurst and Company.

Urban, Greg

1984 Speech about Speech in Speech about Action. *Journal of American Folklore* 94(373):323–344.

1985a The Semiotics of Two Speech Styles in Shokleng. In *Semiotic Mediation*, B. Mertz and R. Parmentier, eds., pp. 311–329. Orlando, Fla.: Academic Press.

1985b Ergativity and Accusativity in Shokleng (Gê). *International Journal of American Linguistics* 51(2):164–187.

1986a Ceremonial Dialogues in Native South America. *American Anthropologist* 88:371–386.

1986b Semiotic Functions of Macro-parallelism in the Shokleng Origin Myth. In *Native South American Discourse*, J. Sherzer and G. Urban, eds., pp. 15–58. Berlin: Mouton de Gruyter.

1988 Ritual Wailing in Amerindian Brazil. *American Anthropologist* 90:385–400.

1989 The "I" of Discourse. In *Semiotics, Self, and Society*, B. Lee and G. Urban, eds., pp. 27–51. Berlin: Mouton de Gruyter.

1991 *A Discourse-Centered Approach to Culture: Native South American Myths and Rituals*. Austin: University of Texas Press.

n.d. Entextualization, Replication, and Power. In *Natural Histories of Discourse*, Greg Urban and Michael Silverstein, eds. Chicago: University of Chicago Press, forthcoming.

Urban, Greg, and Janet Hendricks

1983 Signal Functions of Masking in Amerindian Brazil. *Semiotica* 47:181–216.

Valadão, Virginia, director

n.d. *Waiʔa: O segredo dos homens*. Video. São Paulo: Centro de Trabalho Indigenista.

Vidal, Lux, ed.
1992	*Grafismo indígena.* São Paulo: EDUSP, Studio Nobel Ltda.
Vološinov, V. N.
1973	*Marxism and the Philosophy of Language.* Cambridge, Mass.: Harvard University Press. Originally published in Russian, 1929.
Wagley, Charles
1977	*Welcome of Tears: The Tapirapé Indians of Central Brazil.* New York: Oxford University Press.
Warner, Michael
1990	*The Letters of the Republic: Publication and the Public Sphere in Eighteenth-Century America.* Cambridge, Mass.: Harvard University Press.
Whorf, Benjamin Lee
1956	Some Verbal Categories in Hopi. In *Language, Thought, and Reality,* John Carroll, ed., pp. 112–124. Cambridge, Mass.: MIT Press.
Wilbert, Johannes, ed.
1978	*Folk Literature of the Gê Indians, Volume 1.* Los Angeles: University of California at Los Angeles Latin American Center Publications.
Zuckerkandl, Victor
1956	*Sound and Symbol: Music and the External World.* Translated by Willard R. Trask. Princeton, N.J.: Princeton University Press, Bollingen Series XLIV.

Index

accountability: Bakhtin on, 166; and
elders' speech 161, 164; and myth
telling, 192; and narrative, 139,
168–169; and *warā* discourse,
151, 154
age: and discourse, 84, 142, 149–150,
160–161, 164–166; and lament,
82–83; and status, 97; and *warā*
participation, 150
age grades, 17, 74, 92, 95–101, 109,
118; and *da-ño?re*, 90–91, 110–
112, 114, 117–118. *See also* life
cycle
agency: and discourse, 23–24, 71–72,
141, 224; in historical practice, 23–
24, 29, 42, 55
age-sets, 92–98, 111–112, 114, 117,
147, 258–259n28
ancestors. *See* creators; life cycle
Artaud, Antonin: 220
aspect, 154, 191
audience: and *da-ño?re*, 124; and
myth telling, 8, 192–194; and *warā*
speech, 152, 154, 158–159. *See
also* co-performance
Aytai, Desidério: 11, 257n12, 261n34,
262n39

Bakhtin, Mikhail, 5, 139–141, 145,
166–167, 251n2
Basso, Ellen, 119, 254n19
Bauman, Richard, 5, 8, 143
Brenneis, Don, 144–145

Caton, Steve, 264n65
context: and discourse, 6–8, 167; and
interpretation, 7; and myth telling,
8, 188–197
co-performance, 145, 158–159, 167–
168. *See also* audience
creators, 101, 221; and continuity, 21;
and life cycle, 201; *öwawē-?wa*, 27,
197–198, 221, 223; *Parinai?a*, 3,
188–194, 196–197; performers as,
211–212, 217; Warodi as, 17, 176,
178, 180, 184; Warodi's relation to,
11, 194–206, 215

Da Matta, Roberto, 265n4
dance: choreography, 110–112; and
da-ño?re classification, 65, 79–80;
in dream performance, 4–6, 9; and
gender, 257n20; repetition in,
266n2. *See also* da-ño?re
da-ño?re: composition of, 114, 116–
119, 123, 125–130, 260n11; and
continuity, 114, 116, 125, 128,
130–136; and creativity, 9, 125,
128; classification of, 79–80,
257n12; in dream performance 5,
128–136; formal characteristics of,
112, 118–119, 121–126, 128, 130,
237–238; and individuality, 121,
126, 128, 130; and life cycle, 114–
119, 125, 128–129; movement in,
79–80, 119, 123–125; performance of, 110–112, 114, 117,

122–123, 215–218, 259n3, 261n22, 261n29; and prestige, 128; rehearsal of, 110, 112, 114; and social space, 110–112, 119, 259–260n9; and solidarity, 86, 93, 117–119, 122–130, 136; and subjectivity, 9, 116, 121, 125–130; teaching of, 110, 117, 126, 260–261n21; texts, 119, 123–125, 261n34; and women, 106, 218, 260n11. *See also* dance

deictics. *See* person marking

discourse: accountability and anonymity in, 140–145, 150–152, 154, 165–167, 192; and age, 142, 150–151, 160; and agency, 23–24, 141; and continuity, 6, 17, 24, 63, 92, 168; co-production of, 139–142, 144–145, 153–158, 166; and gender, 142, 150; and identity, 23, 63, 195; ideology of, 140–145, 165, 262n3; and individuality, 149–152, 159–160, 165–166; and intentionality, 140, 165; interpretation of, 7, 15, 179–180; and intersubjectivity, 142, 167; and memory, 16, 18, 101, 135; and power, 71, 142; and prestige, 142, 144, 149–151, 177; and social relations, 140–142, 144–145, 149, 159, 161, 165–166; and subjectivity, 6, 115, 165–166, 195; in *warã*, 149–152, 158–159, 166. *See also* language; performance; speech

disease, 17–18, 28, 35–36, 49

Dixon, R. M. W.: 71

dream performance: role of ethnographer in, 9, 218–220, 224–225; and identity, 3, 4, 202, 207, 217; and intra-village rivalry, 170–171, 215; objectives of, 8, 130, 133, 170–171, 181–182; and Western technologies, 9, 173–174; 214–215, 218–219, 224–225

dreams: and *da-ño?re*, 114, 116–117, 123, 125–127, 129–130, 260n11; discourse about, 115–116; and gender, 114–115; and illness, 101; and immortals, 17, 101, 116, 125, 183; and lament, 83, 114; and life cycle, 114–117, 175, 183; representations of, 5, 9, 114–115; sharing, 5, 11, 89, 108, 115–116, 138, 260n2, 260n13; and sociability, 116; studies of, 5; and subjectivity, 109, 115–116, 138, 260n13; and women's names, 258n24

Du Bois, John, 141

Duranti, Alessandro, 141

economy, 23, 37–38, 42–44, 46, 49; NGO assisted projects, 61–62. *See also* Xavante Project

education, 13, 15–16, 46, 61, 253n30

Eggan, Dorothy, 260n15

elders. *See* life cycle; speech

emotion: and discourse, 80–83, 85–86, 211–212

factionalism: and ceremonial friends, 177; and contact, 35; and *da-ño?re*, 118, 129; and discourse, 149–152, 159–160, 166; and evaluation of speech, 164–165; and fission, 34, 50; influence on fieldwork, 13, 15, 164–165; and life cycle, 97, 176–177; and members' meetings, 87–89, 151; pre-contact, 29–30

falsetto: 78–79, 81, 92

Feld, Steve: 256n2

fission: and *da-ño?re*, 129; and factionalism, 34–35, 50; from Pimentel Barbosa, 39, 50–51, 53, 104, 228; and *warã* discourse, 149; and Xavante Project, 50–51, 53, 55

Flowers, Nancy, 252n24

Freud, Sigmund, 5

FUNAI: and Xavante Project, 44–61; and education, 13, 77; as mediator, 37, 40; dependence on, 24, 47–60; independence from, 61–63; medical assistance by, 49, 53; post chief, 15, 35, 38–40, 45, 103, 159; role in land disputes, 10, 39–41

Gê societies: 25, and gender, 259n30; comparative work on, 11, 252n25; discourse among, 11, 257n12; and myth performance, 262n2; social organization of, 11, 96, 100, 258n23, 265n4; and social space, 99, 257n15. *See also* Indian groups; Xavante communities

gender: and access to expressive resources, 86, 166; and age, 82–83; and *da-ño?re*, 218; and discourse, 84, 142, 150, 257n19; and dreams, 114–115; and immortals, 101; and lament, 82–83, 257n17; and myth, 259n37; in Gê societies, 259n30. *See also* women

Goffman, Erving, 265n7

gossip, 104, 106, 133, 228

greetings, 45, 65, 83–84, 87, 105, 160–161

Gumperz, John, 251n8

Habermas, Jürgen, 140–141, 143, 145, 165–166

Harvard Central Brazil Project, 11, 252n25

health care, 49–50, 61, 255n57

hedza (hymns), 86–87, 231–232, 234, 236

Hill, Jane, and Kenneth Hill, 256n10

Hinton, Leanne, 124

history: agency in, 23–24; colonial period, 25–28; of contact, 10, 22–24, 31–36, 57, 60; learning of, 23, 61; and myth, 29, 57, 254n19

höimana?u?ö (creators). *See* creators

honorifics. *See* person marking

Hymes, Dell, 251n8, 266n1

identity: and *da-ño?re*, 112, 114; and life cycle, 149, 177; and person marking, 179–180, 191, 194–198, 200–201, 203, 205; and quoted speech, 196–197; transformation of 191, 194–198, 200–212

ĩ-hi mrɛmɛ. See speech, elders'

Indian groups: Apinajé, 265n4;

Bororo, 29, 36; Kaingang, 230–231; Kalapalo, 119; Karajá, 28–29; Kayapó, 28, 63; Suyá, 95, 257n12, 258n24, 260n19; Tucano, 99; Tupi, 99; Xerente, 25–26, 28–29; Xokleng 11, 157, 195–196, 265–266n22. *See also* Gê societies; Xavante communities

Indian Protection Service (SPI), 32–37

individuality: and *da-ño?re*, 112, 118–119, 121–124, 128–130; and dialogue, 124; and discourse, 140–145; and lament, 82; and life cycle, 98; role of repetition in, 261n25, 261n26; in *warã* discourse, 149–152, 159–160, 165–166

initiation: 91–92, 97, 101, 116–117, 176, 258n22

intonation: in elders' speech, 84, 108, 161–162, 164; in everyday speech, 84; in myth telling 191, 196; of shouting, 89

Irvine, Judith, 256n10

Jakobson, Roman, 256n10, 260n10

joking, 83–84, 87, 90

Juruna, Mario: 46–47, 57, 171

Keane, Webb: 141

lament, 80–82, 86, 127–128, 257n17, 262n43; and dreams, 114; in initiation, 91; among Kaluli, 257n13

land: disputes over, 10, 36–47, 51; non-Xavante occupation of, 32, 36–37, 41

language: and music, 81–82; and non-linguistic media, 220–221; philosophy of, 140–141, 262n3; as social action, 6; sociology of, 251n8; variants, 258n23. *See also* discourse; speech; speech act; utterance

leadership: and *da-ño?re*, 128; effects of Xavante Project on, 50–51, 55–58; and independence from FUNAI, 61–63; and *warã*, 146, 150–151

Leeuwenberg, Frans, 43
Lévi–Strauss, Claude, 172
life cycle: and *da-ño?re*, 116–117,
    125, 128–129, 260–261n21; and
    dreams, 114–117, 175; and *hedza*,
    234; and immortals, 175–177, 201,
    208; and myth telling, 220; and per-
    formance, 8, 218; phases of, 96–98,
    100–102. *See also* age grades
Lino Tsere?ubudzi, 80, 116, 123, 129,
    162, 253n30
Lopes da Silva, Aracy, 28–29, 31, 35,
    47, 51, 177, 252n24, 253n11,
    254n34

marriage, 67–69, 72
Maybury-Lewis, David: ethnography
    of Xavante, 10–11, 22, 25, 34,
    254n33, 255n36; and Harvard
    Central Brazil Project, 252n25; on
    men's council, 97, 147, 150, 152;
    on social organization, 95, 98,
    252n24
Meireles, Francisco, 33–34, 94.
    See also history, of contact
melody: and language, 81; of
    da-ño?re, 112, 125; of *hedza*, 86;
    of lament, 81
memory: and *da-ño?re*, 128, 135–136;
    and discourse, 16, 135, 185; and
    immortality, 223; and lament, 82;
    and myth telling, 185, 187, 192,
    212, 223; and performance, 6–7,
    81, 223; and technology, 16
Menezes, Claudia, 254n35
men's council: discourse in, 11, 74,
    159–161; participation in, 10, 89,
    97, 184, 106. *See also* speech,
    elders'; *warã*
metadiscourse: and *da-ño?re*, 262n39;
    and elders' speech, 164; as framing
    device, 181–182, 187–188, 265n7;
    in myth telling, 196
metaphor, 143–144, 162, 180
missionaries, 27, 32, 36–37, 53,
    252n24, 254n35

Müller, Regina, 252n24
music. *See da-ño?re*; *hedza*; lament;
    speech, elders'
myth: change in, 8, 185–187, 192;
    dramatization of, 13, 107, 139,
    259n2, 262n2; and gender, 259n37;
    and history, 29, 57, 254n19; and
    memory, 192; of *Parinai?a*, 3, 188–
    194, 196–197; Star Woman,
    259n37, 266n10. *See also* myth
    telling
myth telling: and context, 8, 188–194,
    196–197; and continuity, 8, 185–
    187, 194, 196, 204–207, 224–
    225, 235; and dream performance,
    4–6, 9, 220–223; and identity,
    194–207, 209–212; and immor-
    tality, 194–206, 223–225; and life
    cycle, 8, 193, 220; and memory,
    185–187, 204, 212, 223; and myth
    change, 8, 185, 192, 194; contesta-
    tion of, 8, 185–186; honorifics in,
    200–201; quoted speech in, 190–
    192, 196–197, 205; sound orna-
    mentation in, 190–192, 196

Narayan, Kirin, 252n27
narrative. *See* discourse; myth telling;
    performance

pacification. *See* history; missionaries
parallelism, 112, 161–162, 260n10
Peirce, Charles Saunders, 7, 252n11
performance: among Kaluli 259n4;
    and life cycle, 17, 82–83, 98, 101–
    102; by Riridu, 228–232; rehearsal
    as, 5, 217; scholarship on, 8,
    251n8; and space, 82, 108, 110–
    112, 119. *See also da-ño?re*;
    discourse
person marking: honorifics, 75–76,
    200–201, 256n10, 258n23,
    266n23; and identity, 179–180,
    191, 194–195, 197–198, 200–
    201, 203–205; as social index,
    256n10

Pimentel Barbosa, Génesio, 32–33
Pimentel Barbosa Reserve: and land rights, 37, 39–41; relation to other communities, 23, 35–36, 48, 57–58, 171, 229; relation to outside world, 16–17, 58, 62
pitch, 89–91, 112, 162, 238
polyvocality, 2, 8, 139, 141–142, 168
Portuguese: Xavante use of, 13, 15, 45, 50, 108
prestige: and age, 97, 117; and da-ño?re, 128–130; and discourse, 142, 144, 149–151, 177; of elders, 265n1; and Xavante Project, 51; print, ideology of, 142–143; interpretation of, 16
pronouns, 15, 194–195, 197–198, 201, 223. See also person marking

ranches: and environmental degradation, 41, 43; in SPI era, 35; in Xavante territory, 10, 22, 37–41, 51, 62–63. See also land; settlers
Ravagnani, Osvaldo, 29, 252n24, 253n11
recontextualization, 8, 25, 187
repetition: and continuity, 6, 9, 64; in dance, 266n2; in da-ño?re, 108, 118–119, 121–122, 124, 126; of da-ño?re, 112, 114, 259n3; in discourse, 108, 154, 157–158, 161–162, 164, 166; as parallelism, 260n10; and subjectivity, 196, 261nn25 and 26
resistance, 23–24, 31–32, 51. See also Xavante Project; FUNAI
rhythm: in da-ño?re, 112, 125; in elders' speech, 162; in hedza, 86
Riridu: and hedza, 231–232, 234; use of tape recorder by, 230–232, 235–236
Rondon, General Cândido M., 32. See also history, of contact
Rosaldo, Michelle, 144
Roseman, Marina, 261n26
Rouget, Gilbert, 265n21, 266n3
Russell Tribunal. See Juruna, Mario

Saussure, Ferdinand de, 7
Schechner, Richard, 5, 8, 261n25, 266n2
Schutz, Alfred, 252n13
Scruggs, T. M., 266n3
Searle, John, 140
Seeger, Anthony, 11, 238, 257n12, 260n19
settlers, 28, 32, 35–37, 39–40. See also land
shouting, 64, 78–79, 89–91, 122, 145–146, 148
silence, 65–66, 70–72, 74, 91
Silverstein, Michael, 7, 194, 256n10
sociability: and discourse, 82, 116, 124–129, 143, 151, 195, 201, 206
solidarity, of males: and da-ño?re, 86, 93, 117–119, 122–124, 130, 136; and life cycle, 97–98, 101–102
song: in ceremony, 91, 258n24; and continuity, 21; and creativity, 92; in dream performance, 2, 4–5, 9, 21; learning, 110, 112, 114; provoking lament, 81–82, 262n43; rehearsal, 1, 2, 107–108; and social space, 95, 108; Suyá, 258n24, 260n19; time of, 64–65; and warã, 147–150. See also da-ño?re
sorcery, 29, 34, 50, 104–106, 133
sound ornamentation, 190–192, 196
speech: ability and factionalism, 150–151, 165; and affect, 85–86; elders' 108, 150, 161–165, 235; elicited, 75–76; everyday, 84–86, 162–164; overlapping in, 2, 84, 88, 108, 152–154, 156–158; Portuguese in, 45; quoted, 84, 190–192, 196–197, 203, 205, 265n16; and song, 122; style, 264n55; taboo, 70–77; and trance, 265n21; turn-taking in, 84, 159; volume of, 2, 108, 191, 201. See also discourse; language
speech act: performative, 69; theory, 140–141, 167
status. See prestige
Strathern, Andrew, 144

subjectivity: and discourse, 6, 115, 144, 165–166, 195, 260n15; and dreams, 115–116; *da-ño?re* as expression of, 9, 116, 125, 129

taboo: for novitiates, 97, 264n40; speech 70–77
tape recorder: and composition, 264n65; and dream performance, 9, 107, 173–174, 214–215, 218–219; and translation, 15; Xavante use of, 11–12, 16, 46–47, 77–78, 230–232, 235–236
Tedlock, Barbara, 251n7
Turner, Terence, 256n3
Turton, David, 258–259n28

Urban, Greg, 7, 11, 127, 161, 195–196, 230, 260n10, 261n35
utterance: theories of, 115, 140

vocables, 124–125
voice quality, 122–123, 191, 196, 201
Voloβinov, V. N., 115
Vygotsky, L. S., 166–167

wai?a, 39, 91, 107, 117, 176, 259n1
wapte. See age grades
warã (men's council): as central plaza, 78, 80, 263n38; discourse in, 139–142, 145, 147, 149–154, 156–161, 165–166
Warner, Michael, 16, 142–143, 150

Warodi: and dreaming, 129, 168–169; and dream narrative 2, 138–139, 154–157, 161, 167–169; and immortals, 11, 17, 99–100, 129–130, 132, 169, 176, 178–184, 188, 194, 196–198, 200–206; and Riridu, 230–232; immortality of, 18, 178, 206, 223–225, 236; in men's council, 89, 106, 151
whispering, 191, 201
Whorf, Benjamin Lee, 192, 265n16
women: and age-sets, 95–96; and *da-ño?re*, 86, 106, 260n11; and dream performance, 132, 212, 215, 218; discourse of, 90, 154; immortality of, 266n10; and lament, 82; and names, 218, 258n24, 265n3; role in economy, 43–44; and *warã* participation 147, 166. *See also* gender
writing: and dream performance, 9, 12, 16–17, 106, 172–174; immortality through, 16–17, 225

Xavante communities: groupings of, 36–37, 254n33; pre–contact, 29–32, 35, 41, 254n21, 262n48; population of, 25, 35, 53; relations between, 13, 24, 29, 31, 35–36, 39, 48, 50, 57, 170–172, 215, 229; and Reserves, 25, 36–43, 46, 49, 51
Xavante Project, 24, 36, 44–55, 59–61

Zuckerkandl, Victor, 261n33